ENDING OVERCRIMINALIZATION AND MASS INCARCERATION

Mass incarceration is an overwhelming problem and reforms are often difficult, leading to confusion about what to do and where to start. *Ending Overcriminalization and Mass Incarceration: Hope from Civil Society* introduces the key issues that need immediate attention and provides concrete direction about effective solutions systemically and relationally. Author Anthony B. Bradley recognizes that offenders are persons with inherent dignity. Mass incarceration results from the systemic breakdown of criminal law procedure and broken communities. Using the principle of personalism, attention is drawn to those areas that have direct contact with the lives of offenders and that determine their fate. Bradley explains how reform must be built from the person up, and that once these areas are reformed, our law enforcement culture will change for the better. Taking an innovative approach, Bradley explores how civic institutions can both prevent people from falling into the criminal justice system and help lower recidivism rates for those released from prison.

ANTHONY B. BRADLEY is Professor of Religious Studies, Program Chair for Religious and Theological Studies, and the director of the Center for the Study of Human Flourishing at The King's College. He is also a research fellow at the Acton Institute. He has previously studied ethics at Fordham University and criminal justice at John Jay College of Criminal Justice. He has authored and edited eight books and has written several dozen articles. His writings on religious and cultural issues have been published in a variety of journals, including *Al Jazeera*, the *Philadelphia Inquirer*, the *Atlanta-Journal Constitution*, the *Detroit News*, *Christianity Today*, and *World Magazine*. Professor Bradley has appeared on *C-SPAN*, *NPR*, *CNN Headline News*, and *Fox News*, among others. He is a member of the Academy of Criminal Justice Sciences and the American Academy of Religion.

Ending Overcriminalization and Mass Incarceration

HOPE FROM CIVIL SOCIETY

ANTHONY B. BRADLEY

The King's College

CAMBRIDGE
UNIVERSITY PRESS

University Printing House, Cambridge CB2 8BS, United Kingdom

One Liberty Plaza, 20th Floor, New York, NY 10006, USA

477 Williamstown Road, Port Melbourne, VIC 3207, Australia

314–321, 3rd Floor, Plot 3, Splendor Forum, Jasola District Centre, New Delhi – 110025, India

79 Anson Road, #06–04/06, Singapore 079906

Cambridge University Press is part of the University of Cambridge.

It furthers the University's mission by disseminating knowledge in the pursuit of
education, learning, and research at the highest international levels of excellence.

www.cambridge.org
Information on this title: www.cambridge.org/9781108427548
DOI: 10.1017/9781108611671

First published 2018

Printed in the United States of America by Sheridan Books, Inc.

A catalogue record for this publication is available from the British Library.

Library of Congress Cataloging-in-Publication Data
NAMES: Bradley, Anthony B., 1971– author.
TITLE: Ending overcriminalization and mass incarceration : hope from civil society / Anthony B. Bradley.
DESCRIPTION: 1 Edition. | New York : Cambridge University Press, 2018. |
Includes bibliographical references and index.
IDENTIFIERS: LCCN 2018000204 | ISBN 9781108427548 (hardback) | ISBN 9781108446297 (paperback)
SUBJECTS: LCSH: Criminal justice, Administration of–Social aspects–United States. |
Imprisonment–Social aspects–United States. | Criminal law–Social aspects–United
States. | Law reform–Social aspects–United States
CLASSIFICATION: LCC HV9950 .B693 2018 | DDC 364.60973–dc23
LC record available at https://lccn.loc.gov/2018000204

ISBN 978-1-108-42754-8 Hardback
ISBN 978-1-108-44629-7 Paperback

For David Clyde Jones (1937–2017)

Contents

Acknowledgments

Putting this book together was a team effort. I am thankful for the foundation and donor support from the criminal justice reform program at the Center for the Study of Human Flourishing at The King's College. Donor generosity made it possible for me to assemble a small team of research assistants to help compile some of the data. Matthew Sifert and Taylor Thompson served as principal researchers. They were assisted by Patrick Thomas, Michael Sheetz, and Anthony Barr. I am indebted to the library resources at Fordham Law School and John Jay College of Criminal Justice (CUNY). I received exceptional insights and comments from the students in my course on overcriminalization at The King's College, which improved my overall conception of this book. Nicholas Dunn, a King's College alumnus and philosophy PhD student at McGill University, deserves special recognition for first pointing me to the work on personalism by Christian Smith. My research and writing have not been the same since.

I have the privilege of living in a city where I am in contact with many experts in law, ethics, and criminal justice. I am particularly grateful for the many courses I took at John Jay College of Criminal Justice in New York City that helped me keep the narrative straight in this book. While completing a graduate degree in ethics and society at Fordham University, I took a course with Keith Cruise that served as the catalyst for my research into humanitarian and ethical concerns in the juvenile justice system, which later developed into a broader focus on criminal justice reform at large. This book is an extension of that course. I would also like to thank my colleagues and administration at The King's College who provided me time and resources to complete this project. Without The King's College this book would not have been possible. Lastly, I would like to thank my friends and colleagues at the Acton Institute where I have had the privilege of being a research fellow since 1992. The Acton Institute is where I first learned the importance of keeping the person at the center of constructions of public and economic policy and of civil society institutions.

I would like to thank my editor John Berger at Cambridge University Press who encouraged the vision of this book. John solicited feedback from fantastic reviewers whose suggestions vastly enhanced the scope and content of the book. I wish to thank all of them for their responses, which brought greater clarity to my understanding of where the book should fit in the larger criminal justice reform discourse. Thanks also to Danielle Menz at Cambridge University Press who patiently waited on me and answered my questions through two software crashes.

Finally, I would not be where I am today if it were not for the consistent love and support of family and friends. You know who you are. Your life-giving support allows me to do work like this when others doubt me.

Introduction

There are too many Americans in jails and prisons. Mass incarceration must end, but it is hard to know where reform should begin. This book explores possible starting points for reforming the criminal justice system. This book is introductory in nature for those who have read a few things or watched documentaries and are focusing their attention on how to bring about effective solutions. There are many books that rant against overcriminalization and mass incarceration, and now is the time to mobilize and direct our efforts to a few areas that need immediate attention. The explosion of prison populations in America happened for a reason, and direct action can be taken to end the problem. Our task, of course, lies in sorting out the right causal mechanisms and variables, implementing realistic solutions, and properly going through the process of scaling down the numbers of incarcerated people. Criminal justice is an area that needs consistent advocacy for modernization. There are inherent complexities to the subject, which allow problems to last longer than they need to. Normal law-abiding citizens do not always feel the need to engage with an issue such as handling those that were not able to follow the rules. It is this disparity of human connection that is the first obstacle to overcome in our journey toward bringing down the incarcerated population.

This book is the direct result of assigning and reading the work of five legal scholars in a course I offered at The King's College on mass incarceration and overcriminalization; those five legal scholars are Michelle Alexander, Douglas Husak, John Pfaff, James Forman, Jr., and Stephanos Bibas.[1] After reading Michelle

---

[1] Michelle Alexander, *The New Jim Crow: Mass Incarceration in the Age of Colorblindness* (New York, NY: New Press, 2010); Douglas Husak, *Overcriminalization: The Limits of the Criminal Law* (New York, NY: Oxford University Press, 2008); John F. Pfaff, "The War on Drugs and Prison Growth: Limited Importance, Limited Legislative Options." *Harvard Journal on Legislation* 52, no. 1 (2015): 173–220; James Forman, Jr., "Racial Critiques of Mass Incarceration: Beyond the New Jim Crow." *New York University Law Review* 87,

Alexander's book *The New Jim Crow* in the course, my eyes were opened to a problem that I had previously overlooked: we have an incarceration problem in the United States. Alexander's basic premise is that the War on Drugs drives America's prison explosion. Additionally, her thesis presses the point further that the increased focus on locking up low-level drug offenders disproportionately, and maybe intentionally, landed thousands of black men and women under the control of the criminal justice system. Alexander's thesis made complete sense to me. I was ignorant of the data, and the way she connected the dots seemed plausible. I then joined the national resistance to "do something" about changing drug laws so that we can reduce prison numbers. Then I stumbled upon Pfaff, Forman, and Bibas, and discovered that Alexander got the narrative wrong. I even enrolled in a criminal justice master's degree program at the John Jay College of Criminal Justice in New York City to make sure I was getting the story straight. When I looked at the data it quickly became clear that our "mass incarceration" problem could not be reduced by the so-called War on Drugs. For me this meant that neither Alexander's thesis nor the Netflix documentary *13th* was pointing in a direction that would lead to real progress at dismantling America's exploding prison population.[2] That is, we could legalize all drugs and release everyone from prison incarcerated for a drug-related charge and America would still have a mass incarceration and overcriminalization problem. In fact, the problem with our overly punitive criminal justice system is much worse. We overpunish in the United States and it is neither because of drug offense nor as a proxy conspiracy against people of color. America got into this mess for several other reasons. Our prisons exploded largely because of anthropological reasons. As Elizabeth Hinton suggests, it is better for us to frame our current crisis as a "war on crime" rather than a consequence of the War on Drugs.[3] America has declared war against "criminals," and that label is assigned to a class of persons in ways that redefine the humanity of the offenders and create the context for being overly punitive. This book is about those other anthropological, systemic, legal, social, and political reasons. Legal scholars like Pfaff and Forman encourage us to ask deeper and broader questions about our prison crisis.

According to John Pfaff, drug offenders make up only about 16 percent of a state prison population and explain only about 20 percent of prison growth since

no. 1 (2012): 21–69; Stephanos Bibas, "Prisoners without Prisons." *National Review* 67, no. 17 (September 21, 2015): 27–30.

[2]   In fairness, what Alexander and the New Jim Crow theorists get right is that our drug laws are overly punitive toward disadvantaged minorities, but the data does not support this as the primary causal story of how our prison populations exploded after the 1960s. Again, the War on Drugs and racial bias exacerbate a systemic problem and make the negative externalities even worse.

[3]   Elizabeth Kai Hinton, *From the War on Poverty to the War on Crime: The Making of Mass Incarceration in America* (Cambridge, MA: Harvard University Press, 2017), 25.

1980 during the much-demonized Reagan era.[4] Pfaff highlights the following data points that begin to question Alexander's telling of the story:

> First, the sharp relative rise in drug offenders begins about five to ten years after the slow, steady rise in incarceration began. Second, the relative peak of drug incarcerations, in 1990, approximately 22 percent of all inmates were drug offenders – or, phrased more starkly, over three-quarters of all state prisoners were serving time primarily for non-drug offenses. And third, since about 1990, even as prison populations continued to rise, the share of drug inmates has actually slowly declined, hitting about 17 percent by 2010.[5]

What was responsible for America's prison boom? Property crime and violent crime tell the actual story. These offenders contributed more than two-thirds of America's prison growth. On the race issue, Pfaff presses the point even further. If we were to release every inmate serving time for a drug offense in 2010, the total prison population would fall from 1,362,028 to 1,125,028, and the percentages of the white/black/Hispanic population would change from 34.4 percent/38.1 percent/21.2 percent to 35.5 percent/36.7 percent/21.5 percent. In other words, observes Pfaff, "[T]he percent of the prison population that is black would fall by only 1.4 percentage points (from 38.1 percent to 36.7 percent), and the white–black gap would narrow only slightly, from 3.8 percentage points (34.3 percent vs. 38.1 percent) to 1.2 percentage points (35.5 percent vs. 36.7 percent)."[6]

James Forman, Jr. observes that Alexander's thesis is flawed largely by what it obscures. In addition to getting the narrative wrong about drug-related incarceration, Alexander obscures the black community's support for tougher law and increased law enforcement in predominantly black neighborhoods, especially in black majority jurisdictions, and it obscures that "mass incarceration" avoided the black middle class.[7] In *Locking Up Our Own*, James Forman highlights that black people are in the criminal justice system as police officers, prosecutors, judges, correction office, probation and parole officers, and "tough on crime" community activists.[8] The Nixon Era in the early 1970s was largely focused on decriminalizing marijuana, and it was black church leaders who stopped it and called for more punitive drug laws.[9] It was black political leaders like Detroit's first black mayor Coleman Young who fought against gun control proposals in Michigan.[10] Major US cities and districts like New York, Washington, DC, Atlanta, Chicago, and Detroit had a very

---

[4] John F. Pfaff, *Locked In: The True Causes of Mass Incarceration – and How to Achieve Real Reform* (New York, NY: Basic Books, 2017), 35; Pfaff, "The War on Drugs," 176.

[5] Ibid., 180.

[6] Ibid., 184.

[7] Forman, "Racial Critiques," 115.

[8] James Forman, Jr., *Locking Up Our Own: Crime and Punishment in Black America* (New York, NY: Farrar, Straus and Giroux, 2017), 10.

[9] Ibid., 43–46.

[10] Ibid., 65.

high percentage of black police officers during the "mass incarceration" boom. During the 1980s, it was black leaders who also fought for tougher drug laws, stiffer penalties in sentencing, and mandatory minimums, and tried to do something about "black-on-black" crime.[11] During the crack epidemic, it was cities with top black law enforcement officials and political leaders that clamped down hard on drug offenders. Forman writes that by 1990, "there were 130 black police chiefs nationwide, including the top cops in D.C., New York, Philadelphia, Baltimore, Detroit, Chicago, and Houston" and "more than three hundred African American mayors" in cities like Washington, DC, New York, Los Angeles, Philadelphia, Detroit, Baltimore, Atlanta, and Oakland.[12] Moreover, if one reads the history of how the black middle class, living in large metropolitan areas, perceived the black underclass, the racialized drug war narrative painted by Alexander and others is significantly undermined. In other words, the drug war narrative about mass incarceration, according to the data, gets the larger story wrong. The causes of mass incarceration are much more complex and differentiated. Unfortunately, the racialized drug war narrative will not lead us to solutions that will actually begin to make a difference and dismantle our overly punitive criminal justice system. While it is most certainly the case that drug crime enforcement policies disproportionately impact people of color in disadvantaged communities, it is not the case that solving for that variable will do a whole lot to change the overcriminalizing outcomes of a criminal justice system that is systemically dysfunctional. That is, if the war on drugs had never happened we would likely still be the most incarcerated nation in the developed world.

There is much to do beside changing laws. This book contributes to criminal justice reform by examining moral obligations we have as a collective in making logical civic decisions. Ending mass incarceration has a very practical and simple rationale that anyone can come to logically, and this individual logic must be applied to updating and upgrading our criminal justice system.

Civil society institutions hold a crucial role in the fabric of our society. Typically, the discourse about criminal justice reform revolves around the pursuit of what policy changes need to be made in order to reduce the number of youth, women, and men in America's jails and prisons. Unfortunately, policy alone cannot solve this problem. This book argues that right policies can only bring about criminal justice reform if they work in concert with the other institutions in society that shape human life. The mass incarceration crisis is really a crisis of human dignity. In the criminal justice system, those who break the law are given new labels like "deviant," "offender," "ex-con," and so on. These labels come to define the entire identity of the criminal, and he or she is treated accordingly in

---

[11] Ibid., 126–143.
[12] Ibid., 165.

the system – forever. Criminal justice reform will only be successful if we change it from the person up rather than simply from policy outward.

There are two main concepts which characterize the arc of this book. The first relates to the true meaning of a civil society; the second is that of personalism. The London School of Economics defines civil society in the following terms:

> Civil society refers to the arena of uncoerced collective action around shared interests, purposes and values. In theory, its institutional forms are distinct from those of the state, family and market, though in practice, the boundaries between state, civil society, family and market are often complex, blurred and negotiated. Civil society commonly embraces a diversity of spaces, actors and institutional forms, varying in their degree of formality, autonomy and power. Civil societies are often populated by organizations such as registered charities, development non-governmental organizations, community groups, women's organizations, faith-based organizations, professional associations, trade unions, self-help groups, social movements, business associations, coalitions and advocacy groups.[13]

Civil society institutions fill in the gaps where public policy is not designed well, or where the expertise or equipment is lacking to meet the differentiated needs of criminal justice reform.[14] For those that are considered offenders or ex-offenders, the flourishing of these civil institutions are vital for the enabling of all criminal justice stakeholders. What tends to be lacking in the criminal justice reform conversation is the necessary role of civil society, or mediating institutions, to do the work of human formation at the level of the individual human person, which public policy is ill-equipped to fulfill. The second concept governing this book is the philosophy school on personalism, which will require a more robust explanation.

The perspective in this book draws heavily on personalism as used in the work by Christian Smith, Thomas Rourke, and Rosita Chazarreta Rourke, as well as the philosophical framework of overcriminalization by Douglas Husak.[15] As such, this book argues in favor of decentralizing the dominant political and economic institutions of criminal justice and reorganizing criminal justice reform with the person as the center of focus.[16] Criminal justice reform should be centered on what is good for the person as the integrating principle of the common good and the

---

[13] "Civil Society," T. Romana College, www.trcollege.net/faculty/directory/teaching-staff/46-staff-directory/29-mawia (accessed July 15, 2011).

[14] Anthony B. Bradley, *The Political Economy of Liberation: Thomas Sowell and James Cone on the Black Experience*, vol. 12, Martin Luther King, Jr. Memorial Studies in Religion, Culture, and Social Development (New York, NY: Peter Lang, 2012), 135–136.

[15] Christian Smith, *To Flourish or Destruct: A Personalist Theory of Human Goods, Motivations, Failure, and Evil* (Chicago, IL: University of Chicago Press, 2015), 1; Christian Smith, *What Is a Person? Rethinking Humanity, Social Life, and the Moral Good from the Person Up* (Chicago, IL: University of Chicago Press, 2010); Thomas R. Rourke and Rosita A. Chazarreta Rourke, *A Theory of Personalism* (Lanham, MD: Lexington Books, 2005); Douglas Husak, *Overcriminalization: The Limits of the Criminal Law* (Oxford: Oxford University Press, 2008).

[16] Rourke and Chazarreta Rourke, *Personalism*, xi.

entire social order. As the criminal justice system became more centralized, criminal law evolved into a depersonalized process, with a focus on the abstractions of criminal law procedure, rather than the costs to human persons (victims and offenders) and local communities.[17] By keeping the person at the center, perhaps we can arrive at a criminal justice reform framework that reduces criminal activity and dismantles recidivism. Incarceration should be the last resort for keeping communities safe, rather than a knee-jerk response to violations of the social contract.

What is personalism? There are both religious and nonreligious conceptions of personalism that developed in the West during the twentieth century that could be useful for the various contours of criminal justice. For the purpose of this book I am drawing heavily from nonreligious sociological and political accounts of personhood as a way to create space for a common entry point into the discourse from various and diverse perspectives. Rourke and Chazarreta Rourke explain that immediately after World War I, personalism caught on as a movement intellectually led by philosopher Emmanuel Mounier.[18] Personalism arose to challenge the depersonalizations and dehumanization of war and a social order that was becoming more and more urbanized, mechanized, and industrialized. A person had become a means to an economic and political end rather than an individual. Rourke explains, "for Mounier, a person was a living center of creative activity, communication, and commitment who comes to know himself across the bridge of action. Free, creative, and acting persons were to unite with others to create in which the structures, customs, and institutions are rooted in and revolve around the person as the center."[19]

This is a realist view of a person that assumes human action, motivations, intentions, and ontology matter for conceptions of justice and human flourishing. Smith argues that human flourishing must orient its discourse around three central questions: What are the interests and motivations that drive human action? What are true human goods? What can account for the existence of evil?[20] According to Smith, when conceptualizing human flourishing, much of sociological thought is unconcerned with human motivations or the "microfoundations" of human social interaction beyond a "rational-choice perspective."[21] Smith highlights the importance of human motivations, saying that if humans lack motivations, "then their status as particular objects is diminished. People become mere subjects."[22] The issue of motivation has direct consequences for how humans are treated in society.

---

[17] William J. Stuntz, *The Collapse of American Criminal Justice* (Cambridge, MA: Belknap Press of Harvard University Press, 2011), 287–312.
[18] Rourke and Chazarreta Rourke, *Personalism*, 7.
[19] Ibid.
[20] Smith, *Flourish*, 1.
[21] Ibid., 2.
[22] Ibid., 3.

Furthermore, Smith explains the need to address human goods and determine what human needs are in the interpretation of what is good for the person and for society. He critiques the Western displacement of good with right, arguing that true human interests must be understood in order to actually prefer liberal values over antiliberal values. The fact stands that there are set human values that must be explored and pursued. Finally, Smith insists that sociological accounts must address the reality of evil and human failure. Theories that fail to address the problem of evil must either embrace moral relativism or skepticism.[23] As such, from a personalist perspective, criminal justice reform must keep the person at the center while considering the interests and motivations that drive human action, the true "good" nature of humans, and what can account for the existence of evil.

Personalism understands humans to be "natural-goods-seeking persons."[24] We need to therefore understand what it means to be a person that wants to make radical progress with criminal justice reform because offenders are persons before they are anything else. Smith correctly observes that only by understanding the personhood of human beings will we adequately be able to understand and explain people and their social relations, because humans cannot be properly understood apart from their personhood.[25] Personalism demands an account of who persons are and that account will necessarily have profound moral, political, and social implications.[26] Furthermore, personalism advances a theory of human good and happiness that draws on ancient accounts of human flourishing. Smith argues that there are "multiple, basic human motivations for action," and these motivations inform the teleology of the person.[27] These motivations are important to consider because they shape how we come to understand deviance. Understanding these motivations will allow us to create realistic goals for offenders in the criminal justice system during and after incarceration ends. Personalism believes that people, by extension, do have an ontology.[28]

Human beings depend on their social lives for their existential development but are ontologically dependent on no one for their personal being. Smith observes, personalism recognizes that "all persons are radically dependent upon the social for their existential development and flourishing, but persons are not dependent on the social for their ontological personal being."[29] Essentially, humans do not need anything from society to be persons, but they do need society's help to flourish and to fully self-actualize. This distinction requires an understanding of the differences "between being and becoming, ontology and existence, the real and the

---

[23] Ibid., 4.
[24] Ibid., 8.
[25] Ibid., 9.
[26] Ibid.
[27] Ibid., 10.
[28] Rourke and Chazarreta Rourke, *Personalism*, 27.
[29] Smith, *Flourish*, 10.

actual, full potential and variable realization."[30] Human action and practices are driven, then, by "real motivations and interests that are grounded in the nature of reality"[31] and a necessity to identify and understand if we wish to comprehend and explain social life, social structures, and how we need to reform the criminal justice system. Furthermore, personalism reintroduces morality into social science, and "it rejects the modern divorce of *is* from *ought*, fact from value. It recognizes that many descriptive claims entail concepts and ideas that raise ... normative claims."[32] Finally, personalism revives the tension between the good and evil elements of human existence and reconciles the increasing divide between modern optimistic and pessimistic accounts of social life. The very ideas and judgments about why society must reform the criminal justice system presuppose some notion of what is good and right for offenders, in relation to which "other things are judged to be exploitative and oppressive."[33] These matters demand that we know something about human nature and under what circumstances we thrive, as well as those circumstances that undermine human flourishing. These questions provide a map for the kinds of policies we need to legislate, and a map for seriously considering the expertise and limitations of various spheres in civil society with respect to what realistic role they can play at preventing crime and reforming offenders who violate the social contract and cause harm to their neighbors. These questions do not necessarily translate into specific public policies, but rather they appeal to the need of prudential judgment that investigates whether or not our criminal justice reform proposals take human motivations, the nature of good, and the reality of evil seriously as a lens through which we determine if a policy or program is best, given the ontology of the human person.[9] Personalism helps us consider criminal justice reform on an individual level as well as the level of reciprocity found among members of a community.

The notion that men, women, and youth are potentially being exploited or oppressed by the criminal justice system presupposes notions of what is good and right with human beings, what it means to be human, what is beneficial for humans, what is harmful to humans, and so on.[34] Again for Smith and others in the personalist tradition, ontology, by extension, cannot be dismissed. Every theory about human flourishing presupposes some ontology about people; however, what matters is whether or not those presuppositions are explicitly articulated at the outset. Criminal justice reform will not make much progress moving forward unless all interested parties are willing to bring their ontological assumptions about the personhood of offenders and victims out into the open and test them openly with what human persons are actually like. Following Smith, this book takes a critical

---

[30] Ibid., 10.
[31] Ibid., 12.
[32] Ibid., 13.
[33] Ibid., 24.
[34] Ibid., 17.

realist approach to criminal justice reform. Critical realism believes that much of reality exists and operates independent of human experience, that human knowledge about this reality is always historically and socially situated and conceptually mediated.[35] Therefore, says Smith, "we must inquire into matters such as what human beings are, ontologically, what causes their actions, and what is in fact good and bad for humans to the limits of our ability to understand such concerns."[36] Personalism, then, is driven by a realist account of what persons are ontologically, what persons are capable of causally, how finite persons are limited in their causal capacities, and what personhood entails as genuine goods to pursue teleologically. In personalism, the natural character, capacities, tendencies, interests, and ends of humans, and the constructed cultural and institutional outcomes to which those naturally give rise, are what organize and shape how personalism describes and explains human life. The cultures and the social, economic, and political institutions and structures, or processes that people develop and pass on, are first and ultimately made sense of by the nature, capacities, goods, and limits of human persons.[37]

Personalism, then, rejects any individualistic account of human life. Individualism reduces the notion of our common human flourishing as mere means of attaining an individualistic, if not a narcissistic, pursuit of what is good.[38] Moreover, individualism in both economic and political theory states that the good of the whole is defined by what is good for individuals disconnected from the good of others combined with the false notions that humans are autonomous and can thrive as independent individuals free from the active participation of others.[39] It must be understood and accepted that humans are not merely individuals. Humans are ontological persons who are dependent on others for their social fulfillment, which leads to individual flourishing. Rourke and Chazarreta Rourke argue that "as a social being, the human person requires a civil life within which he realizes his proper nature as oriented to community. The person needs to live well, not simply in his capacity as a private individual but precisely as member of the community."[40] The community has a need to thrive and flourish in solidarity with all of its members. Criminal law, and criminal justice reform by extension, should direct the offender, as a person, to realizing his or her place as a contributing member to the community. It is the emphasis on community that is required of our civic institutions. Reforming criminal procedure statutes and adjudication processes alone are inadequate for properly recognizing the full humanity of those who receive the interventions of crime prevention as well the reform proposals of ex-offenders. The

[35] Ibid., 13.
[36] Ibid., 13.
[37] Ibid., 30.
[38] Rourke and Chazarreta Rourke, *Personalism*, 55.
[39] Ibid., 55.
[40] Ibid., 67.

criminal justice system cannot address the ontological and teleological needs of the human alone. A primary presupposition of this book, based on personalism, is that persons are free centers of responsible activity and can be intrinsically interested in helping others in the community flourish as well.[41]

What is a person? The definition of what it means to be human is central to criminal justice reform if those reforms point us to what is best for people integrally interconnected with others in the community. This book uses Smith's definition of what it means to be human as its operational anthropology. For Smith:

> By person I mean a conscious, self-transcending center of subjective experience, durable identity, moral, commitment, and social communication who – as the efficient cause of his or her own responsible actions and interactions – exercises complex capacities for agency and intersubjectivity in order to develop and sustain his or her own incommunicable self in loving relationships with other personal selves and with the nonpersonal world.[42]

It is the beyond the scope of this book to unpack the details of Smith's account of this definition, but for the purposes of this book I want readers to understand that when I talk about human persons I mean something specific. This book presupposed that human beings have certain capacities and are, by definition, dependently social creatures "steeped in personal social relationships as a good end in itself, because that is what any normal, thriving person is and does."[43] The purpose of our humanity is to develop and unfold our personhood that move us toward, argues Smith, "personal excellence, thriving, flourishing."[44] In our uniqueness, particularity, and historical situatedness, we are "unrepeatable and inalienable."[45] The dignity of persons demands, I argue following Smith, that reducing prison population numbers is not enough, nor is it a good goal. Criminal justice reform is but one variable in the equation of what is necessary for human flourishing because persons are dependent members of a community. Our imagination for reforming the system must begin with human dignity, which will include policy changes but also many other considerations that require the expertise of the institutions of civil society because humans are inherently social creatures, according to the definition I am using in this book.

Why does anthropology matter? Anthropology matters because our criminal justice devolved into a labeling system that redefined the humanity of people who broke the law. Once new labels were assigned to criminal deviants, they then became much more complacent about using the law to control "criminals" to keep our communities safe. Once offenders lost labels associated with human dignity,

---

[41] Ibid., 68.
[42] Smith, What Is a Person?, 61.
[43] Smith, *Flourish*, 47.
[44] Ibid., 52.
[45] Ibid., 53.

social decision-makers, lawmakers, and voters at-large became increasing agnostic and disinterested, following the social turbulence of the 1960s, about the quality of our criminal justice system. The level of contempt and disdain for offenders has a long history in American society. As a society, we have very little patience for deviance and people who make unwise decisions, so if criminals end up in a dysfunctional and oppressive criminal justice system, "well, so be it," as some might argue. "Criminals are getting what they deserve." Jails and prisons, then, are places where we lock up the "rabble." The "rabble" are the deviants in our society. John Irwin famously categorized them as people who are detached and held in disrepute.[46] Criminal deviants are detached from and not well-integrated into the prosocial norms of conventional society, and they are disputable because they are evil, disgraceful, inhumane, offensive, dangerous, threatening, untrustworthy, rabble-rousing, unruly, treacherous, destroyers of the common good, and so on. And we must do whatever we can to keep our communities free of them and our children as far away from them as possible. Therefore, we lock up the rabble as we have always done in America since the nation open prisons first established by Christians.[47]

OUTLINE OF THE BOOK

The book is divided into two parts. The Part I explores the policy challenges many have suggested are a necessary part of criminal justice reform that need immediate attention. The first of the book is introductory in nature and serves to provide the larger historical context that others have highlighted consolidated into a single location. Chapter 1 opens the book by stating the problem and challenges with overcriminalization. The chapter includes a discussion of the expansion of the definition of "crime" without exacting requirements of intentionality, and the power of state and federal agencies to send someone to prison for infractions that would not constitute individual crimes. Chapter 2 offers a discussion about the role of prosecutorial discretion in the juvenile and adult criminal justice systems. The chapter highlights, among other things, that prosecutorial overreach disproportionality affects those living in rural and urban settings. Chapter 3 addresses the role of judicial discretion. The chapter wrestles with the question: "Do our punishments fit their crimes?" Across this country defendants are condemned to years, decades, or even life in prison for minor infractions because of minimum sentencing statutes. Giving judges more discretion in sentence can alleviate the burdens of mass incarceration among other things. Chapter 4 explores the disparities in the quality of criminal defense, especially for the criminals who are economically challenged.

---

[46] John Irwin, *The Jail: Managing the Underclass in American Society* (Berkeley, CA: University of California Press: 2013), 2.

[47] Harry Elmer Barnes, "Historical Origin of the Prison System in America." *Journal of the American Institute of Criminal Law and Criminology* 12 (1921): 45–50; Irwin, *The Jail*, 3–8.

Defendants who are on the lower end of the socioeconomic scale find themselves at the mercy of public defenders who are swamped with cases and are often disinterested and unqualified. Research shows that even before mass incarceration accelerated in the 1980s, overburdened systems of indigent defense struggled to meet the Sixth Amendment constitutional mandate. States are unable to fund adequate indigent defense systems or provide sufficient resources for oversight, training, and management of cases.

Part II of the book expands the discussion beyond the issues related to the adjudication process to include the role of civil society institutions like education, the family, nonprofit organizations, and models of reform that are working well in some states. Chapter 5 explores the connection between education outcomes as a predictor of deviance, especially in low-income communities. Nationally, on any given night, approximately 81,000 youth are confined to juvenile facilities and 10,000 children are held in adult jails and prisons. Approximately one in ten young male high school dropouts is incarcerated or in juvenile detention. For African Americans, that number is one in four. Increasingly, school districts are arresting children for behavior problems that are not criminal. For example, research shows that just over 2 million youth under the age of eighteen were arrested in 2008. Of these 2 million, about 95 percent had not been accused of violent crimes. In 2010, of the nearly 100,000 youth under the age of eighteen who were serving time in a juvenile residential placement facility, 26 percent had been convicted of property crimes only, such as burglary, arson, or theft. Chapter 6 highlights an often-missed variable in the reform discourse, namely the social, moral, and economic costs of overcriminalization and mass incarceration. This chapter explores how overcriminalization significantly undermines human flourishing and social well-being by harming the family, social networks, social citizenship, and removes capable men and women from using their creative capacities in the marketplace. Chapter 7 profiles a number of states that are moving in helpful directions. Since nearly 90 percent of all prisoners in the United States are in state facilities, the work that states are doing to reduce their prison populations is the foundation to reform. This chapter highlights a few effective reform initiatives from a number of states across the country. Chapter 8 provides examples of the role that nonprofits are playing in keeping people out of the criminal justice and, once in, keep offenders from reoffending and trapped in cycles of offending, incarceration, probation, and parole. This chapter highlights a number of the most progressive civil-society and nonprofit solutions to overcriminalization that are making a real difference. These are the types of programs that need to be replicated throughout the country.

The problem of overcriminalization will be solved through a thorough examination of the nexus of individual and societal interests and concerns. Trends of industrialization within the criminal justice system must be offset by a new and enlightened evolution of the role of civil society in implementing both civil systems *and* government policies which intersect to define our modern civilization.

We often celebrate the successes of our society in technology advancement, competitive endeavors, cultural wonders and international dominance in military and economic affairs. Bringing down the jail and prison population is possible, immediately necessary, and a responsibility for all of us to understand and support. Analysis of each major component of the criminal justice reform issue provide excellent strategies for taking apart the system that is casting a shadow on the potential of some of our most dynamic populations of citizens.

PART I

1

An Overcriminalized America

At the end of 2014, there were 1,561,500 individuals held in prisons in America.[1] Ninety-six percent of those individuals had terms that were longer than twelve months. At year-end 2013, there were an estimated 6,899,000 individuals in correctional systems across America.[2] One in thirty-five adults was under some form of correctional supervision in 2013.

The percentage of imprisoned Americans may not seem high, but it is indeed extremely high. The United States accounts for about 22 percent of the world's prison population.[3] To help bring this number down, some have suggested that the American justice system must focus on reducing mandatory minimums, reforming laws currently on the books, and eliminating unnecessary laws. With so many laws on both a state and federal level, the harsh reality seems true to the words of Joseph Stalin's chief of police, Lavrentiy Beria: "Show me the man, and I will find you the crime." In the United States especially, we have a misconception that justice is common, and that we have the fairest justice system in the world. However, this is not the case. With harsher criminal laws and overly punitive statutes beginning in the 1970s, the United States greatly increased its prison population and its attitude toward offenders, leading to massive increases in the number of Americans in the criminal justice system.

Lost in the nightmarish procedural malaise, millions of lives are destroyed because of overcriminalization. When voters think of criminal laws and offenders, they perceive citizens that are better off being removed from society. As a result, offenders have lost their humanity and their identity. The fact remains that it is

---

[1] "Prisoners in 2014," Bureau of Justice Statistics, published September 2015. www.bjs.gov/content/pub/pdf/p14.pdf.

[2] "Correctional Populations in the United States," Bureau of Justice Statistics, published December 2014. www.bjs.gov/content/pub/pdf/cpus13.pdf.

[3] "World Prison Population List," International Centre for Prison Studies, published September 30, 2013. www.prisonstudies.org/sites/default/files/resources/downloads/wppl_10.pdf.

incredibly hard for offenders to find jobs after being released from prison. After all, who would want to employ a convicted felon when there are plenty of other citizens in the job market?

This attitude inevitably leads to discouragement among offenders, leading to additional criminal behavior. If they are not able to find a job or receive student and housing loans, what incentive is there for them to stop committing crimes? If anything, the cultural and economic ostracization of these citizens directly leads to them committing more crime. Thus, the first step is to incentivize individuals to commit less crime. While this is the goal, the War on Drugs levies extremely harsh penalties against all offenders without hope of successfully reintegrating into society after their release. In this way, the War on Drugs accomplished its goal of imprisoning drug offenders, but it gave them no hope of achieving a normal life outside of prison. Thus, the ex-convicts became reoffenders, entire communities were decimated, and generations of families were destroyed. The punitive disposition toward offenders, especially in low-income communities, has ultimately created a permanent underclass that will only grow and continue the pattern of incarceration, cyclical drug use, low education, and underemployment.

For example, if a youth commits a nonviolent drug-related crime, he or she will most likely have multiple opportunities stripped away from them, many of them permanently. American youths with criminal records in some states can have extreme limitations on their voting rights, educational opportunities, and employment by the time they are adults. If the goal of criminalization is to encourage better behavior, we should not be taking away the very qualities that are meant to help our young adults succeed in society.

Another damaging aspect of overcriminalization is the effect on the family. On the level of the offender, he or she is negatively affected by being apart from their family. The intention here is that the offender is punished for their actions. But this also punishes the offender's family. For many families, especially single-parent families, this individual is the only source of income. Imprisoning the parent removes the only source of income and increases the chances that the kids will get into trouble as well as perform poorly in school.

When we look at the purpose of law, we see there are five reasons why we punish offenders: deterrence, incapacitation, rehabilitation, retribution, and restitution. As we have learned from the outcome of the failed War on Drugs, deterrence has completely failed. Another area where our system has failed is in rehabilitation. We can now see the damage done to countless American families not only because of drugs but also because of the lack of success in rehabilitating individuals who wish to recover from drugs. Even thirty years after we began strong drug criminalization, the United States has not found a way to successfully rehabilitate drug users and reintegrate them back into society. In fact, what we have done is simply used the threat of incarceration as a means of social control in our society, targeted at those groups that the middle and upper classes tend to label as problems in need of containment.

We have also failed with retribution. Retribution, ideally, removes the desire to commit future crimes by removing the need for personal vengeance. However, many offenders are left with nothing after they are removed from prison. Many return to deviance and crime because they have no hope of achieving success after their sentence. How can we expect offenders to contribute to society if we remove the tools that enable them to succeed? If we strip them of their personal liberties, such as their ability to vote and receive student and property loans, we are incentivizing these former offenders to return to crime. In their eyes, criminality is the only activity they can pursue. This is the opposite of the retributive approach that the law ought to create.

The systematic bureaucracy continues to strip offenders of their civil liberties because we often feel like these people have not paid restitution to society. Somehow we believe we have lost something when these individuals commit crimes. In some cases, we do, such as when murderers take lives, or robbers take property. However, a drug offender's biggest offense is against themselves. More importantly, why do we believe these offenders ought to pay so much restitution for offenses that they are committing against themselves? Society's perception of offenders is often dehumanizing. Rather than approaching offenders with hopes of reintegration, we treat them like badly behaved house pets who need to be yelled at, or at worst punished with physical pain.

Incapacitation, which prevents crime by removing the offender from society, is the only area where we have succeeded as a society. Many people believe that offenders have broken the rules, and so they must be kept away from law-abiding citizens. Even then, we have not accomplished our goal. With minimum sentencing laws, we must remove many offenders for a mandatory amount of time. But what if sentencing would not benefit a particular individual? Should we not judge each case on the merits of the specific circumstances? It would make much more sense to employ the punishment to commit the crime, rather than blanketing all offenders with minimum laws that may or may not help the individual.

The purpose of incapacitation is to remove the offender from society so they do not cause harm. However, if this is the case, we cannot expect them to contribute to society after release. Most often, prisons are located far outside urban areas, away from families and institutions that can assist offenders in rehabilitation. If we remove individuals because they are a threat to society, we ought to do a better job of encouraging them to contribute to society in productive ways rather than moving them to the outskirts of society. We cannot expect offenders to successfully participate in society after such a banishment.

WHAT SHOULD WE CRIMINALIZE?

We have shown that overcriminalization is a major issue in our society. But what should we criminalize, and are there any laws that should be decriminalized? In order to discover what laws are efficient, we can look to the costs and benefits of the law. If the costs outweigh the benefits of a particular law or individual prosecution, it is inefficient. Many nonviolent offenders could be put into this category. Is it more efficient to lock these people up? Or would it be more efficient to establish a treatment program so that they could succeed and move past the problems that led them to crime? We should be able to devote resources to methods that are successful. When treatment becomes a priority, the institutions that are best at delivering effective treatments over the long-run must be used. With drug offenders making up close to half of the US federal prison population, this approach would significantly reduce the inefficiency of the federal prison system.

Paul Larkin argues that overcriminalization is manifested in unnecessary criminal statutes.[4] He posits that some of these statutes are either redundant, not historically blameworthy, or simply increase the penalty for an act that is already outlawed. However, he argues that legislators and the creation of new criminal laws are the biggest factors to blame for overcriminalization. When it comes to new criminal legislation, the cost of creating new laws is relatively low. Making an activity illegal does not mean that the legislator has to learn anything about the specific act. Often, it is other agencies or bureaucrats that create the legislation, and legislators simply vote on it.

One main reason legislators are now accountable for the creation of new laws is that prisoners and felons cannot vote. Because felons are stripped of their voting rights, there is little accountability for the legislators to act in the interest of helping the population of offenders reintegrate successfully. Legislators, who are interested in getting reelected, usually only appeal to people who have the ability to vote for them. Because felons are not a part of the voting populace, legislators have no incentive to appeal to felons.

Additionally, many legislators feel pressure from the voting populace when it comes to criminalization. No legislator wants to be known as "the man who let felons go free" or "the woman who decriminalized something and *x* happened as a result." For legislators, it is much safer to continue criminalizing. From their perspective, they wonder why they should fight for offenders when they are degrading to society. Why help the small number of people who are hurting the rest? These are the types of questions legislators asks themselves, disregarding the rights and dignity of offendors in the process.

---

[4] Paul J. Larkin, "Public Choice Theory and Overcriminalization." *Harvard Journal of Law and Public Policy* 36, no. 715 (2013): 736.

In early November 2015, the Department of Justice released nearly 6,000 nonviolent drug offenders. *The Washington Post* called it the largest one-time release of federal prisoners.[5] Many hope this will be the first domino to fall in the game of crime reduction. It is clear that this is a bipartisan issue, much like the War on Drugs was a bipartisan issue in the 1980s. Republicans and Democrats had agreed that there should be a War on Drugs, but now the majority of representatives in both parties agree that the penalties are too harsh and that we need to temper the law with prudence. When deciding what to criminalize, many believe that legislators should focus more on tangible change rather than on the harsh punishments now in place. In the past, the law has not been flexible enough to take into account certain details regarding individual circumstances surrounding criminal behavior. There is a stronger movement now to correct these injustices so that offenders who are seen as low risk are able to be released from prison sooner so they can reintegrate and begin contributing to society again.

It is important that people have the proper motivations to make contributions to the common good and the prosperity of their communities. This cannot happen with offenders in prison serving sentences that are disproportionate to their crimes. In order for society to be more efficient and for a greater amount of social welfare to come about, we should be striving to help our offendors reintegrate into society. At the moment, offendors are disconnected from society when they are released from prison. The combination of isolation and lengthy prison sentences makes for culturally illiterate offendors who have little hope of becoming normal citizens.

For most offenders, prison does nothing to help them personally. To the contrary: the harsh environment creates new stresses that are debilitating and accelerate the problems which led to incarceration. Prison is a place where offenders lose their humanity in ways much worse than prior to entering the system. A strong case could be made that most nonviolent individuals are better off staying in society and participating in a civil-society program rather than being alienated from other people and quarantined with violent offenders. Some have made the case that the incarceration of nonviolent offenders could actually be disallowed under the Eighth Amendment and the "cruel and unusual punishment clause."[6] A further analysis of the Eighth Amendment would give more power to the courts in their ability to deem certain incarcerations cruel or unusual punishments for a given crime.

The biggest catalyst for overcriminalization is nonviolent drug offenders. Scholars and social justice advocates consistently point to nonviolent offenders as the segment that should be decriminalized the most. This is because their negative effect on society is much more indirect and hard to realize. In addition, it is hard for the

---

[5] "Justice Department Set to Free 6,000 Prisoners, Largest One-Time Release," *The Washington Post,* published October 6, 2015. www.washingtonpost.com/world/national-security/justice-department-about-to-free-6000-prisoners.

[6] Paul J. Larkin, "Strict Liability Offenses, Incarceration and the Cruel and Unusual Punishments Clause." *Harvard Journal of Law and Public Policy* 37, no. 1065 (2014): 1105.

government to produce a tangible reason, backed up with a common law under-standing, of what these nonviolent offenders are doing wrong. In the eyes of many, these nonviolent offenders are breaking the law, but are not offenders.

John Pfaff and others make the case that the narrative regarding our prison growth explosion occurring on the heels of the War on Drugs is an error. In his 2015 article "The War on Drugs and Prison Growth: Limited Importance, and Limited Legislative Options," Pfaff highlights that overall only 17 percent of prison-ers are serving time for drug offenses and that drug offenders in prison only explains about 22 percent of prison growth. In fact, if all black drug offense prisoners were released today, the black prison population would drop by 1.4 percent. According to Pfaff, it is the conduct of prosecutors that has driven prison growth in recent decades, not drug policy. Prosecutors have been much more aggressive in "throw-ing the book" at people, and that has had significant consequences. Pfaff and others observe that while the War on Drugs may not have grown the prison population it may have created more collateral social and economic costs such as reducing health outcomes for the poor, removing men from the labor market, destabilizing families and social networks, and destroying civic participation, which induces antisocial and criminal behavior. In the end, the War on Drugs has clearly undermined civil society and made many low-income communities much worse off.

In addition, more than one-third of imprisoned nonviolent drug offenders are first-time offenders. The real question we should be asking is whether these individuals should truly be classified as offenders or not. Insofar as these individ-uals are breaking penal code, they are offenders. However, *ought* they to be called offenders? If the penal code is unjust, those who are punished under that code will have been punished unjustly. With such a high number of nonviolent offenders in prison, we need to revisit our criminal laws and seriously consider what we deem to be punishable by law and what we believe ought to be criminal law.

DEFINING OVERCRIMINALIZATION

Overcriminalization is a relatively new term for American citizens. Many commen-tators on criminalization and criminal justice have outlined the problems of mass incarceration. In a sense, the problem of mass incarceration is caused by overcriminalization.

Overcriminalization can be understood in several ways. Douglas Husak argues that there are multiple ways that overcriminalization is unjust. The first is the criminalization of things that should not be criminalized. Husak argues that we use punishments to a level that is unjust for many people who break the law. Rather than enforcing justice through the law, we are enforcing the law, absent of any objective sense of justice. The second way we can understand overcriminalization is the sheer number of criminal laws. Husak argues that we have far too many laws. The sheer scope of criminal laws is unjust.[7]

Overcriminalization is a new term because it is hard to compare it against an objective standard. How many laws are too many? Objectively, we may claim that we have many laws, but we cannot say there are too many, because we have no way of substantiating these claims with data. Husak suggests a theory of criminalization which argues that we indeed have too much criminalization.

The fact is that philosophers and legal scholars do have a standard for criminalization: justice. However, this is not a concept that is objective when it comes to voters and legislators. This makes it even more difficult to enforce laws based on a standard of justice, as it is not objective in the eyes of voters and legislators. Thus, the burden of proof is on those who claim that we indeed have overcriminalization. It is up to those individuals to prove that America has more criminal laws than necessary. A standard must be formed if there is to be a case made that our nation is overcriminalized.

In 2014, 612 individuals were imprisoned per 100,000 residents. Thus, one in 163 American citizens is in prison every year. While this simple statistic may not be enough to prove that we are overcriminalized, it does seem to be a shockingly high number. At that number, every American should know someone who is in prison. It has also been shown that minorities are more statistically represented in prisons. The statistics get even worse when it comes to minority males. At year-end 2014, imprisonment rates for blacks were 3.8 to 10.5 times higher than for whites and 1.4 to 3.1 higher for Hispanics and any given age group.[8] This shows that minorities are disproportionately represented in prison populations, both federally and on a state level. What is shocking is that many of these imprisoned minorities are young people. According to the Bureau of Justice Statistics (BJS), black males aged eighteen to nineteen are ten times more likely to be imprisoned than whites (1,072 prisoners per 100,000 black males as opposed to 102 per 100,000 whites).[9]

There are also a large number of individuals who are under the jurisdiction of the criminal justice system, mainly probation and parole, not just prisons and jails. According to the BJS, 6,899,000 persons were supervised by correctional systems across America. That translates to one in thirty-five Americans, or 2.8 percent.[10] Many Americans ignore probation and parole because they do not see this as punishment in a strict sense. They see it as lenient and more rehabilitative than

---

[7] Douglas Husak, *Overcriminalization: The Limits of the Criminal Law* (New York, NY: Oxford University Press, 2008), 17, 31.
[8] "Prisoners in 2014," Bureau of Justice Statistics, published September 2015. www.bjs.gov/content/pub/pdf/p14.pdf, 15.
[9] "Correctional Populations in the US, 2013," Bureau of Justice Statistics, published December 2014. www.bjs.gov/content/pub/pdf/p13.pdf, 8.
[10] Prisoners in 2013," Bureau of Justice Statistics, published September 2014. www.bjs.gov/content/pub/pdf/p13.pdf, 1.

punitive. American society as a whole has a skewed concept of punitive action when it comes to parole and probation. In addition, the punishment for violating parole or probation is incarceration. Rather than encouraging good behavior and discouraging bad, we seem to only be concerned with preventing more bad behavior, which often backfires.

Since the 1970s, the number of individuals in the justice system has continued to grow. The size of the American prison population has increased nearly 400 percent since 1980.[11] This unprecedented expansion is a telling trend of overcriminalization. While it is not a strict definition of what overcriminalization is, it does quantify that we are criminalizing more than ever before. We also detain more individuals than other international countries. America is responsible for 22 percent of the world's prison population. The United States has an incarceration rate nearly five times higher than any other Westernized industrial country in the world. Husak asks a critical question that can frame this discussion: "[W]hy [do] we resort to punishment more readily than other countries generally and Western Europe in particular?"[12] Our tendency toward harsh criminalization and a greater number of criminal laws in comparison to European justice systems sheds light on the fact that the United States is guilty of overcriminalization.

Americans understand prison, parole, and probation as necessary evils. Yet we are not upset by prison rape culture, which is more likely to be the punchline of a joke than a serious topic for discussion. Americans seem to think that because the individual is in prison, they deserve anything that happens to them. Yet, implicit in this assumption is that everyone who is in prison deserves to be there. This is an incorrect, and dangerous, assumption. Many assume that the vast amount of criminalization is good because it provides a social good, improving the lives of law abiding citizens. However, the case can be made that an increase in criminalization is actually detrimental to society. As some point, we will not be able to adequately manage our prison populations. Many make the case that this has already happened and that we no longer efficiently control our criminal justice system.

Unfortunately, we tend to throw away human dignity in favor of getting tough on crime. Nothing is inherently surprising about this reaction, unless our beliefs of what offenders deserve is not actually what they deserve. The problem is not that our sense of justice tells us that they should be punished, but rather the way in which we go about punishing offenders. Punishment ought only to be served when it is just and if it is not, it is therefore unjust. The goal here is to show that many of the punishments we hold now are indeed unjust and do not adequately reflect or fulfill the purpose of punishment.

---

[11] "Trend in US Corrections," The Sentencing Project, Updated 2015. http://sentencingproject.org/doc/publications/inc_Trends_in_Corrections_Fact_sheet.pdf, 1, 2.

[12] Husak, *Overcriminalization*, 5.

Even if one is not convinced by the moral argument here, there is a cost analysis that is compelling as well. Everyone almost always considers the costs of any decision, whether they are explicit or implicit. This is often reflected in the price of a good. It is necessary for consumers to know the cost of goods to make choices and decisions. Almost all people would argue that we should try to be more efficient with any resources that we have. The justice system should be no different. If we could be more efficient with dollars spent on our justice system, by all means it is imperative that this become a priority. In 2011, the fee to cover the average cost of incarceration for federal inmates was $28,893.40.[13] On a state level, the average annual cost per inmate is $31,286.[14] In New York, the cost per inmate is more than $60,000. Most citizens would agree that these costs are extraordinarily and surprisingly high. In 2014, the median household income was $53,657.[15] This means that for New York, as well as many other states, the cost of maintaining prisoners is higher than or nearly as high as the median income of an average citizen.

As the number of federal prisoners grows, increasing tenfold since 1980, the Department of Justice will continue to spend more and more money on housing federal prisoners. Currently, 25 percent of the DOJ budget is spent on taking care of federal prisoners. This takes money away from other programs that could be contributing to progress in our society. In addition, the fiscal impact of an increasing prison population has ballooned federal and state budgets. By 2020, an estimated $6.9 billion will be spent by the Bureau of Prisons (BOP), which is nearly 30 percent of the Department of Justice's budget.[16] This trend is only rising; every year, a greater percentage of the DOJ's budget is spent by the BOP. This is a testament to how an increasing amount of money is required for prison upkeep. This decreases the amount of money that can be allocated for other critical parts of the DOJ budget, such as allocations for probation and parole.

---

[13] "Annual Determination of Average Cost of Incarceration," Prisons Bureau, published March 18, 2013. www.federalregister.gov/articles/2013/03/18/2013-06139/annual-determination-of-average-cost-of-incarceration.

[14] "The Price of Prisons: What Incarceration Costs Taxpayers," VERA Institute of Justice, updated July 20, 2012. www.vera.org/sites/default/files/resources/downloads/price-of-prisons-updated-version-021914.pdf, 9.

[15] "Income and Poverty in the United States: 2014," United States Census Bureau, issued September 2015. www.census.gov/content/dam/Census/library/publications/2015/demo/p60-252.pdf, 5.

[16] "The Growth and Increasing Cost of the Federal Prison System: Drivers and Potential Solutions," *Urban Institute*, published December 11, 2012. www.urban.org/research/publica tion/growth-increasing-cost-federal-prison-system-drivers-and-potential-solutions/view/full_ report, 2.

MOVING TOWARD A THEORY OF CRIMINALIZATION?

There are several questions we can ask to discover a theory of criminalization and determine what is and is not a crime.[17]

- Is the act inherently wrong and ought it to be prohibited in every circumstance? Does the act threaten the public or individuals?
- Would civil penalties be effective in deterring the act?
- Do the costs to the taxpayers of investigating, prosecuting, charging, and imprisoning the individual outweigh the benefits to society?
- Was there intent to commit the crime?
- Must the individual be incarcerated, or would probation, parole, or a drug court be more fitting and proper for the individual's case?
- Is the act a misdemeanor or a felony, as felonies create a restriction of constitutional and personal liberties?

These types of questions can launch a more robust understanding of what a crime is and how we go about punishing crimes and penalizing offenders.

Douglas Husak argues that overcriminalization is objectionable precisely because it produces too much punishment. While overcriminalization affects other citizens in society, the primary victims of overcriminalization are "persons who incur penal liability."[18] When punishments are enforced for conduct that fails to meet the standard of criminalization, this is considered overcriminalization. According to this standard, many laws in America would be unjust because of their failure to satisfy the hypothesis of overcriminalization.

In addition to producing too much punishment, overcriminalization can also include problems regarding the proportional punishment of crimes. Husak calls this the *principle of proportionality*, which states that the acuteness of the sentence should correspond with the severity of the crime. Under this thesis, disproportionate punishment is unwarranted and therefore unjust. Husak argues that because justice system has no principle of proportionality, a large number of injustices have taken place in the system. Overcriminalization ensures that this trend will continue unless attention is brought to this issue.

In a simple, direct correlation, as laws increase, punishment increases. If Husak is correct, too many laws result in too much punishment. His philosophical and moral justification for this is that "we should care about injustice and its victims."[19] Really, we should wonder why this has not become a more prevalent issue prior to this crisis point. Husak first questions what factors created this

---

[17] "Criminalizing America – How Big Government Makes a Criminal Out of Every American," *American Legislative Exchange Council,* published November 12, 2013. www.alec.org/article/criminalizing-america/, 9.

[18] Husak, *Overcriminalization,* 14.

[19] Ibid.

problem, and second, he wonders why academics have been so quiet about this obviously unsustainable predicament.

It is very troubling the level to which criminal justice has become a political issue. More and more we expect our problems to be solved by the government. As we trend toward more government intervention, we expect the government to intervene in many areas of life where personal responsibility and civil engagement should be paramount. The criminal justice system is no different. The nature of our criminal justice has certainly been effective in locking away those who are dangerous to society but has also done a lot of harm to families and individuals who need help instead of punishment. Americans continue to seek out political answers for a deeper problem that should be solved through civil institutions. Like many issues in our modern society, we mistakenly turn to the government to answer our prayers. One of the hardest things about overcriminalization in particular is that there is not a lot of scholarly research on the topic and there are few who can present an accurate, adequate argument for a particular action. This has led to politicians taking a "better more than less" approach to law enforcement. By casting a wide net, the government has caught many individuals who are offenders, but also some who do not deserve to be punished harshly, and in some cases, not at all. The justice community in government has also made the net tightly woven, leaving little room for judicial discretion and personal, circumstantial defense. Harsh policies and sentences have been implemented to such a significant degree, the criminal justice system has caught a lot of small fish who do not belong in the net.

Unfortunately, penal populism has led to Republicans and Democrats competing for who is going to have a larger role in being harsh on crime. Since the 1980s, both Republicans and Democrats have fought over who will win the battle of being tough on crime and proving that they have a proven track record of being tough on crime. Ironically, over thirty years later, both Republicans and Democrats are fighting who will take the biggest steps in addressing mass incarceration and overcriminalization. As drug use in America grew, the public became increasingly concerned that crime was out of control and that drugs were rampant. The legal, legislative, and economic apparatus in this country overreacted and created an environment of mass punishment and incarceration. America's understanding of drug criminalization and the justice system has now swung to the other extreme. Now, more light is being shed on the justice system and the perception that the law is being applied unfairly and unjustly.

RISK PREVENTION

There is a strong public misperception that heavier criminalization will result in less crime, because theoretically it would deter more people from committing crimes. Yet it was only in 2013 that for the first time there were fewer than 10 million crimes committed in the United States, according to the FBI.[20] Obviously strong criminalization has not been a strong deterrent for offenders, as it has taken over thirty years for the crime rates to decrease nationally. It is clear that there is no strong correlation between an increase in criminalization and a decrease in crime rates. Despite finally having less crimes committed than we have had in the last four decades, we still criminalize at historical rates.

Lawmakers continue to criminalize, not because it has been proven to work, but because it is far easier, both legislatively and politically, to criminalize. It is much harder to pressure a politician for criminalizing than for decriminalizing. Politicians know what they're getting with criminalization. The same cannot be said for decriminalization. Politicians are often afraid to be the first person to propose something new for fear they will be voted out of office. Many would prefer not to test the political waters regarding criminalization. With criminalization as a significant topic for the last forty years in American society, politicians find it much easier to avoid the topic of decriminalization and focus on the politically comfortable alternative of criminalization. It is the path of least resistance that makes voters feel safe, even if in error.

There is a growing frustration in the world of both intellectual scholars as well as the common citizen regarding overcriminalization. In Texas, for example, a local news source reported that a woman was arrested for an overdue library book.[21] Prosecutor turned commentator Tony Blankley wrote that the criminal code used to be a clearly delineated forest of "tall oak trees," but it is now a vast plain of "blades of grass" that continue on and on and are unavoidable.[22] Mark Levin of the American Bar Association posits that we should "analyze before we criminalize."[23] It is up to the lawmakers, he says, to evaluate the law on both a micro and macro level and determine what ought, and more importantly what ought *not*, to be criminal law.

Only recently has focus shifted from encouraging criminalization to pointing out the vices. With the introduction of the SAFE Justice Act, introduced by Representatives Jim Sensenbrenner and Bobby Scott, our legislators have shown that overcriminalization is a bipartisan issue. They have also shown that there are legislators who are willing to support the rights of offenders and work toward reducing overcriminalization. The legislation has been tested on a state level and has been shown to improve both the costs of the justice system and the welfare of inmates. The act

[20] "United States Crime Rates 1960–2014," *Disaster Center*, Published 2014. www.disastercenter .com/crime/uscrime.htm.

[21] "Texas Woman Arrested for Overdue Book," KWTX.com (June 29, 2006), http://tinyurl.com/ awrtou.

[22] "The Criminalization of (Almost) Everything," *Cato Inst. Book Forum* (October 1, 2009), http:// tinyurl.com/b555jty.

[23] "At the State Level, So-Called Crimes Are Here, There, Everywhere," *American Bar Association*, published Spring 2013. www.americanbar.org/content/dam/aba/publications/criminal_ justice_magazine/sp13_state_level.authcheckdam.pdf, 3.

improves both front-end sentencing and back-end release policies.[24] The law would also limit federal mandatory minimum drug sentences to only the most severe offenders. This will ensure that lower level drug possessors will not *have* to receive a certain amount of punishment. The SAFE Act will reduce costs that prisons incur as well as save money for reinvestment in law enforcement needs. The introduction of this bill shows how Congress is putting more effort and attention into criminal justice reform. Although this bill has not become law, it is the type of reform our country needs to enact a more efficient and fair justice system.

Many experts argue that adding additional time to sentences of prisoners does very little to deter future crime. Criminals that are serving longer terms are not incentivized to obtain any skills or continue any education in prison simply because they will not have much opportunity or time to use them once upon release. As a result, adding more time onto sentences is a high-cost, low-result operation.

Overall, states' incarceration rates have decreased 4 percent in the last ten years. A large part of this drop can be attributed to state-level reforms that have occurred across the country. Over two dozen states have enacted reform that has helped both crime and prison population rates decrease. Several states have been productive in getting the ball rolling for a solution to overcriminalization. Acting as Brandeis' "laboratories of democracy," states have been able to learn from each other and the federal government should leverage this experience to increase efficiency and attainment of desired outcomes.

ANCILLARY OFFENSES

Ancillary offenses are offenses that serve as replacements for a primary crime. They are often related to the primary crime, but somewhat indirectly. Ancillary crimes are often charged if the primary crime cannot be proven, and the prosecution wants to charge the defendant with *something*. For example, if the prosecution cannot prove that the defendant killed the victim with the particular weapon, but they know that the defendant had an unlicensed firearm, they could charge them with weapons charges and the like instead of the murder charge, which would require more, and less circumstantial, evidence. Yet, instances like this have led to ancillary offenses becoming *complementary* instead of *supplementary*. As a result, many prosecutors charge defendants with the ancillary offenses in addition to the primary offense. Because these ancillary offenses are rather new to the legal world, prosecutors have a broad range of interpretation when it comes to these offenses. This has resulted in an increase of severity in punishment for crimes. For prosecutors, they are able to define these ancillary offenses as they wish, which creates an attitude of sweeping,

---

[24] Bobby Scott, "Sensenbrenner, Scott Introduce Bipartisan, State-tested Criminal Justice Reform Legislation", published July 25, 2015. https://bobbyscott.house.gov/media-center/press-releases/sensenbrenner-scott-introduce-bipartisan-state-tested-criminal-justice.

subjective generalizations which can lead to dangerous interpretation of what is in the best interest of the public. Husak makes the case that these ancillary offenses are both unnecessary in criminal law and actually do more harm than good. It is unlikely that these offenses will help provide more justice in the system.

As it stands now, prosecutors have a great amount of leeway when it comes to prosecuting offenders. Often prosecutors charge the defendant based on what the prosecutor wants them to plead guilty to. They have the freedom to interpret the law fairly broadly and essentially *make* the defendant guilty. There are no statistics on how many innocent people are in prison, but if wrongfully convicted, it is difficult to prove innocence unless new evidence comes to light. If you put yourself in the shoes of the defendant, it would be better to plead down to a smaller punishment that you didn't commit rather than being convicted on a full charge for a crime you didn't commit. This highlights the problem with overcriminalization from the side of the prosecutors. The power they have over the defendant is both legal and financial.

It is often the case that the prosecutor has the legal power behind him or her to enforce the full extent of the law on the defendant. This is a good thing when the prosecutors are focused on justice and ensuring that the community is better off. However, there are often outside incentives that push the prosecutors to seek higher imprisonment rates rather than justice. This pursuit of imprisonment may or may not be malicious. On the one hand, prosecutors want to keep their job, and in order to keep their job, they must be successful in putting defendants away in prison. But on the other hand, prosecutors are incentivized to push the full extent of the law on defendants and show very little care for individual defendants.

Prosecutors also have the financial budget of the city, state, or federal government behind them when in court. Most defendants do not have any resources to hire an attorney to carry on a trial. This can also lead to the defendant pleading down to less prison time, even though he or she may be innocent. Rather than proving guilt, the prosecution can carry out trials for months in the hope that the defendant exhausts their resources and cannot continue the trial. This is a large negative incentive that is provided for the prosecutor, as they are focused more on imprisoning the defendant than the defendant receiving help or curving their behavior. It is easy to put yourself in the position of a defendant who has little chance of surviving a trial of any significant length. The incentive structure for prosecutors must be changed if there is any hope in curbing our rates of criminalization, on both a state and federal level.

Prosecutors seem to have no limit to what they can charge. If a defendant is cleared on one offense, it is easy for prosecutors to go down the line and charge the defendant with the next most serious crime. There is no limit to the offenses that the prosecutors can charge, as long as they can connect the defendant to a crime. Some may respond that the Fifth Amendment protects the defendant in this case: "[N]or shall any person be subject for the same offence to be twice put in jeopardy of life or limb." While this ensures that no person is charged for the same offense twice, prosecutors can often find loopholes to escape this. They can find new evidence, witnesses, or testimonies that can reopen cases. It is also easy for the prosecutor to go after the next best thing, namely, not the same offense, but a different offense that carries a slightly less severe punishment. Again while each individual is protected by the Fifth Amendment, it is a simple task charging the defendant with a different crime.

As former US Attorney General Robert Jackson states, "the prosecutor has more control over life, liberty, and reputation than any other person in America. His discretion is tremendous ... While the prosecutor at his best is one of the most beneficent forces in our society, when he acts from malice or other base motives, he is one of the worst."[25] Our judicial system relies heavily on the role of the prosecutor. Yet there is very little accountability when it comes to prosecutors on the state and federal level. It seems that in the pursuit of justice, it matters very little if the prosecutors themselves are just or not. Even if misconduct is found, there are varying and disjointed punishments for prosecutors, as each state has their different offenses. Very few prosecutors actually face sanctions from appellate courts. This environment has been the foundation of institutional bias toward the accused and created an overly aggressive atmosphere in most prosecutors' offices.

When it comes down to it, prosecutors and police have the most power when it comes to punishment in the criminal justice system. It is the police who investigate and arrest the individuals and the prosecutors who charge the defendant with a crime or crimes. The extent to which defendants will be punished is ultimately up to these two parties. Husak points out that the powers of these two groups are almost wholly discretionary.[26] Since the decisions are so discretionary, it is often very difficult to appeal or review a particular case. Rather than having a set rule to fall back on, officers and prosecutors are given more leeway, and this makes it difficult to hold them accountable.

Husak observes that if every defendant took his or her case to trial, we would not have the resources to hear and decide every case, let alone in an efficient manner. However, this incentivizes the state and federal prosecutors to negotiate for bargains and deals. Thus, the growth of the power of the criminal justice system has revolved around these basically forced negotiations. The vast majority of cases are designed to create a plea bargain and to put pressure on the defendant to skip the trial and accept a plea bargain. Some say that up to 95 percent of adjudicated cases result in plea bargains.[27]

---

[25] Robert Jackson, *Address at Conference of United States Attorneys, Washington, D.C.* (April 1, 1940).
[26] Husak, *Overcriminalization*, 21.
[27] Rachel E. Barkow, "Separation of Powers and the Criminal Law," (2006) 58 *Stanford Law Review* 989, 1047 n. 310.

These plea bargains also defend and protect the prosecutors involved. Once a case is closed, it stays closed, for the most part. These plea bargains ensure that the defendants cannot be acquitted by juries. And yet, acquittal is the best chance that defendants have for having their case decided in their favor. This overreach on behalf of the prosecutors is one area where there must be significant reform. With an increasing amount of statutory overcriminalization, prosecutors are armed and ready to defeat as many defendants as they can.

When we examine the motivation of the prosecutors, they have all the incentive to charge individuals with crimes on the books and have them incarcerated. This is largely a part of their job description. Various community stakeholders have raised their voices and said that they don't like offenders making their neighborhoods unsafe. They wanted something done about crime. Prosecutors listened to these fears, as they took their marching orders from legislators at the state and federal level. We have legislated with increasing severity, and this has only fanned the flames of mass incarceration and overcriminalization. Crimes that are not seen as very serious carry surprisingly heavy consequences and remarkably severe punishments. From an outsider's perspective, even though many of these individuals commit only one crime, the prosecutors of the state and federal government carry a heavy stick and they are aggressively and actively looking for opportunities to use it as much as possible. These offenses allow prosecutors to swing their sticks freely and repeatedly by stacking charges one on top of the other. As we discuss later, prosecutors have all the freedom and incentive to place multiple charges on defendants. Even though defendants are protected by the Double Jeopardy clause of the Fifth Amendment, it is not completely robust in its enforcement. Prosecutors are certainly limited by this, but they also have ways of avoiding and getting around it. For example, the ruling in the 1983 case *Missouri v. Hunter* allows for multiple punishments for the same offense if so ruled by the legislature. In many instances, specifically with drug offenses, the legislature is more than willing to grant additional charges.

Unfortunately, it seems our judicial system has grown so reliant on guilty pleas that we cannot longer avoid them. While a sound understanding of overcriminalization cannot completely eliminate the issues with plea bargaining, we could certainly limit the injustice surrounding prosecutorial overreach and our reliance on plea bargaining, as later chapters will highlight.

CRIMINALIZATION AND THE ANTHROPOLOGICAL QUESTION

Different societies and cultures throughout history have had different methods of crime and punishment. From Hammurabi's code to public hangings to our current mass imprisonment, every group of people has some punishment for when a member of their society commits a crime. In America, there is a strong perception among some that our criminal justice system is just and fair. However, this perception is skewed. There is also a strong sense of complacency when it comes to our justice system as well. We consistently add laws, but as a society we have not thought about nor critiqued how many laws we have and why we have them. If we are to solve the problem of overcriminalization and mass incarceration, we must first realize that it is indeed a problem. We have to argue why we should not be complacent and that we should indeed push for more justice in our criminal justice system that maintains the human dignity of offenders and victims. Criminal deviance is often clearer to discern, but it is time that we focus more on the justice system. It is obvious that we should punish offenders. Our founding fathers set up helpful ways to accomplish this, but we have failed the well-being test for victims and offenders alike for the past several decades. With the combination of the executive, legislative, and judicial branch, we have several different avenues of creating, executing, and enforcing laws in the United States.

But why *should* we punish? We must distinguish between law breakers, wrongdoers, and offenders. As it stands, on the basis of overcriminalization, not all lawbreakers are wrong doers. Too many individuals are being punished for breaking laws with punishments that are meant for wrongdoers. This distinction can be seen with the example of the Nuremberg Trials. For example, at the time, the Nazis could do whatever they wanted to their prisoners because it wasn't against the law. However, the atrocious actions of the individual Nazis were obviously evil and wrong. Even though their actions were wrong, they were not against the law. This brings up the question of whether justice is in the law or in what behavior in its citizens the law should be encouraging or discouraging.

The central question of over criminalization that needs to be answered is, who should be punished? Many of the problems that our justice system faces revolve around the issue of who the justice system *ought* to punish. It also does not help that we disagree over who to punish. Many proponents of "law and order" would argue that all the rabble and offenders ought to be punished to protect and deter. But many did not realize that by criminalizing so severely and by "cleaning up our streets," we permanently damaged the lives of so many Americans. So yes, our streets have been cleaned up, so to speak. But we have done irreparable damage to our society and to the lives of many. It is the task of our current leaders to ensure that we do not continue to damage lives in this way.

It is easy to say that we should punish offenders, but a tougher question has arisen: Who is a criminal? As has been explained, we ought to revisit our definition of criminal and whether a law-breaker is a criminal. It is possible that our definition of criminal is correct, but it is the law that needs redefining. If it is the law that needs redefining, there must be a strong public and legislative push for laws that enact justice. Contrary to the typical thinking that we should help the afflicted in our society, we have not yet reformed this part of our society, even though it clearly needs reforming.

A significant aspect of the criminal justice system is *how* we punish our offenders. There are several facets of punishment, as has been discussed earlier. On a level of principle, we should punish individuals as persons. If we are going to further enact justice in our society, we should have a better idea of what justice looks like for our society on an individual basis. It is not a wild claim that our current criminal reform system does not work as well as it should. Obviously, there are individuals who are in prison that ought to be there. This fulfills the incapacitation component of criminal justice. But there are also individuals who are incapacitated who ought not to be there. This is obviously wrong and does not fulfill anyone's sense of justice. As a result, we must criminalize in a way that is efficient and does the best at ensuring fairness.

CONSEQUENCES OF PROSECUTION

There are many layers to the consequences of prosecution. There are several spheres that are negatively affected by unjust prosecution. Problems arise that create structural imbalances in society. They revolve around felonies, parole, families, and community.

Prosecution for a felony is a serious offense. Most felonies have to do with a personal, direct attack, or offense of another person, such as murder, robbery, or kidnapping. However, with an increase in drug criminalization came an increase in drug "felonization." In an effort to make drug use a serious offense, lawmakers enacted strict rules against the use of drugs. This included the increase of many drug crimes, which would typically be misdemeanors, to felonies. This action has had snowballing negative effects. One negative has been the effect on the individual. With a felony on his or her record, the individual must disclose that information to a potential employer. Doing so greatly decreases the likelihood that this individual will receive the job.[28] This alone has many other negative effects on the individual and his or her family, as well as the economy, to the tune of $57–65 billion. Felonies are one of the major barriers to education, skills, and work, and having one causes irreparable damage to the individual and his or her family. The issue is especially compounded when it is a male who goes through these troubles. Male offenders make up 90 percent of convicted felons. The number of felons is also estimated to be between 12.3 and 13.9 million. These numbers seem particularly high, and any citizen should be concerned about the negative effects on our economy and our society. A push toward more thoughtful criminal laws would help reduce the inefficiency in our economy and society and have a greater positive impact on the lives of many of our citizens. Researchers have found that "80 to 90 percent of employers said they would hire 'former welfare recipients, workers with little recent work experience or lengthy unemployment, and other stigmatizing characteristics,' but only around 40 percent said they would consider hiring job applicants with

---

[28] "Ex-offenders and the Labor Market", *Center for Economic and Policy Research*, published November 2010. www.cepr.net/documents/publications/ex-offenders-2010-11.pdf, 7.

criminal histories."[29] The fact that individuals have been to prison has a strong stigmatizing effect on employment and other opportunities. Felonization quickly degrades an individual's human and intellectual capital. The ability to partake in education, work experience, and skill accumulation is greatly reduced by being convicted of a felony. Felony charges can impact some or all of the following: voting rights after release, federal student loans, private employment, public housing, weapon possession, and public office. These are just the biggest ways that felons can be stripped of their liberties and ability to create a successful life for themselves after being released.

It is easy to believe that felons are only a small part of society. However, felons make up roughly 7 percent, or one in fifteen, of working-age adults in the United States. Even when felons complete their sentences, it is difficult to reintegrate into society. If their debt has been served, one would think that we should do our best to bring them back into society. However, the message that is sent to felons is that they still have not repaid their debt. This problem is exacerbated when felons search for housing and apply for loans and education grants. From an employer's perspective, not hiring someone because they are a felon makes sense most of the time. Obviously, a bank would not hire someone who has committed fraud. However, there is a great disservice done to the community and to the economy because of this. Even though many employers are only trying to protect themselves and their business, there is no doubt that most felons would be benefited by reliable employment. Vladimir Beaufils, chairman of the Capital Region Ex-Offenders Support Coalition, argues that recidivism is so high because "you end up going back to the path of least resistance. You have every good intention, and then reality smacks you in the face."[30] We must also keep in mind that some corporate insurance policies forbid the hiring of felons. This reality that Beaufils mentions is the change in the mindset of the felon. Why struggle to find a house and a job when I can just commit more crime at a low cost? Once arrested, charged, and processed, there is little chance that a felon's life will go back to being as good as it was. That individual will forever be marked a felon. After being released, a felon faces an uphill battle toward normalcy. The sad reality is that it is far easier to fall back into crime and prison than it is to find a sustainable job and living situation.

With a strong stigma against ex-felons, we should move toward policies that create a sustainable atmosphere for felons to succeed. No ex-felon should be punished for the entirety of his or her life, especially after they have gone through the legal system to pay their debt to society. When corporations restrict an ex-felon's ability to be employed, this is punitive. This can often drive the ex-felon to feel more animosity

---

[29] "Study Shows Ex-offenders Have Greatly Reduced Employment Rates," *Prison Legal News*, published Dec 15, 2011. www.prisonlegalnews.org/news/2011/dec/15/study-shows-ex-offenders-have-greatly-reduced-employment-rates/.

[30] "Felons Struggle after Paying Debt to Society", *Associated Press*, published March 10, 2012. www.pennlive.com/midstate/index.ssf/2012/03/felons_struggle_after_paying_d.html.

toward our society, culture and the business who rejected them. The least we can do is give felons a chance to succeed at being fully human and exercising agency toward their own good and the good of their neighbors. As it stands now, the deck is stacked against them. If we can give ex-felons a chance to live, work, and contribute to society, we may be surprised by the result.

The second area where offenders face great challenges is parole. The majority of prisoners, approximately 80 percent, will ultimately be subjected to some sort of parole. There is a common assumption that parole works as a better alternative than continuing to imprison someone. However, supervision via parole has little effect on the rearrest rates of released prisoners. Parolees often fare no better than prisoners released without any supervision.[31]

At a core level, the theory of parole is sound. By slowly reintegrating a prisoner back into society, he or she will be better able to produce and thrive in our culture. Parole is used as both a monitoring service and a social service. Parole officers are able to keep their eyes on the parolees and hopefully keep them in line. At the most basic level, parole is designed to reduce more serious crimes being committed by individuals who have already committed in the past. Parolees are exposed to society again and ideally will successfully reintegrate. Parole is often used as an instrument to engage prisoners in goal-driven work and treatment that will hopefully help their reentry process.

With a growing parole population, there is concern that we are not providing enough services to parolees. With each additional parolee, the quality of service decreases. This is troubling because one of the goals of parole is to reduce recidivism in country. A BJS study found that less than half of parolees successfully completed their parole without committing another offense or violating their release policy.[32] A separate report by the BJS also found that 67.5 percent of prisoners are rearrested within three years.[33] This tells us that the criminal justice system is likely not doing a good job. At the very least, it is certainly failing when it comes to rehabilitation. Studies show that the offenders who benefit the most from parole are offenders who have had the least interaction with the justice system.[34] The individuals who benefit the most are low-risk, low-level offenders, as they are the most responsive to sanctions given by their supervisors.

On the other hand, those who benefit the least from parole supervision tend to be offenders who have been arrested several times and convicted of drug charges or

---

[31] "Does Parole Work? Analyzing the Impact of Postprison Supervision of Rearrest Outcomes." *Urban Institute*, published March 2005. www.prisonlegalnews.org/media/publications/urban%20institute%20study%20on%20parole,%202005.pdf, 1.

[32] "Trends in State Parole, 1990–2000", Bureau of Justice Statistics, Published October 2001. www.bjs.gov/content/pub/pdf/tspoo.pdf.

[33] "Reentry Trends in the U.S.: Recidivism," Bureau of Justice Statistics, 2005, www.bjs.gov/content/reentry/recidivism.cfm.

[34] "Does Parole Work?," www.prisonlegalnews.org/media/publications/urban%20institute%20study%20on%20parole,%202005.pdf, 11.

violent offenses. Thus, the most serious offenders are the least likely to benefit from parole supervision. Parole is only helping the people who are the least likely to commit crimes again. If the goal of the prison justice system is focused on reducing overall crime, and specifically the recidivism rate, the justice system should specifically target the individuals that are being drawn back into crime. As it stands currently, the people that are needing help are not receiving it, and especially not through the criminal justice system.

There are multiple reasons why parole may not be as effective as it could be. The first is that there is not nearly as much supervision as there ought to be if we want parole to be effective. Many caseworkers have large caseloads and can only meet with each parolee for a limited amount of time, often only monthly. If we want parole to be more effective, more direct supervision and emphasis on a hands-on approach will be needed. Parole officers are often separated from parolees by large cultural or contextual divides. This keeps the officer from relating with the parolee on the best level. By introducing a more local parole process, both parole officers and parolees would be benefited. The largest problem with parole is that its function has moved from service-oriented to surveillance-oriented. Parole officers are now charged with monitoring many different offenders, rather than trying to directly help them. In order to return to a service-oriented approach, both surveillance and treatment will be necessary. This approach will likely be more effective than telling parolees what they can't do.

There is an especially strong ripple effect with incarceration that affects the family. With many fathers being imprisoned, this leaves many families with only a mother to support them. As a result, many kids have no father figure to look up to. This also exacerbates the crime problem. Many young teens feel that they now have to be the man of the house and provide for themselves and their families. This can often lead to many young males turning to gangs and drugs in order to provide some security, income, and protection. These families, often low-income black families, end up being stuck in a rut of incarceration and imprisonment. This problem perpetuates itself as generations grow up in fatherless, low-income homes. Many young black males are forced to grow up too early and try to provide for their family. This can halt their education, which ultimately limits them and their capacity to maximize their potential.

Even though drug laws are meant to target offenders, they ultimately target the family and create a network of cascading collateral social costs, especially for low-income families in urban and rural areas. Reports show that 52 percent of state inmates and 63 percent of federal inmates are parents. It is the family that ends up doing the time for the father's or mother's crime. The BJS has found that the nation's prisons have held about 744,200 fathers and 65,600 mothers at midyear 2007.[35] These parents have approximately 1,706,600 minor children, which

---

[35] "Reentry Trends in the U.S.," Bureau of Justice Statistics.

accounts for 2.3 percent of the US resident population under age 18. There is no question that the removal of one or both parents has a massive negative effect on a child. Without a parent, the child is forced to become independent and grow up in a way that is unhealthy to themselves and their family. When a parent is arrested, the child is immediately thrown into a financially tumultuous situation. For younger children, many either stay with family, such as aunts or grandparents, or are forced to enter some sort of welfare system. Roughly 10 percent of children enter the foster system when their mother is incarcerated.[36] When mothers and fathers are torn away from their children, children often react as though their parent has died and are exposed to experiences that have no place in the home.[37] Lengthy sentences often last for the totality of the child's childhood, so in a sense, their parent has effectively died for the time being. For older children, they are forced to make a decision of whether they will continue their education, do their best to work, or find income through other means, such as selling drugs or involving themselves in gangs.

Finally, there is also a large degradation to the community as a whole. Specifically in urban areas, where crime is more present, it is common to know someone who is in prison. Over half of state prisoners reported that they had a family member who was incarcerated This problem of incarceration is indeed perpetuating itself, but it is also perpetuating in specific communities. At yearend 2014, 37 percent of the prison population was black and 22 percent was Hispanic. There is always much talk that minorities are disproportionately represented in the prison population and it does seem as though it is true. Whites make up 77.4 percent of the US population, with Latino (17.4 percent) and black (13.2 percent) the next highest proportionally.[38] And yet, over 50 percent of our prison populations are represented by minorities. This shows how the criminal justice system affects minorities differently as those who disproportionately live in areas of high arrest rates, like urban centers.

OVERCRIMINALIZATION AND THE JUVENILE JUSTICE SYSTEM

One way in which the government has undermined the family is through the criminalization of behavior in high schools, which will be covered in more detail Chapter 5. Naturally, parents are very supportive of their children attending school and getting an education. Parents want their children to thrive and most parents know that education is the key to upward mobility. Many scholars argue that

---

[36] "Caught in the Net: The Impact of Drug Policies on Women and Families", Common Sense for Drug Policy, November 4, 1987. www.csdp.org/research/final-caught-in-the-net-report.pdf, 50.

[37] "Why Punish the Children?: A Reappraisal of the Children of Incarcerated Mothers in America," *National Council on Crime and Delinquency*, January 1993. www.nccdglobal.org/sites/default/files/publication_pdf/why-punish-the-children.pdf, 16.

[38] "Overview of Race and Hispanic Origin: 2010," United States Census Bureau, Published March 2011. www.census.gov/prod/cen2010/briefs/c2010br-02.pdf?cssp=SERP, 4.

completing high school is crucial for employment, and a college degree is key to upward social mobility.[39] Yet truancy laws take absence too far. Truancy laws are designed to force children to go to school by threatening imprisonment, fines, or other punishments.

In 2015, several outlets reported the case of Julie Giles of Georgia, who was arrested because her son, who was on the honor roll and "Student of the Month," had nine unexcused sick absences when the school only allowed six. Economist Milton Friedman wrote in his 1980 book *Free to Choose*,

> [It] is far from clear that there is any justification for the compulsory attendance laws … research has shown that schooling was well-nigh universal in the United States before attendance was required. In the United Kingdom, schooling was well-nigh universal before either compulsory attendance or government financing of schooling existed. Like most laws, compulsory attendance laws have costs as well as benefits. We no longer believe the benefits justify the costs.[40]

Despite Friedman's warning, the United States shot off in the other direction. Legislatures toughened school attendance laws under the guise of promoting stricter education laws and encouraging kids to go to school. Both Republicans and Democrats are at fault for creating such harsh truancy laws. Horror stories pour in from all around the country with disaster tales of how truancy laws have gone wrong. The addition of criminal and civil penalties has led to results that are opposite of what the government intends. If the problem is that kids aren't showing up to school, why would you imprison them or create civil penalties?

There will be, however, problems that public school systems cannot solve because they are not designed or equipped to do so. There are other institutions in society better equipped and designed to effectively perform certain tasks that are naturally outside the expertise of the education sector. Issues at home and with any given individual student are problems that the school system cannot control. Issues with the family could stem from a number of breakdowns: neglect, abuse, substance usage, lack of interest on the part of the parents, or financial distress. These types of issues are often the root cause of deviant behavior and low academic performance. If the child is worried about home life, it becomes difficult to concentrate and focus on schoolwork. The child may believe there is no hope or no purpose in educating themselves, especially if their family sets a bad example. Some children believe they will end up like the rest of their family no matter what, so they don't see the purpose in trying at all. The student may be struggling with a number of personal issues as well, such as low self-esteem (which ties in with poor grades), untreated mental health issues or disabilities, abuse, substance abuse, or lack of drive. If we want our

---

[39] "Thirteen Economic Facts about Social Mobility and the Role of Education," *The Brookings Institution*, June 2013. www.brookings.edu/research/reports/2013/06/13-facts-higher-education.

[40] Milton Friedman, *Free to Choose: A Personal Statement* (San Diego, CA: Harcourt Brace Jovanovich, 1990), 162.

kids to do well in school, we should be focusing on providing the best environment we can for them. Truancy is often an early sign of a child engaging in other negative behaviors such as alcohol or drug use. Truancy can often be seen as a "gateway" to some of these other activities that may result in the student dropping out of school.

So how should our justice system go about truancy? As we will see later, we must acknowledge that truant behavior is not criminal behavior. In some states, both students and parents could possibly be locked up for the child failing to attend school. By intervening immediately, reengaging with youth, and decriminalizing truancy, we can help our kids stay out of trouble and in school. Increases in youth crime rates are also the result of locking up teens for petty offenses. Many petty offenses are criminalized just as heavily as more serious offenses. Youths are tasked with knowing what is against the law, as well as numerous "status offenses," offenses that are illegal to youths and not adults. Teenagers are culpable if they break any law in our extensive legal code or any number of status offenses, such as drinking alcohol underage, using tobacco products, staying out too late, or having sexual relations. All of these latter actions are legal for adults but not for youths, and we must ask if it is humane to criminalize these types of teen activities given the fact that a teen is much more likely to be arrested for such an offense if he or she is a minority and disadvantaged living in dense neighborhoods than being middle-class or higher living in a neighborhood with high property taxes. This is not to say that we should let youths run rampant, but we should understand the amount of heavy criminalization that we place our juveniles under. We should stop criminalizing the teenage years. Eric Luna argues that the criminal justice system somewhat plays the role of the father. He says that the "paternalistic goals of the state" may result in involuntary confinement, just like offenders.[41] In their own way, youths are incarcerated in our society. If they do certain things that adults do, there are serious repercussions. By forcing juveniles to obey extensive laws, we have already imprisoned them.

CONCLUSION

By now we can see that mass incarceration and overcriminalization is indeed a problem in the United States. What personalism reminds is that any justification of criminalizing deviant behavior must keep an emphasis on the person at the center of whatever theory of punishment we use to adjudicate criminal offense because of the consequences of punishment for human persons and those connected to them. The widespread enactment of drug criminalization has had negative effects on our society as a whole, but also on poor, minority, low-income individuals in particular. With more and more people speaking up about perceptions of racial inequality and police brutality, overcriminalization reform could be a big step in increasing social

---

[41] "The Overcriminalization Phenomenon," *American University Law Review*, Published 2005, http://digitalcommons.wcl.american.edu/cgi/viewcontent.cgi?article=1707&context=aulr, 706.

mobility for these aforementioned groups. At the very least, we should strive to have our justice system treat victims and offenders with the highest level of human dignity with prison numbers that reflect our efforts. For instance, rather than having as many as one in three black men imprisoned over the course of their lives, we should push to have that number closer to one in nine, which is the incarceration rate of white males. This is not to say that one in nine is the ideal; it is by no means a goal but perhaps it could serve as a benchmark for where we should start in order to pursue even lower ratios. Rather than aiming for a certain ideal number, citizens and legislators alike should push for prudent reforms that make what ought to be a crime a crime and what is not a crime not a crime – and respect human dignity in the process. And that process includes examining prosecutors more closely.

2

Prosecutorial Overreach

The three half-brothers had spent decades in prison waiting for just this very moment. One of the two brothers still living, Robert Hill, was the first to be heard in court. He walked with a cane because of his multiple sclerosis, and his lawyer made the case against the main witness used in his conviction. "The conviction of Mr. Hill was based primarily, almost entirely, on the testimony of a witness who we now feel to be extremely problematic," claimed the assistant district attorney. Hill's two half-brothers were put behind bars in a separate murder case with this very same witness, and he was convicted by this witness's testimony the second time he was accused of murder by the same prosecutor. The man who had put them behind bars was a discredited New York prosecutor with fifty-seven former cases under review; he had repeatedly used the same witness in separate trials. The brothers were all exonerated of their charges, one posthumously, but not after spending decades of their lives behind bars.[1]

It is very easy for the public to forget that the high percentage of mistakes in criminal justice have devastating effects which no average individual could endure or even fathom. Government inefficiency is a common fact in American life. Citizens expect for the US Postal Service to operate at a slow pace; government offices and bureaucratic functions are slow. Imagine the criminal justice system, where the public priority and exposure of the government function is the absolute lowest priority. The abuse and neglect that occurs is dehumanizing and must be eliminated in each state. This government function must not only be reformed but modernized and optimized to leverage the skills of the dedicated criminal justice professionals in the system.

---

[1] Stephanie Clifford, "Judge Voids Murder Convictions for 3 Half Brothers Linked to Brooklyn Detective." *The New York Times.* May 06, 2014. Accessed August 01, 2017. www.nytimes.com/2014/05/07/nyregion/brooklyn-judge-vacates-murder-convictions-of-3-half-brothers.html?_r=0.

It is harder for many people to afford private attorneys to represent them against elected prosecutors and cases such as the brothers who lost their lives to misconduct are very common. The role of these prosecutors for a long time was undocumented and unchecked. Numerous studies existed examining many different factors contributing to mass incarceration, but no research studies existed on the influence of prosecutors. John Pfaff of Fordham Law was one of the first to realize this omission from the studies, and he told *The Atlantic* in an interview: "We have no data on prosecutors. The studies kind of skipped over that. That struck me as a problematic omission. I decided to figure out what role prosecutors play. I saw that we needed to add them back in."[2] He did just that and found huge changes in how DAs were charging cases across the country. From the 1990s to the 2000s there was a jump in felony charges: one in three arrests in 1994 were felonies. By the late 2000s that became two out of every three arrests. The Prosecutors had immense power over this change. In short, Pfaff found that "[r]oughly speaking, half of this increase in felony filings comes from cases of misdemeanors being charged as felonies." With this realization, prosecutorial transparency became another factor in the criminal justice reform debate. Criminal justice reform must start with taking a close look at the role of prosecutors.

DEFINING THE PROBLEM

Certainly not all prosecutors are out to imprison the most people that they can at any cost. However, just as there are police officers that use excessive force, there are prosecutors that abuse their power. Many are familiar with the term mass incarceration, but fewer are familiar with overcriminalization and prosecutorial overreach. The purpose of this chapter is to explain prosecutorial overreach and show how it affects both overcriminalization and mass incarceration.[3] Chapter 1 demonstrated that the established culture and mechanisms of the criminal justice system create unfair, redundant, or unjust results. But it is also true that many of these laws are enforced and implemented in a way that is unfair and unjust. Despite what criminal laws state, prosecutors are free to enforce and charge defendants with the crimes as they see fit. Eric Luna writes that the greatest asset to law enforcement is its professional and structural demeanor.[4] Like law enforcement, prosecutors are given a great amount of power in our criminal system and are tasked with enforcing justice. The public trusts officials to operate with an impartial professionalism across

---

2 Juleyka Lantigua-Williams, "Are Prosecutors the Key to Justice Reform?" *The Atlantic.* May 18, 2016. Accessed August 01, 2017. www.theatlantic.com/politics/archive/2016/05/are-prosecutors-the-key-to-justice-reform/483252/.

3 John F. Pfaff, *Locked In: The True Causes of Mass Incarceration – and How to Achieve Real Reform* (New York: Basic Books, 2017), 1.

4 "The Overcriminalization Phenomenon", *American University Law Review*, Published October 2, 2005, 722. www.wcl.american.edu/journal/lawrev/54/luna.pdf.

each of their tasks. Yet, like any other human being, some prosecutors yield to perverse incentives and motivations that undermine the public interest. Prosecutors are a very unique group of professionals; their success is determined by number of convictions, which fundamentally skews their activities and motivations. Luna speaks candidly, stating that district attorneys are not reelected for letting cases slide or "shrugging off acquittals."[5] Prosecutors can pick and choose the cases they want to pursue, often only cases they can win in order to prove they as individuals are great at their jobs. The perception is that public safety requires everyone found guilty of crimes to be put in jail or prison. Justice is applied in unfair and inequitable ways due to perverse incentives in an ambitious and competitive environment. William Stuntz, the late Harvard Law professor, goes as far to say that the current criminal justice climate is lawless and diseased.[6]

John Pfaff argues that prosecutors are the primary drivers of prison growth in America, which explains why the prison population rose while crime went down. There was a decline in crime and a rise incarceration rates, according to Pfaff, the rate at which prosecutors filed felony charges against arrestees ballooned between 1994 and 2008.[7]

> Yet while arrests feel, the number of felony cases rose, and steeply. Fewer and fewer people were entering the criminal justice system, but more and more were facing the risk of felony convictions – thus prison. Between 1994 and 2008, the number of felony cases in my sample rose by almost 40 percent, from 1.4 million to 1.9 million … In short, between 1994 and 2008, the number of people admitted to prison rose by about 40 percent, from 360,000 to 505,000 and almost all of that increase was due to prosecutors bringing more and more felony cases against a diminishing pool of arrestees.[8]

> America's prison populations ballooned during a period decreasing crime as prosecutors are incentivized to prosecute heavily and defendants are encouraged to plead guilty. Prosecutors have the full power and resources of the state master experts at putting people behind bars, going up against defendants who are usually completely ignorant regarding legal matters and financially poor. Defendants also face an increased punishment for taking their case to court. Charge stacking and increased penalties push defendants to roll over rather than fight their case. This reaction tells the prosecutors that they should push for more and more jail time; the success of their job is based on the incarceration rates.

5 "The Gatekeepers," *The Marshall Project*, published March 16, 2015. www.themarshallproject .org/2015/03/16/the-gatekeepers#.PFOa400Qj.
6 William J. Stuntz, *The Pathological Politics of Criminal Law. Michigan Law Review*, Vol. 100, Available at SSRN: https://ssrn.com/abstract=286392 or http://dx.doi.org/10.2139/ssrn.286392 (2001), 523–526.
7 Pfaff, *Locked In*, 72–74.
8 Ibid.

The prosecutorial system is set up where prosecutors have the ability and incentive to overly incarcerate with impunity. Luna points out that as a result of the incentives that the criminal justice system provides, law enforcement and prosecutors are not impartial to the results of the case.[9] To the contrary of public interest, prosecutors are directly affected by the results of arrests and convictions. It is in their self-interest to seek the incarceration of more and more people. Defendants often see no other way of escaping unscathed, so they plead down to what they think is the best deal, leading to more convictions and incarcerations. As a result, prosecutors, law enforcement, and legislators are all satisfied with themselves because they have "taken criminals off the street" when in fact they are innocent, or guilty of a lesser crime than they serve time for. Pleas are drawn out of defendants, who are fearful to defend themselves because if they fail, mandatory minimums will force them to serve much more time than if they just submit to the will of the prosecutor. The reality is that prosecutors have unchecked power in our criminal justice system and can, at critical times, supersede what is reasonable and fair for defendants. The concepts of innocent until proven guilty, trial by jury, and proof beyond a reasonable doubt are often myths. This restriction of rights must be recognized as a problem and dealt with accordingly. Luna observes that defendants may in fact be punished for exercising their rights guaranteed to them in the Constitution.[10]

Part of the problem when it comes to understanding prosecutorial overreach are misunderstandings or misconceptions of terms of their responsibilities. It is likely that many citizens understand the job of the prosecutor in a way that is different from reality. Television shows perpetuate the myth that crime is rampant throughout our country. Even if the TV shows are fictional, what often follows is a general desire to prosecutors to "do something" about crime. The high volume of police or law shows create an idea in the minds of the American people that crime is a large part of our society and that we need people to protect us. Entertainment shapes cultural prejudices. We are also much more willing and forgiving when it comes to abuses from prosecutors. Some believe that it should be prosecutors that lead our justice system away from mass incarceration and overcriminalization.[11] There will always be crime, but prosecutors should not engineer criminalization and mass incarceration. We must ensure incentives that lead away from mass incarceration and overcriminalization. Rather than prosecutors ensuring convictions and long sentences, as we often do today, they ought to prosecute in a way that reduces recidivism and is aimed at benefiting our society to reduce future crime. Out of sight prisoners are a problem for every state, rotting the core of mostly poor urban and rural communities. Recognizing the fact that crime and violent crime have decreased significantly in

---

[9] Luna, 724.
[10] Ibid., 735–736.
[11] "The Gatekeepers," *The Marshall Project*.

the last thirty years,[12] we must ask ourselves if the need for prosecutorial leveraging is still necessary for our justice system to do its job well.

According to a report by the National Registry of Exonerations, 42 percent of exonerations since 2004 were due to official misconduct.[13] Prosecutors have the power to simply suppress evidence that does not meet their storyline of a crime, very rarely being held accountable for their misconduct.

INCENTIVES AND ACCOUNTABILITY

When it comes to prosecuting defendants, prosecutors have no real risk of punishment if they bend their power. There is no limit to the creativity of prosecutors who believe that a defendant is guilty. With no repercussions for heavily charging defendants, prosecutors have no limit to the amount of charges they can bring. With such broad powers, prosecutors are free to bring any somewhat reasonable charges they wish without it serving any useful purpose other than to inflict pain on the defendant and glorify their own legal skills.

Many indictments list dozens of charges against a single individual. The defendant must make a choice if he or she wants to plead down to a smaller sentence from any number of charges or fight all of the charges in court. Fighting these charges cost what low-income defendants can't afford. Thus, many defendants choose to plead guilty. Prosecutors who have perverse interests in mind have no restriction on the charges that they can bring against a defendant.[14] While there are limited restrictions on the charges that prosecutors can bring, it must also be noted that they also have an advantage that defendants do not. There is a general perception that prosecutors are defenders of public justice, with the number of laws now, the average American commits three crimes *per day*. The combination of the number of laws and the ways they are used to prosecute citizens results in a criminal justice system diseased by illogical systems. If we are truly just in our criminal justice system, prosecutorial discretion and behavior must be modernized. The injustices of some prosecutors must be reeled in by our commitment to a fair American legal system.

Glenn Harlan Reynolds argues that prosecutorial discretion is becoming such a big issue that it may have a negative effect on due process rights that are guaranteed

---

[12] "United States Crime Rates 1960–2014," *The Disaster Center*, Published 2014. www.disastercen ter.com/crime/uscrime.htm.

[13] "Exonerations in the United States, 1989–2012", The National Registry of Exonerations, Published May 2012, 22. www.law.umich.edu/special/exoneration/Documents/exonerations_ us_1989_2012_full_report.pdf.

[14] "Our Criminal Justice System Has Become a Crime," *USA Today*, Published March 19, 2014. www.usatoday.com/story/opinion/2014/03/19/law-enforcement-clue-jury-criminal-column/ 6490641/.

to citizens.[15] He argues that because of the unrestrained nature of overcharging and plea bargains, the act of prosecuting a defendant has become all the more important and yet more and more unconstrained. Reynolds notes that former Supreme Court Justice Robert Jackson once commented that if prosecutors are able to choose their cases, they will be able to choose their defendants. Essentially, prosecutors will only pick cases that they know they can win. This results in a dangerous misappropriation of responsibility and duty: prosecutors will prosecute the people that they *think* they can get a guilty verdict for, not people that *are* guilty. With an increase in laws and legislation, the ability for prosecutors to abuse their power has become much easier. Not all prosecutors are abusing the power, but too many are. We must recognize the dangerous reality, and potential, that rests in the hands of imperfect human beings who are as fallible as any of us but have much greater incentives to be overly punitive. With our extensive criminal code, prosecutors will always have the ability to abuse their power.

Some opponents would claim that the increase in prosecutorial power has benefitted the criminal justice system. The causality between the two is not direct.

ENCOURAGEMENT OF OVER-PROSECUTION

Unfortunately, there may be misconceptions about our justice system that give the average person a different idea about how justice is applied our society. Prosecutors decide to charge or not charge any particular defendant with any crime. John Pfaff views this as matter of serious concern: "prosecutors have the unreviewable ability to decide whether to file charges against someone who has been arrested, and they face almost no oversight about what charges to file if they decide to move ahead with the case."[16] This adversarial system means that each party, prosecutor and defendant, are represented in court before an impartial judge. Lynch believes that the principle generally means that judges in the courts are not the investigators of cases. Judges do not determine the truth of the evidence nor provide ultimate justice to either party. The court's job is to settle the admissible differences between the prosecutor and the defendant. Judges take a secondary role and can only review the evidence that has been presented to them by the two parties, they can only review the case insofar as specific evidence has been presented to them. It is the prosecutor's responsibility to investigate the defendant, acquire any evidence, as well as pursue any line of questioning with the defendant. This means that the prosecutor has a fairly large say in what evidence is brought before the court and what information is shared with the defending party and to the judge.

---

[15] Glenn Harlan Reynolds, "Ham Sandwich Nation: Due Process When Everything Is a Crime," 113 *Columbia Law Review*. (2013): 102, www.columbialawreview.org/ham-sandwich-nation_ Reynolds.

[16] Pfaff, *Locked In*, 130.

Prosecutors have their own individual, outside incentives to take legal action or to attempt some sort of plea with a defendant. Plea bargains are debated and negotiated outside of the courtroom; the judge has no say in the negotiations and no way of investigating the matter further, unless further evidence arises. If the plaintiff and defendant agree about the degree of punishment, Lynch says, there is nothing the courts can do to affect their decisions. This gives a great deal of power to the prosecutors, who know that often the defendants cannot afford a trial, and are scared of going to jail for a long time. In the end, prosecutors wield a sharp and dangerous tool, even if they usually just use it to threaten people. Lynch claims that the role of the prosecutor is pivotal in our criminal justice system, their client is not just a single individual, but society as a whole.

Stephanos Bibas argues that we must fear what "idiosyncratic prosecutorial discretion."[17] He proposes that some amount of discretion is good, but that it must be moderated and mediated by other parties so that prosecutors do not control all of the power. In order to discourage prosecutors from acting in their own interest, we must remove as many private interest incentives as possible.

It is critical to understand the extent of prosecutorial discretion in our country. Rebecca Krauss writes that the American criminal justice system has allowed prosecutors their free reign when it comes to prosecuting criminals. She says that federal laws, mainly the separation of powers, require that the decisions of prosecutors are not subject to review. Also, the laws and the justice system itself encourage the practice of prosecutorial discretion. Krauss goes on to cite the 1978 Supreme Court case *Bordenkircher v. Hayes*, as well as *Wayte v. United States*, in which Justice Powell delivered the opinion, saying, "[S]o long as the prosecutor has probable cause to believe that the accused committed an offense defined by statute, the decision whether or not to prosecute, and what charge to file or bring before a grand jury, generally rests entirely in his discretion."[18]

Historically, the courts, including the Supreme Court, have upheld the notion that public prosecutors have ultimate discretion whether or not to pursue charges with any individual who has been accused of a crime. It is also worth noting that the prosecutor can also choose not to charge someone with any given crime, even if there is evidence against the individual. *Bordenkircher* notes that while prosecutors cannot pursue charges in a vindictive way, where the defendant is punished for exercising their constitutional right to due process, there is nothing to be said about negotiations that could take place in a plea bargain scenario.[19] Even if one has great faith in the federal and state prosecutors, one must admit that they have a great deal

---

[17] "The Need for Prosecutorial Discretion", *University of Pennsylvania Law School*, (2010) 370, 371. http://scholarship.law.upenn.edu/cgi/viewcontent.cgi?article=2428&context=faculty_scholarship.

[18] US Supreme Court. "*Wayte v. United States* 470 U.S. 598 (1985)." Justia Law. Justia, 19 March. 1985. https://supreme.justia.com/cases/federal/us/470/598/case.html.

[19] See *Bordenkircher v. Hayes*, 434 U.S. 357, 364 (1978).

of freedom when it comes to pursuing charges against defendants, and we must eliminate elements of the practice which are blatantly unjust. With little restrictions of prosecutors, their free reign is too often dangerous and worrisome. While most prosecutors to not act in a vindictive way, we must acknowledge that these prosecutors will be inclined to mistakes, anger and temptations resulting in defendants' lives being ruined and the community paying a hefty price.

ACCOUNTABILITY

The lack of structural accountability of prosecutors within the criminal justice system creates an inherent disincentive when it comes to accountability. It is usually up to the District Attorney's office to sanction their own prosecutors according to the law and their own ethical code. While this happens occasionally, abuse of power is subject to interpretation. Occasionally crossing the line is rewarded rather than discouraged. Any organization holds a bias toward its own employees, especially employees who are tasked with enacting justice. The great power of a prosecutor's office comes with great responsibility, there are difficult moral and ethical quandaries that come with the job. Accountability between coworkers is challenging in a normal work environment, let alone in a stressful position that pertains to upholding and defending the law.

As the American founding generation understood very well, humans are imperfect. We expect each other, at some level, to transgress the law. The Constitution intentionally gives strict and powerful checks against powers because the consequences of getting it wrong are substantial. The best to ensure the enactment of justice is through accountability between several offices and multiple individuals all of whom have independent roles and priorities. If we are to resolve some of the problems revolving around prosecutorial misconduct, we must realize that there are disincentives currently in place. By implementing external checks to the offices, we can protect prosecutors from themselves.

It is very difficult to quantify which prosecutors, and how many, are partaking in misconduct. The amount of discretion is well protected, there is no institutional or structural civic oversight into the details of prosecutors make decisions. Pfaff observes, "despite the power of prosecutors, there is almost no data or research on what drives them."[20]

Even if they are discovered by a colleague, there may be professional consequences and political scenarios that come into play which protect the prosecutor as is noted in the 2011 Yale Law Review article, *The Myth of Prosecutorial Accountability After Connick v. Thompson*.[21] Keenan, Cooper, Lebowitz, and Lerer note in the

---

[20] Pfaff, *Locked In*, 134.
[21] "The Myth of Prosecutorial Accountability After *Connick v. Thompson*: Why Existing Professional Responsibility Measures Cannot Protect Against Prosecutorial Misconduct", *Yale Law*

article is the fact that many of the known cases of prosecutorial misconduct only become known when there is a long trial or court proceeding.[22] Combined with the fact that the vast majority of cases end in plea bargains, it is likely that most prosecutorial misconduct goes unnoticed and uninvestigated. This leaves many defendants at risk of prosecutorial overreach and abuse. Finally, the authors note, the people that are best able to recognize and investigate misconduct are judges, prosecutors and fellow attorneys, all individuals who are concerned about being involved with a misconduct case and the political ramifications that it may have on their careers.[23]

From a defendant's point of view, it seems utterly hopeless and pointless to go after the prosecutor on any charges of misconduct. The complaint itself could in fact make the situation worse for the defendant, as they would be provoking the prosecutor to find additional charges and longer sentences of incarceration. Defendants usually possesses very little legal resources and are not in a place to defend their position with much credibility. Compared to many other professions, rarely is a prosecutor's job on the line for how they perform. There has been a history of treating different prosecutors preferentially when it comes to cases of misconduct. Punishment for misconduct, if any, is selectively applied. The lack of uniformity in punishment negatively affects incentives.

Stuntz argues that there is a specific prosecutorial bias toward the poor. He believes that it was unfair for prosecutors to go after the poor just because they did not have the money to afford better attorneys. Prosecutors know that they have the advantage when it comes to prosecuting poorer defendants. In a written dedication to William Stuntz, Douglas Martin, writing for the *New York Times*, points out that Stuntz believed that the important question of guilt or innocence could get lost when it comes to the prosecution of defendants.[24] He argues that for people who can afford expensive lawyers, trials often proceed in a way that does not focus as much on the substance of the case. With trials involving lower-income defendant's, plea bargains are really only bargains for the prosecutor and end up being more like scams for the defendant. It seems as if Stuntz believes that the job of the prosecutor has morphed into something that it was created to fight. Rather than pushing for judicial justice, prosecutors are now focused on putting people in prison in order to pursue their own success and develop their own careers.

Journal Online 203 (2011) 201, www.yalelawjournal.org/forum/the-myth-of-prosecutorial-account ability-after-connick-v-thompson-why-existing-professional-responsibility-measures-cannot-pro tect-against-prosecutorial-misconduct.

[22] Ibid.

[23] Ibid.

[24] www.nytimes.com/2011/03/21/us/21stuntz.html?mcubz=0.

Stuntz recognized the role of the prosecutor has evolved from striving to enact justice to trying to lock people up.[25] He also pointed out that defendants were usually poor, and prosecutors hesitate to bring charges against individuals who could afford better attorneys. By having more skilled attorneys the constitutional literacy of the defendants create a scenario more balanced and fair. There is a much greater risk in prosecuting such a case, and it is much less likely that such a case would result in a plea, as the defendant would be able to expend resources in their defense.

One example of this broken system made national news back in 2012 when entrepreneur and web developer Aaron Swartz committed suicide due to impending charges against him. In 2011, Swartz was arrested on Harvard University's campus after using a laptop to illegally download academic journal articles over MIT's network. Eventually, Swartz was indicted on thirteen different felony charges by federal prosecutors. This carried a maximum sentence of fifty years in prison and up to $1 million in fines. Swartz and his attorneys were later able to talk the prosecutors down to a six-month sentence in a low-security prison, as long as Swartz plead guilty on all 13 felonies. After JSTOR, the academic journal source, and MIT declined to pursue civil litigation, and with incarceration pending, Swartz was found dead in his apartment of apparent suicide by hanging.

Harvey Silvergate, writing for *Massachusetts Lawyers' Weekly*, argues that US Attorney Carmen Ortiz took the case in order to "send a message" to Swartz and his team. Several sources stated that federal, not local, prosecutors had been taking over the prosecution of the case. Ortiz's office released a press release in July 2011, saying, "If convicted of these charges, Swartz faces up to 35 years in prison, to be followed by three years of supervised release, restitution, forfeiture and a fine of up to $1 million."[26] At the time justice officials had argued that Swartz had indeed stolen materials and should not be treated any different than any other criminal. However, the Department of Justice later admitted that they had specifically targeted Swartz for his activism and outspokenness regarding access to materials.[27]

Doug Lieb, in a recent *Yale Law Journal* article, writes that prosecutors in the Aaron Swartz case appeared to be "aimed at making the defendant suffer a severe price" for actions that, in a normal circumstance, would not have been punished the same way.[28] It is tempting to look at a high profile case like Swartz's and understand that the Attorney's Office wanted to make an example out of him. This approach to prosecutorial discretion was encouraged in this case and obviously had negative

[25] William Stuntz. *Collapse of the American Criminal Justice System* (Cambridge, MA: Harvard University Press, 2011) 2, 7, 13.
[26] "Alleged Hacker Charged with Stealing over 4 Million Documents from MIT Network," *The United States Attorney's Office Massachusetts*, July 19, 2011. www.justice.gov/archive/usao/ma/news/2011/July/SwartzAaronPR.html.
[27] "DOJ 'Admits' to Targeting Aaron Swartz Over His Activism," *Russian Today-United States*, edited December 24, 2013.
[28] "Vindicating Vindictiveness: Prosecutorial Discretion and Plea Bargaining, Past and Future," 123 *Yale Law Journal* 1014 (2014): 1016–1089.

consequences, not just because the defendant was guilty, but because of the severe and harsh penalties that were going to be levied against him. This did not go unnoticed by the public. By attacking such a public figure, it worked against the Attorney's office and is now an example for critics of increasing prosecutorial power. Many agree that prosecutors pursued Swartz with too much vengance. The law allows for the severe punishment of defendants going to trial, and Swartz ended up with a severe sentence. The US Attorney's office clearly used prosecutorial discretion in determining that Swartz was a high-profile individual who needed to be punished. By using this power aggressively, prosecutors have shown that they can fall victim to their own interests and many people found their actions dishonorable and vindictive. The treatment of Swartz sheds light on the problem of vindictive power and strength by prosecutors.

PLEA BARGAINING ABUSE

The frequent use of plea bargaining is a fairly recent legal phenomenon.[29] The justice system has evolved to where the vast majority of cases today are resolved with plea bargains, undermining the ability for a defendant to fully exercise his or her rights, especially at the state level. According to George Fisher, caseload pressure and sentencing guidelines have stripped judges almost entirely of the power of leniency.[30] In recent decades, according to William Stuntz, guilty pleas are easily induced when the law that defines crime is both broad and specific, leaving little room from defense arguments that might lead to jury acquittals, which gives prosecutors an enormous amount on influence on the outcome of the case.[31] Guilty pleas in most states have become the preference of prosecutors which unfortunately collapsed into more guilty pleas and harsher sentences.[32] Lieb argues that our current environment and attitude toward the judicial system has invited further thought and investigation into whether plea bargaining and the power of prosecutors should be more closely scrutinized.[33] In the last several years, the Supreme Court has established that the best method of combating these pleas is to empower the defendant with effective counsel. Ideally, this would ensure that the proceedings of the case happen in a way that is fair to the defendant. Lieb points out that by pushing for this type of initiative, they are admitting that there have been some decisions or pleas that have been inappropriately decided. He pushes the reader to consider about what constitutes a just or unjust bargain. Why is this an issue? Because guilty

---

[29] George Fisher, *Plea Bargaining's Triumph: A History of Plea Bargaining in America* (Stanford, Calif.: Stanford University Press, 2003).
[30] Ibid., 220–221.
[31] Stuntz, *Collapse*, 257.
[32] Ibid. 259.
[33] Lieb, 1016–1019.

pleas, thanks to plea bargaining, are now easier to extract and are crucial to the massive increase in America's prison population.

Because there has been more and more evidence that prosecutors are abusing plea bargaining, Justice Anthony Kennedy in *Missouri v. Frye* argued that plea bargaining "is not some adjunct to the criminal justice system; it *is* the criminal justice system."[34] So, while the court increasingly wants to regulate plea bargaining, there is evidence to suggest that plea bargaining is a primary means of adjudicating cases, not adequately examining the guilt or innocence of the defendant. It is wrong to encourage plea bargaining to increase efficiency. The justice system's job is not to pick its battles, but rather to do their best to enforce justice in every single. Plea bargaining is not the optimal way to enforce justice, and it is inherently unjust that 95 percent of cases end this way. According to Pfaff, "thanks to the plea process, the public never sees how prosecutors actually deploy it ... [p]lea bargaining not only shields prosecutors from accountability, it also makes them more powerful by allowing them to process more cases per year."[35]

Defendants are encouraged to plea to whatever crime they are charged with, regardless of innocence or guilt. This is outside of the concept of being innocent until proven guilty. Lieb notes that the worst part of the rise in plea bargains is that they have become the rule rather than the exception and that no restriction on plea bargains has been established.[36] The Supreme Court has made slight attempts at regulation, but methods are indirect due to the structure of the legal system. Plea bargains also help prosecutors around weaknesses in their cases. Pfaff observes, "even if the main claim is weak, a prosecutor can come up with a set of charges and sentences that are more appealing to the defendant than the risk of something worse at trial."[37]

Prosecutors have the least accountability and the most control over the fates of the defendants. A Florida man, Shane Guthrie, was arrested for assaulting his girlfriend and threatening her with a knife. The prosecutor in the case offered Guthrie a plea bargain of a two-year prison sentence, plus probation. After Guthrie denied the offer, the prosecutors later offered a five-year plea deal. Again, Guthrie denied it. The prosecutor, reacting to Guthrie's desire to exercise his right to a trial, filed another charge that came with a maximum punishment of life in prison. This process is called "legal vindictiveness," defined by the Supreme Court as the act of a prosecutor retaliating against a defendant for exercising their legal right to a trial, thereby denying the defendant their due process rights as defined in the Constitution. Guthrie should be punished, but not for exercising his right to due process.

---

[34] *Missouri v. Frye*, 132 S. Ct. 1399, 1407 (2012).
[35] Pfaff, *Locked In*, 133.
[36] Lieb, 1039–1045.
[37] Pfaff, *Locked In*, 133.

Prosecutors control plea bargaining, as judges are not capable of creating pleas, and defendants have no choice in the pleas offered. Lieb notes that there is no mandate for prosecutors to make plea bargains with defendants, but there has still been a growing legitimacy to the conception that the offer of a plea bargain has become standard practice. Even though plea deals are common, they are not a right of the defendant. Plea bargains are not woven into the fabric of legal history. Legal precedence and values contradict the concept, Lieb observes. Since there is no constitutional right to a plea bargain, it is the prosecutors who are left holding all the cards. Lieb notes that even though this may seem uncontroversial at first glance, it does show that plea bargaining is a significant deviation from the norm in legal history. Lieb's point is to show that if plea bargaining is such a large part of our legal system there should be (1) precedent for such a strong presence and (2) strong legal precedent that justifies plea bargaining.[38]

Judicial actors are unable to grant the right of uniform plea deals across the board. This is because the power of discretion lies with prosecutors, not judges and juries. The perceived *modus operandi* is that trials are the criminal justice system, rather than plea bargains. To continue to ignore the relevance and importance of plea bargaining in the American legal system would guarantee that the problem of mass incarceration will grow. Justice Lewis Franklin Powell, in *Wayte v. United States*, stated that "This broad discretion rests largely on the recognition that the decision to prosecute is particularly ill-suited to judicial review."[39] Law should not be a matter of convenience; from a personalist perspective, we are talking about the lives of real, flesh-and-blood people. Persons are not reducible to their cases. Although prosecution is difficult and slow for prosecutors, it does not mean that we should circumvent our system. As a collective we ought to care much more about whether people pleading are actually guilty or not.

Plea bargaining is cheaper for state and local court systems than jury trials and is one of the main reasons these deals occur at such a high rate. Prosecutors have woven plea bargaining into the identity of the legal process. If our legal system was truly dedicated to the balance and separation of powers, the discretion of the prosecutor would be reviewed by another party. The reality is that we are promoting a tainted method of legal practices. Thus, as Lieb, Pfaff, Stuntz, and others have observed, prosecutorial discretion needs more accountability.

PROSECUTORIAL DISCRETION

In most criminal cases, the defense lawyer meets with his or her client shortly after the client is arrested. In the beginning, the defense lawyer is at a significant disadvantage to the prosecutor. The prosecutor has access to the police report,

[38] Lieb, 1058–1069.
[39] *Wayte v. United States*, https://supreme.justia.com/cases/federal/us/470/598/case.html.

witness interviews, and evidence. The defense and the defense lawyer are restricted by visiting hours and other restrictions at jails. This also gives the prosecutor confidence on the strength of his or her case, as Ted Rakoff notes in his article "Why Innocent People Plead Guilty."[40]

When the defense attorney meets with the prosecutor, there is a clear misalignment of leverage, information, and power. The prosecutor is holding all the cards and can keep the defense from accessing important information. The prosecutor will explain to the defense that, unless they accept a plea bargain, the government can charge the defendant with the most serious crimes. This scare tactic is extremely effective, as the defense attorney likely will advise the defendant to take the plea deal. From the position of a prosecutor, it is critical that the defense agree quickly to a plea bargain, saving the prosecutor time, legal resources, and money. If the defense continues to push for a trial, the prosecutor sees no other option than charging the maximum. The defendant and his or her counsel are their energy responding to gamesmanship of the prosecutor, rather than focusing on facts and the law.

The prosecutor knows they can leverage the defendant into a plea. Grand juries will likely be biased toward the prosecutor's side, and likely agree with any position that the prosecutor holds, as he is a representative of the local, state, or federal government. Statutes like mandatory minimum sentencing have compromised the criminal justice system. Rakoff notes that prosecutors have the ability to create and configure the charges brought against the defendant by how the charge is described. Prosecutors are able to use mandatory minimums as an institutional threat against defendants. The prosecutor makes the charging decision, but also essentially the power of sentencing as well.

Both the defense attorney and their client are at the mercy of the prosecutor. The defense is fighting an enormous uphill battle. In most cases, the best-case scenario for the defense is that they are offered a plea bargain that lacks any heavy sentence, understanding that the prosecutor would like the defense to plead early. For the defense, even if the plea bargain is unfair in their eyes, there is not much they can do to curb the effects of the prosecutor's offer. Legal precedent has some effect when it comes to sentencing, but the reality is that many defense attorneys advise their clients to take what they can get. For the client it is much better to plead guilty and serve minimum time than be proven guilty and serve extended time in prison. Rakoff argues that appeals to the prosecutor's boss are not often successful, especially since they are "on the same team."[41] If one puts themselves in the shoes of the defendant, it is easy to see that serving a year term, for example, would be much better than being found guilty and serving a ten-year sentence.

---

[40] "Why Innocent People Plead Guilty," *The New York Review of Books*, November 20, 2014. www.nybooks.com/articles/2014/11/20/why-innocent-people-plead-guilty/.
[41] Ibid.

Prosecutors' hefty power leads to considerable overpunishment and abuse. Few regulations restricting the power of the prosecutor and there is no appeal process for the defense to use if the prosecutor is using the discretion indiscriminately. No other office has such a large and still unchecked power over another human being in the twenty-first century in practice.

Rakoff admits that there may be arguments against such a strong condemnation.[42] He argues from a cynic's perspective, saying that crime has declined in the last fifty years and that most citizens feel much safer than they did just a few decades ago. The idea here is that with the increase in prosecutorial discretion and power, prosecutors are now able to control our streets with an unchecked iron fist and that they are succeeding at reducing crime.

Rakoff's counterargument begins with the Jeffersonian idea that a government-run criminal justice system will eventually lead to abuse and possibly tyranny. With the amount of the control that the prosecutors have over defendants, Jefferson's warning does not seem like that outlandish of a claim.[43] Rakoff examines three supports for Jefferson's claim. First, the criminal justice system is lopsided in favor of the government. Even though our justice system is founded on the principle that each defendant will have their opportunity in court, many do not see any time in the courtroom because of plea bargaining. The guarantee in the Fourteenth Amendment that the government shall not "deprive any person of life, liberty, or property without due process of law" has been circumvented by prosecutor's ability to use plea bargains. Rakoff argues that as our founders tried to move away from the "rigged British system of colonial justice," so too should be move from the overreaching power of prosecutors in our justice system. Second, plea bargaining is largely hid from judges, juries, and the public eye. Most pleas take place between the prosecutor and defense attorney behind closed doors. The problem here is that the deals are not subjected to any third party or any outside eyes. Rakoff points out that the results of many of these meetings are arbitrary and defense attorneys are left with no leverage. Third, there is a serious collapse of justice when it comes to plea bargaining. The prosecutor dictates the offense and the sentence, and "wins" when the defendant is sentenced and imprisoned, regardless of whether or not they actually committed the crime. One could see how it would make more sense to plea to a crime you did not commit than be convicted for a crime you did not commit. Even though a defendant may be innocent, the likelihood of being convicted for a serious crime carries the sentence of a serious crime. While this number is not incredibly large, it is statistically significant across the millions of those that are incarcerated, and it is especially significant to families and communities that have suffered from overbearing and powerful prosecutors.

---

[42] Ibid.
[43] Ibid.

The combination of limited resources and overbearing caseloads stack the odds against the defendant. The defendants can clearly see that successfully defending themselves is unlikely and will result in a heavier punishment. When the plea bargain is introduced, in the mind of the defendant that deal represents the best option with the least amount of destructive capabilities. Even when not guilty, Rakoff notes it is still rational to take the plea bargain offered by the prosecutor.

Theoretically, Rakoff argues, this problem should be solved when the judge questions the defendant on the facts of the case. The judge may question the defendant, but, operating on the assumption that the defendant has already admitted and plead guilty, the judge will likely not linger on the defendant's case. Even if 4 percent of convicted felons are innocent, that would mean that over 80,000 felons are innocent of their crimes. That is a staggering and unacceptable number.

Prosecutors, as well as those who advocate for them, argue that discretion and immunity is crucial to their roles as public servants. They argue that regulations from the state bar associations are enough to keep prosecutors in check. The problem is that there is very little evidence to show that the actions of state bar associations are deterring misconduct among prosecutors. In a profession that is about justice, there is too much allowance for misconduct and unfair actions by prosecutors. The job of the prosecutor is arguably the most powerful public service position, and yet not many are raising it as an issue. Prosecutors have the power to ruin lives, end them, and tear apart families and communities, and yet there is no regulation on their actions. If we are to start trusting our legal system, we must hold prosecutors accountable for their actions when they abuse discretion.

PROPOSALS FOR SOLUTIONS

In his article *The Pathological Politics of Criminal Law,* William Stuntz argues that the solution for prosecutorial discretion reform can be aided by resurrecting or expanding court powers that are now held by prosecutors.[44] As noted by Richard McAdams, Stuntz argues that where an individual violates a law that would not be seen as criminal, the government would have to show and prove that the particular individual deserves to be punished.[45] Stuntz also believes that certain laws should be eliminated from legal code if they have not been enforced in a certain amount of time. The courts are not incentivized to send more people to jail like prosecutors are because judges are not promoted for convicting more citizens. These suggestions would help with the negative incentives that prosecutors have, and defendants would be given a much fairer trial by judges who are neutral and impartial to the

---

[44] Stuntz, William J., The Pathological Politics of Criminal Law. *Michigan Law Review,* Vol. 100, December 2001. Available at SSRN: https://ssrn.com/abstract=286392 or http://dx.doi.org/10.2139/ssrn.286392.
[45] "The Political Economy of Criminal Law and Procedure: The Pessimists' View," *The University of Chicago Law School,* October 2008, 5.

outcome of the case. The national goal in prosecutorial transparency reform is to limit the ability of the prosecutor to act freely in the system. As Misner states, "the sentencing powers of the judge have not been constrained through sentencing guidelines or sentencing minima, the prosecutor's authority is theoretically subject to greater control."[46] Judicial powers have generally taken a backseat in the plea-bargaining process, and prosecutors filled that void. If courts played a more active role in sentencing, more plea bargains could be prevented, and prosecutors would be tasked with proving guilt rather than just assuming or creating it.

Another necessary reform is increasing the investigations that bar associations perform regarding prosecutorial misconduct. Overzealous prosecutors are not often punished for their misconduct; they believe there is no party to police them. Prosecutors primarily regulate themselves with a small amount of accountability to bar associations. Increasing the activity of the bar in regard to prosecutors will help curtail misconduct.

Reforms in the plea-bargaining process will greatly aid defendants in their right for a fair trial. Another necessary reform in this area would be to require prosecutors to prove and provide documentation for any claims that they make allowing defendants to honestly assess their situation and take a look at their case. More transparency from prosecutors will ultimately allow us to instill more justice in our justice system. Many states have emphasized reform as "laboratories of democracy," as Justice Brandeis said, for the government to examine and judge. Some states have pushed discretion from the back-end to the front-end, meaning that rather than parole officers and administrators making decisions on treatment, judges have the power to interpret the law as well as the offense and make a determination of guilt and sentencing *before* the defendant goes to prison.

The criminal justice system has changed massively over the years and will take many years to enact the kind of reform that could solve the problems that our justice system deals with. Robert Misner notes that the current push toward the "federal-ization" of crime is not the best way to implement real change, primarily because it is the state and local governments that are best able to enact change that is effective.[47] Misner argues that in order to institute effective change in policy, we must identify what needs to be changed, and how we can change it. Risner makes the case that we should take away the prosecutor-centric vision of criminal justice. Since a large portion of the criminal justice problem is paying for the maintenance of criminals, he suggests putting the power of the finances into the hands of the legislature, so that there is more outside accountability.

---

[46] "Recasting Prosecutorial Discretion", *Journal of Criminal Law and Criminology*, Spring 1996, 755, http://scholarlycommons.law.northwestern.edu/cgi/viewcontent.cgi?article=6876&context=jclc.

[47] Robert L. Misner, *Journal of Criminal Law and Criminology*, Vol 86.3, Spring 1996, Recasting Prosecutorial Discretion, 763.

Prosecutors must be more accountable and operate with transparency. This is easy to say but a hard policy to implement. When civic institutions at the local level enforce accountability to bar associations, legislators, and citizens, prosecutors will act more responsibly and there will be less disastrous incarcerations. Prosecutors must bring down crime rates by having criminals stop offending. Programs other than incarceration serve the community by not creating angry vindictive criminals who are permanently emotionally scarred from the mental and physical horrors of incarceration. The parole system must be modernized so that people can get the community assistance they need to be productive citizens rather than feeling helpless and resort to crime in order to meet basic needs of food, clothing, and shelter.

We can improve the quality of our justice system by encouraging prosecutors to participate in sentencing alternatives. Risner creates a tangible list of items for states and localities when implementing prison reform. The first is creating more communication between prosecutors and the prisons that they are sending people to. Inventory and other data should be shared between the state and the general public, transparency within the system will allow prosecutors and others to understand the effects their actions have on the lives of defendants and individuals in prison.

Sonja Starr argues in favor of sentence reduction. Trial and appellate courts should be granted the ability to reduce sentences in order to check the power of the prosecutor. By giving defendants more guidance, a steady interpretation of the law could be taken and there would be more flexibility when it comes to sentencing. It is important to note that not all cases or sentences would be subject to these purposes. It will likely not be the sole remedy for prosecutorial misconduct, but it could help those who are being prosecuted unjustly or being given too long of a sentence.

Third-party civil institutions are vital in keeping prosecutors accountable. Adam Gershowitz suggests that the third party would be neutral and not likely to be swayed by political interest.[48] Gershowitz points out that publicly identifying these prosecutors would likely have a serious effect on their behavior. By naming the prosecutors committing unacceptable behavior, the public could show that they have the right to a fair trial and will not stand for any misconduct. Gershowitz begins his piece by pointing to the fact that judges do not name the prosecutors who have committed misconduct in a trial. Their names are redacted to keep their identity secure, even though they are engaging in illegal misconduct. Every normal defendant is subject to disclosure and the negative aspects of public knowledge that they have been accused of a crime. Prosecutors should be held accountable for misconduct, which will drastically improve our society as a result.

---

[48] "Prosecutorial Shaming: Naming Attorneys to Reduce Prosecutorial Misconduct", *College of William and Mary Law School*, 2009, 1064, http://scholarship.law.wm.edu/cgi/viewcontent.cgi?article=2287&context=facpubs.

Finally, John Pfaff recommends that prosecutors should be better regulated and held accountable for their actions by adequately funding public defenders and other indigent defense counsels. The presence of these legal professionals encourages prosecutors to focus on more serious offenses. Programs must gather data regarding the decision-making processes and practices of prosecutors. Intelligent plea-bargaining guidelines must be created and enforced. Prosecutors must be incentivized to employ probation, parole, and treatment. Cost structures within states must be changed so that county-elected officials are not sending prisoners to state-funded prisons. Prosecutors must live in the communities of those they are prosecuting, closing the proximity gap. Local residents must have more power to monitor and be knowledgeable of what prosecutors are doing and have the ability to remove them from their positions.[49]

CONCLUSION

Prosecutorial overreach and misconduct is at the root of the general distrust in the judicial system by communities that are targeted by overzealous actors. The lack of community-positive incentives and weak accountability allow for many prosecutors to consistently abuse their power. Like many painful truths with nefarious embedded interests, prosecutorial misconduct is consistently swept under the rug out of the public eye. It is just one area where criminal justice reform could take place. It is the task of the chapter to prove that it is indeed a problem, and a problem worth solving.

Prosecutors are not immune to personal incentives and self-interested goals. There must be restraints and checks on the power of prosecutors, especially when caseloads of defendants for every prosecutor are large. Prosecutors should not be rewarded for the amount of people that they put behind bars. Whether through sentencing or plea bargain, punishing individuals to the furthest extent of the law creates more crime. Lives are being ruined because of the severity of punishment. It is too easy for prosecutors to pursue maximum punishment. The law intended to keep society in check being misused to ensure success of federal, state, and local prosecutors. Society should encourage and promote prosecutors who can be merciful to those who deserve it.

With unlimited legal resources, it is in the prosecutor's interest to charge maximum punishments against defendants and in the interest of the defendants to plead guilty. The way our justice system is set up allows for the continuing infringement of rights by prosecutors. As Luna pointed out, prosecutors are not immune from being biased toward the outcome of the case. When prosecutors

---

[49] Pfaff, *Locked In*, 206–217.

engage in serious misconduct, it is not only the defendants who lose their dignity, our system and "ideal of justice does as well."[50]

Reform to control overzealous prosecutors will better the lives of thousands, especially at the state level. To properly limit of prosecutorial misconduct, there should be more open communication between judges, prosecutors, legislators, and prisons as to the administration of justice. The purpose of the system is indeed to provide justice, not to lock people up. The justice system is working against large segments of society, creating major social problems.

Applications of personalism and civil institution engagement will unleash the professional potential of this group of attorneys because we must remember that they are only humans themselves and need to be given the right incentives to promote the dignity of victims and offenders alike. The competitive nature in which they thrive can be applied to a system that utilizes that energy for net gains in the community, not for the hemorrhaging of lives. Reform and modernization of prosecutorial procedures will make the criminal justice system improve and better utilize the individual talents of prosecutors and judges. Because of legislative measures to control crime, the role of judges in adjudicating justice has been undermined by politics. Judges need to have their discretion, under the rule of law, returned to them.

---

[50] "Are There Viable Solutions for Prosecutorial Misconduct?", apublicdefender.com, Published March 9, 2015, http://apublicdefender.com/2015/03/09/are-there-viable-solutions-for-prosecutorial-misconduct/.

3

Judicial Discretion

Eric Patrick Wright will spend the next two decades in prison. According to reports in a local Florida newspaper, he fired a gun when an angry ex-girlfriend forced her way into his fiancée's home.[1] He never shot at her; a shot was fired by him into the ground in an attempt to scare her off. Florida's mandatory minimum sentences for aggravated assault left the punishment out of the judge's hands, who was openly critical of the law and sentence.

Mandatory minimum sentences fail to give the discretion necessary for the judiciary to look at cases within their individual context, and often do not give any option other than prison for the accused. Many judges would like to provide alternative sentencing, but laws are created by legislators. Mandatory minimum and three-strikes laws are easy to sell to voters, but often create extreme injustices. Rehabilitation and alternative forms of punishment are often more appropriate. It is a problem that relates both to proportionality of punishment to the crime, and for judges to be able to exercise their own judgment, not be forced into a decision required automatically by law without consideration for the specific facts of that case. There needs to be a change to this process that sentences people to prison without any accommodation for judicial discretion or proportionality.

A 2016 study by the Brennan Center for Justice appeared in *The Atlantic* and highlighted the scale of this problem.[2] There are more prisoners in America than there were in the Soviet gulags at their peak, and a greater proportion of black Americans are imprisoned now than black South Africans during apartheid. The study found that up to 39 percent of these people may be "unnecessarily

---

[1] "Florida Judge: 20-Year Sentence for Firing Gun an Injustice." NBC-2.com. August 01, 2017. Accessed August 01, 2017. www.nbc-2.com/story/36022466/florida-judge-20-year-sentence-for-firing-gun-an-injustice.

[2] Matt Ford. "A *Blueprint to End Mass Incarceration*." The Atlantic. December 16, 2016. Accessed August 01, 2017. www.theatlantic.com/politics/archive/2016/12/mass-incarceration-brennan-center/510749/.

incarcerated." The conclusion: "576,000 inmates currently locked up for crimes ranging from mail fraud to simple burglary could be swiftly released without endangering their fellow Americans." Addressing the problem from the start would help keep some of these people out of prison for petty crimes and restore some normalcy to the criminal justice system. Proportionality and increased judicial discretion is immediately necessary.

The legal system is an intricate, complex, and misunderstood pillar of modern society and the American republic. The role of precedent and legal interpretation is something the average individual is never trained to comprehend, which exacerbates the normal question that often arises during the criminal justice reform debate: "Does the punishment fit the crime?" The answer to that question is often a resounding no within the court of public opinion; however, the legal system is designed to exist outside of public opinion. Understanding the confluence of the legal system and public outrage is something vital to instrumental advancement of prudent judicial discretion.

Due to thresholds of mandatory minimum statutes, defendants are condemned to years, decades, or life in prison for minor infractions. The mundane and technical process of legal proceedings also frequently confuse poor and uneducated defendants, leading to thousands of mismanaged cases. Often because they do not understand their rights, innocent individuals are behind bars for long periods of time. Many believe that increasing judicial discretion in sentencing would mitigate weaknesses of the criminal justice system, ultimately decreasing the negative effects of overcriminalization.

When we think of a judge, there is a common respect and admiration for proper and fair decision making. As individuals, good judgment is celebrated, and the wisdom judges possess are a key component in the mind of the citizens regarding how the criminal justice system is able to function fairly. If we want to make immediate gain at reforming the criminal justice, we must also start by closely examining the role of judges.

JUDICIAL DISCRETION: AN INTRODUCTION

For centuries around the world in traditionally centralized legal systems, courts have struggled with the role of judges and the concept of judicial discretion. There is always clear merit for the use of some judicial discretion, as it increases fairness and equality for defendants. By allowing judges to apply their own personal judgment in the interpretation of facts, citizens have a higher likelihood of receiving a fair and just outcome. The greatest concern against large degrees of discretion is that it is subjective, and its misuse can poison the judicial process by unfairly destroying the people that it is supposed to protect. Prosecutorial discretion is something deeply ingrained in the legal system, and proponents of judicial discretion highlight that judicial oversight is much more protected and structured in the scope of the damage it can do compared to prosecutorial discretion. The purpose of this chapter is to introduce how an increase in judicial discretion would benefit both the legal system and the citizens that the system is designed to protect.

America's constitutional law is such that judicial discretion is necessary to maintain the separate but equal functional branches of government. It is not realistic for members of Congress and state legislators to write laws which address every possible crime. There are numerous scenarios that appear in the judicial process which require the interpretation of the law by a judge. As an observer that is independent of interest in an outcome, it is important that judges be granted the discretion to interpret and apply the intent of the law to circumstances presented in legal proceedings. The proper application of legal standards does not mean that strict guidelines must be provided to judges in order to resolve disputes.

The American conception of judicial discretion has fluctuated since the beginning of the judicial branch of government. In 1824, when American legal tradition was being established, Chief Justice John Marshall directly addressed the issue of judicial interpretation of the law: "Courts are the mere instruments of the law, and can will nothing. When they are said to exercise a discretion, it is a mere legal discretion, a discretion to be exercised in discerning the course prescribed by law; and, when that is discerned, it is the duty of the court to follow it."[3]

Many argue that extending judicial discretion increases the power of the individual judge and could contradict the laws passed by legislative branches, circumventing the will of the people. The error in this assessment is that judicial power is given in order to implement justice on the part of the legislative branch. While the legislative branch makes the laws, it is the responsibility of the judges to interpret the will of the law and implement rulings that reflect the legislative branches intentions.

The largest misconception about judicial discretion is that judges have wide variations of their rulings, essentially able to change the law. This is not true. Instances where judges have discretion do not negate the processes and guidelines of the law, or allow judges to ignore or change precedent. Instances of judicial discretion appear much more in cases that have a lack of precedence, or there are loose statute or regulations. It is in these instances where judges are most useful and able to apply their legal skills and experience to ensure a responsible rendering of justice under the law. It makes the most sense to give judges discretionary power in many situations, as they are elected by citizens and appointed by executives specifically on the merit of their ability to apply proper standards to legal proceedings.

Another common critique of judicial discretion is that the judge's discretion will have great variation in the subjective application of the law. The fear is that there will not be consistency, and that justice will not be evenly administered. A judge's individual discretion is feared because decisions could be impacted by external

---

[3]   *Osborn v. Bank of the United States* 22 U.S. 738 (1824), Page 22 U.S. 866.

factors such as past decisions, personal bias, or religious beliefs. This fear insinuates that judges have free reign, which is not true. A discretionary ruling is still able to be found in error and ruled against in the appellate process.

Appellate courts can review several areas of the judicial process: the merits of the case, if the judge trying the case has misinterpreted or misunderstood the specific law at hand, if the ruling was unreasonable or irrational, and whether the ruling was made based on incorrect findings. The ultimate power of appellate review (and check on unwarranted judicial discretion) is throwing out the case and the previous decision because of the mistake of the judge.[4]

Judicial discretion can be traced back to the beginnings of America's legal system and is in line with common law standards. However, this use of discretion has been taken for granted.[5] As Yale Law professor Kate Stith observes, "in the modern era, we have grown suspicious of discretion. To a formalist, discretion seems the very antithesis of law."[6] For many, the idea of discretion is scary because it allows for people to be treated differently. What must be accepted is that this difference in treatment does not inherently imply a lack of justice for anyone. No two cases are the same, and thus defendants must be treated and sentenced differently depending on the judge's individual interpretation regarding the circumstantial merits of their case. Stith makes the case that our modern age has aimed to reduce the discretion of government officials across the board. Many are afraid that "discretion" will be used to *not* exercise the proper interpretation of the law.

In order to limit the role of judicial discretion in sentencing, mandatory minimum sentences were created. Mandatory minimums take away large powers of discretion by judges and institute mandatory time ranges of sentences for defendants that are found guilty or plead guilty to a crime. The idea was that mandatory sentencing would further codify the law and punishments of criminals. Each felon would be treated and punished equally in the eyes of the law. Examples of this are three-strikes laws and sex offender registries. If one is a convicted sex offender, it is mandated that their status as a sex offender be made public, as they are branded a danger to society. A similar sentiment revolves around three-strikes laws, which state that if an individual is convicted of three crimes, they will receive a severe sentence, regardless of the crimes. Mandatory minimums make certain across the board assumptions about the effectiveness of punishments handed down by the courts.

In the case *Ewing v. California* (2003), Gary Ewing stole three golf clubs valued at $399 each from a pro shop at an El Segundo golf course in California.[7] Ewing slid the clubs down the leg of his pants, before he was noticed hobbling out of the store

---

4   Thomas A Zonay. "Judicial Discretion: Ten Guidelines for Its Use." The National Judicial College. The National Judicial College, 21 May 2015.
5   Kate Stith. *"The Arc of the Pendulum: Judges, Prosecutors, and the Exercise of Discretion,"* www .yalelawjournal.org/pdf/691_2w13sx9h.pdf, 422.
6   Ibid.
7   *Ewing v. California* 538 U.S. 11 (2003)

by a shop employee, who then called the police. Ewing was convicted of grand theft of personal property for stealing the three golf clubs. In the eyes of California law, felony grand theft is subject to discretion from both the judge and the prosecutor. Counsel agreed to reduce the classification of the crime to a misdemeanor. Although Ewing asked the court to exercise discretion in his favor, which would eliminate the effect of the three-strikes law, the judge declined this request, in part because of past criminal history. Due to previous burglary and robbery charges, the judge imposed a twenty-five-to-life sentence under California's three-strikes law. Ewing appealed his conviction to California's appellate court which rejected his argument that his twenty-five-year sentence was disproportionate to the crime. This case would ultimately rise to the Supreme Court, where the court would uphold the ruling. In a similar case, *Lockyer v. Andrade* (2003), a defendant was found guilty of stealing $150 of video tapes from a pair of California department stores. Because of the California three strikes law, the defendant was sentenced to 50 years in prison. Like *Ewing v. California*, *Lockyer v. Andrade* was decided in favor of the prosecution and resulted in severe jail time for the defendant.

The reality is that prosecutorial discretion is much more widespread and impactful than even the perceived role of judicial discretion. With respect to mandatory sentencing, there has been a significant shift from judges to prosecutors, who are enormously invested in the decision of the case, for better or for worse. It is prosecutors and not judges who are capable of seriously affecting the length of a sentence, simply through the method in which they file charges against an individual. Even when a judge believes leniency should be applied, there are strict restrictions, simply because of the method and procedure utilized by prosecutors given to them by laws of their state and federal government.

Judicial discretion about sentencing is not a specific legislation or policy, only an opinion of who should be making the decision about sentencing. As retired Judge Nancy Gertner writes, "[judicial discretion] simply describes who ought to make the decision about sentencing, *not what the decision should be*."[8] While it is in the self-interest of some prosecutors to pursue the most severe punishment, it is not so with the judge. The prosecutor receives direct benefit in the outcome of the case, as they advance in their career for their win-loss record in court, often leading to more financially lucrative professions. Judges do not receive professional ratings or advancement based on the outcomes of cases they preside over. The potential danger in giving judges more discretion is lower than allowing prosecutors to have the amount of discretion they currently have.

One of the most important issues within the realm of judicial discretion is that of the rehabilitation of defendants sentenced to incarceration. It is not in the direct interest of the prosecutor whether the felon is rehabilitated or not, their sole objective is to secure a conviction and incarceration. It is the burden and

---

[8] Nancy Gertner, *Federal Sentencing Reporter*, Vol. 28, No. 3, 165–166.

responsibility of the judge to ensure that the defendant has his or her rights preserved and protected, taking into consideration the life of the defendant. The judge is the last opportunity for the dignity of the person to be protected. The judiciary can be used to carefully "consider alternatives to incarceration, creative sentencing options, the insights of neuroscience, or evidence-based practices."[9] This creates an important role for the judge when considering sentencing. Judge Mark W. Bennett observes, "those complicit when a social function becomes unjust often explain their involvement by describing their limited role – they were simply 'following the orders' of others. So it is with the drug war."[10] This creates scenarios where judges are issuing sentencing rulings that they do not agree with, allowing them no discretion at all.

Part of the need for increased judicial discretion stems from the control that Congress and the Sentencing Commission have in creating strict laws. The creation of harsher sentences by these two institutions makes them partially responsible for the explosion of incarcerated felons. After its founding in 1984, the Sentencing Commission has continued to use its discretion to increase sentences and keep felons behind bars longer. The Sentencing Commission's Guidelines continue to increase sentences, while rarely reducing them. Marc Miller goes so far as to say, "the federal system ... would make administrators of the Gulag jealous."[11] This quotation is a testament to the difficult situation that judges are put in. Even "evidence presented by the judiciary, the defense bar, and others who advised against its proposals" was ignored in favor of giving more sentencing power to the Sentencing Commission.[12] As the Sentencing Commission is directly responsible for the guidelines which increased the severity of sentences, reform to reduce mass incarceration, and certainly overcriminalization, must begin here as well.

In examining the possible causes of mass incarceration and overcriminalization, it is necessary to examine certain initiatives that were passed through Congress. The biggest and most pronounced initiative was the growth of the role of mandatory minimums. Mandatory minimums are activated based on the crime an individual is charged with – which is directly determined by the prosecutor. The prosecutor also controls what facts are charged and presented, which is the basis that mandatory minimum requirement is based on. Prosecutors have the power to enhance the sentence of the felon if they so choose binding judges by charging defendants that

---

[9] Ibid.
[10] Mark Osler and Mark W. Bennett. "A "Holocaust in Slow Motion?": America's Mass Incarceration and the Role of Discretion," *DePaul Journal for Social Justice* Spring 7.2 (2014): 117–78. Accessed April 28, 2016.
[11] Marc L. Miller, "Domination & Dissatisfaction: Prosecutors as Sentencers," 56 *Stanford Law Review* (2004): 1211, 1222.
[12] Amy Baron-Evans and Kate Stith, "Booker Rules," *University of Pennsylvania Law Review* 160 (2012): 1631, 1634.

carry mandatory minimum sentencing. With the strength of prosecutorial discretion, judges have no discretionary power in these common circumstances.

It is confusing, and dangerous, to put power in the hands of "adversarial judges . . . rather than in the hands of a dispassionate judge."[13] Additionally, this gives the prosecutor a new weapon: bargaining power. Osler and Bennett note that in narcotics cases, mandatory minimums almost always come into play. One could see how prosecutors could use this minimum as a threat against the felon to rat on his accomplices or plead guilty to a different charge.

Mandatory sentencing guidelines are an additional restriction of judicial discretion that has been placed on judges. Similarly to mandatory minimum sentencing, mandatory guidelines restrict judicial discretion and tie the hands of judges. Mandatory guidelines take into account not just the offense of the felon, but the "relevant conduct" as well. This conduct is anything that the prosecutor cares to bring to light about the felon. This could be anything that relates to the personal character of the witness that is not included in the charge itself. Needless to say, much of the information presented to the court to create what could lead to this mandatory sentence directly comes from the prosecutor. In *Booker v. United States*, the Supreme Court ruled that the Mandatory Guidelines were to be advisory rather than mandatory. This did help recede the power of the prosecutor, but unfortunately it still leaves intact the guidelines as the method for sentencing.

The purpose of this book is to raise awareness and provide guidance toward tools for change and reforms that can help people across the country. A major victory and milestone in the reformation of arcane criminal justice sentencing was the Fair Sentencing Act that President Barack Obama signed into law in 2010. This law reduced the sentencing disparity between crack and powder cocaine significantly, from a 100:1 ratio to a ratio of 18:1. In the last several years, there have been more legislative bills drafted and debated that are aimed at solving the problem of mass incarceration and overcriminalization, particularly within the realm of drug reform. There is consensus throughout the federal branch of government that change is necessary. Former Attorney General Eric Holder has stated, "that too many Americans go to too many prisons for far too long and for no truly good law enforcement reason."[14] Reform needs to extend beyond drug crime.

Providing greater discretion to judges would have a significant impact in solving the problem that Attorney General Holder mentions. Until the 1980s federal judges had the discretion to sentence felons to probation or the maximum punishment. There were only a few punishments that carried mandatory minimum sentences. According the United States Sentencing Commission, "Since 1991, the number of

---

[13] John Conyers, Jr., "The Incarceration Explosion," *Yale Law and Policy Review* 31 (2013): 385.
[14] Eric Holder, Address at the Annual Meeting of the American Bar Association's House of Delegates (August 12, 2013), www.justice.gov/isolopalag/speeches/2013/ag-speech-130812.

mandatory minimum penalties has more than doubled."[15] Looking over a similar timeline, there is a correlation between the number of mandatory minimums and the increase in the amount of federal and state prisoners. The federal population ballooned from 25,000 prisoners in 1980 to over 218,000 in 2012.[16] Since the Sentencing Guidelines have been in place, most federal sentencing judges handed down sentences strongly in line with the guidelines. Osler and Bennett argue that there are several reasons for nearly universal adherence to the guidelines. Many judges have never *not* had the guidelines. This implies that judges are not using discretion because the possibility has been removed, and they simply, do not know how. The guidelines have been in place for so long judges are not familiar with how to rule outside of them. Although the guidelines have been made advisory rather than mandatory due to the *Booker* ruling, many judges know only that they feel safe with them and are not comfortable ruling outside of their normal actions. This phenomenon is characterized by Osler and Bennett as "cognitive anchoring," research suggests that the ranges put in place by the Guidelines anchor the judges to any potential sentencing.[17] The danger here is if judges really are anchored to Guidelines, there could be large errors in judgment, insofar as there is any judgment at all. The strong influence of the guidelines greatly limit the role of judges, stripping them of their individuality and power in the courtroom, in essence relegating the judge to a simple administrator.

Passing legislation that reduced mandatory minimums on a congressional level would significantly affect federal and state law and in turn remove the restrictions placed on judges. An added bonus of this is that it would also incentivize and encourage state legislatures to pass laws that would have similar mitigating effects on overcriminalization. Members of Congress must take the first steps followed by state legislators in order to show initiative on criminal justice reform. As most felons are held in state prisons, these types of legislations would also have the biggest impact on the improvement of cities and communities.

WHAT JUDGES HAVE TO SAY

Judges, legal scholars, and members of the criminal justice system are beginning to raise concerns about the rampant problems with lack of judicial discretion. More and more, judicial discretion is being highlighted on a national level

---

[15] US Sentencing Commission, Report to the Congress: Mandatory Minimum Penalties in the Federal Criminal Justice System (2011) 71–72.

[16] Nathan James. The Federal Prison Population Buildup: Overview, Policy Changes, Issues and Options, *Cong. Research Serv* (2013) 2

[17] Mark W. Bennett, "Confronting Cognitive 'Anchoring Effect' And 'Blind Spot' Biases In Federal Sentencing: A Modest Solution for Reforming A Fundamental Flaw," *Journal of Criminal Law & Criminology* 104 (2014): 116–26.

as something that needs to be addressed in order to bring about positive change toward a more equitable system.

As concerned citizens, it is important to ask how often judges are forced to hand down decisions they disagree with or wish that they could have more discretion on, not for their own convenience, but for the good of the defendant and community. Judges are too often left powerless because they are not handing down real justice or empowering individuals that made mistakes. Bennett, a federal judge for over two decades, believed that he had often viewed his job as less about presiding than abiding by dozens of mandatory minimum sentences established by Congress in the late 1980s for federal offenses. Those mandatory penalties, many of which require at least a decade in prison for drug offenses, took discretion away from judges and fueled an unprecedented rise in prison populations.

This is the type of situation that judges across the country have to deal with when they hand down sentences. When trying to understand the character of a defendant, judges must have the ability to examine the entire life story and circumstances which led to the offense. This perspective must be embraced if the problem of recidivism is to be reduced. There seems to be a fundamental lack of understanding about the individuals committing crimes and the type of experiences which have characterized their lives. Only with objective and methodical, reasoned understanding can institutional changes designed to help people like Weller. One of these institutional changes could be giving judges like Bennett more discretion in sentencing. This discretion should not undermine the rule of law or its role in deterrence. Judges need to have more of a role in making those decisions.

PROPORTIONALITY

Judges have the unique ability to dictate whether the punishment of a felon fits the crime committed. This issue is one of proportionality. Many make the case that the laws are disproportionate to the crimes which violate laws that are on the books. The main issues with this relate to mandatory sentencing and the motivations of prosecutors. Unfortunately, prosecutors are not terribly incentivized to care about proportionality. It may be in their character to care, but it is certainly not in their job description or the realities of their work environment. Prosecutors often try to push for increasing penalties, not creating leniency. Judges will often use their discretion in sentencing in order to help the defendant get what they need in order to curtail their criminal problems. Examples of providing help to defendants would be sentencing rehabilitation for alcoholics or drug addicts, and psychologists for people with mental disorders. With an increase in mandatory sentencing, this aspect of the law and of the important and influential role of judges is taken away. It is a great irrationality that power is being taken away from judges when they are the ones best in position to provide defendants with the help they need to stop committing crimes.

In the American criminal justice system, there are punishments that are much more severe than the crimes. The justice system and punishment has been used in an attempt to solve a host of other societal and cultural problems. Heavy incarceration breaks up families and communities, and as a result, the people from these broken families and communities are more likely to commit crime, which perpetuates the problem. The public, academics and elected officials must work together to start to shrink this problem. Rather than blindly punishing individuals, their punishments and treatments would be more effective if matched to what they need to become productive citizens. A 2010 estimate puts federal, state, and local expenditures at $80 billion, with most of this spending coming at the state and local level.[18]

JUVENILE CRIME

In addition to heavier sentencing for adult offenders, juvenile offenders have also been targeted for greater punishment. More and more juvenile offenders are being treated as adults. Recently there has been an increase in the number of state statutes that punish juveniles with tougher penalties and reduce the age that juveniles can be sentenced as adults. Along with mandatory minimums, laws have been implemented that increase the amount of crimes that juvenile offenders must serve in criminal court. As a result, the number of offenders has increased because of these technical adjustments.

There are currently forty-six states that give judges discretion in determining which juvenile offenders are sent to criminal court, so long as the automatic transfer to criminal court does not take place. There are noteworthy stipulations in state laws that make certain situations more serious than others: The offender is at least fourteen years of age, the act is "heinous or aggravated," the child is beyond rehabilitation, and the sentence is in the best interest of society; the child is sixteen years of age, committed a serious drug offense (IC 35 – 48-4), and it is in the best interests in society; the child is ten years of age and committed murder; or the child is sixteen and committed a class A or B felony, involuntary manslaughter or reckless homicide, and it would be in the best interests of the community; and last, the youth committed a felony and has been previously convicted of a felony or a nontraffic misdemeanor (IC-30–3-2–6).

Even with this sort of law, judges have the ability to use their discretion on a case-by-case basis in evaluating the defendant. Judges have the ability to take into account the age of the offender, as well as any history of abuse, family neglect, educational level, and other significant factors that may affect people's decisions. This is important because policy makers can use the tendencies of the judges to determine what

---

[18] Melissa S Kearny, Benjamin H. Harris, Elisa Jacome, and Lucie Parker. *Ten Economic Facts about Crime and Incarceration in the United States* (Washington, DC: Brookings Institute, 2014).

success is achieved in the system. It is likely that the judges have the most knowledge of what practices are working and which are not. When legislators want to know what best incentivizes felons to reform and rehabilitate, working with judges has shown to be the most prudent in creating effective policy. Our concern for the end of the book is whether or not this is enough.

In order to evaluate the cases of the defendants, judges look at the situations from which they come. Understanding the life of the offender is important for judges to make smart choices regarding appropriate punishment. This practice, referred to as attitudinal theory, analyzes the attitude of someone is based on beliefs informed by their life experiences. Judges use this to extrapolate the life of the individual to the crime that they have committed. Ideally, judges will take into account the life that the defendant has lived up to this point and determine what level of punishment and rehabilitation is necessary to garner the most improvement.

Attitudinal theory posits that the beliefs and values of the individuals inform the intention of their decisions. The theory suggests that there is a causal link between how the individual was raised.[19] Because attitudes are so important in determining the causes of one's actions, it would be prudent and beneficial for judges to analyze the behaviors of offenders as well as their beliefs, values, and how they were raised. By informing judges with these pieces of data, our justice system will be able to better serve offenders and get them the help they need. We may also start to acquire data on delinquency statistics and information on determining at-risk youths.

Additionally, some researchers argue that trying children as adults has no effect on crime statistics and that transferring juveniles to adult court will actually do more harm than good. In examining the research evidence, Jeffery Fagan finds that rates of juvenile offending are not lower in states where it is relatively more common to try adolescents as adults.[20] Likewise, juveniles who have been tried as adults are no less likely to reoffend than their counterparts who have been tried as juveniles. Treating juveniles as adult criminals, Fagan concludes, is not effective as a means of crime control.

Fagan argues that the proliferation of transfer regimes over the past several decades calls into question the very rationale for a juvenile court. Transferring adolescent offenders to the criminal court exposes them to harsh and sometimes toxic forms of punishment that have the perverse effect of increasing criminal activity. The accumulating evidence on transfer, the recent decrease in serious juvenile crime, and new gains in the science of adolescent development, concludes Fagan, may be persuading legislators, policymakers, and practitioners that eighteen may yet again be the appropriate age for juvenile court jurisdiction. Again, thinking

[19] Jill M D'Angelo, "Juvenile Court Judges' Attitudes Toward Waiver Decisions in Indiana." *Juvenile Court Judges Journal* (n.d.): 1–2. Kaplan.edu. Kaplan, 2006. Accessed May 5, 2016.
[20] Jeffrey Fagan. "Juvenile Crime and Criminal Justice: Resolving Border Disputes." *SSRN Electronic Journal SSRN Journal* 18.2 (2008): 81–118. Campaignforyouthjustice.org. 2008. Accessed May 7, 2016.

of juveniles as persons, we need a better approach to youth offenders than incarceration and leaving them to the care of the state.

ADULT REINTEGRATION: EFFECTIVE SOLUTIONS

Tackling recidivism is important in reducing the debilitating impact of incarceration, and the successful reintegration of offenders into society is vital in order to understand how increased judicial discretion would be an effective method for criminal justice reform. Only recently have there been programs that strive to successfully reintegrate prisoners into society. After decades of prisoner recidivism is there is finally consensus that the prison system is not helping offenders reintegrate. More and more, researchers are investigating important policy implementations that can help felons across the country reintegrate into society. Investigation into more innovative policies and practices will be useful on both a federal and state level when it comes to criminal justice reform. Topics include determining which prison programs work best when it comes to prisoner reintegration, minimizing the negative effect that children face, acknowledging the problem that our society faces with prisoner reintegration, and how to use a comprehensive reform to help individuals.[21] Most importantly, we must recognize that government programs are limited in what they can accomplish.

There are several approaches to helping offenders reintegrate into society. Bazemore and Stinchcomb suggest that communities must commit themselves to breaking down the barriers between citizens and offenders, developing offenders into productive citizens. This social support, they suggest, could significantly improve the lives of ex-offenders. Many dissenting voices to structural reform are worried about the programs that are currently offered to prisoners.[22] Unfortunately, not as much emphasis is put on the back-end of an offender's sentence. It seems most citizens only care about getting the convict off the streets, not back on them. It is this emphasis on punishment and physical revenge against the convict which is at the core of many criminal justice problems. Naturally, the government, both federal and state, should be focused on programs that have proven to be effective. Through the implementation of successful programs, more felons can be helped and communities empowered with productive citizens. Through the utilization of behavioral treatment and therapy which maximize community and family to make decisions, community-based programs are able to treat the problems that these convicts have, not just the symptoms of their problems. Many researchers offer different suggestions in the hopes that the justice system can improve. Most recognize the contribution

[21] Candace Smith, "Rising to the Challenge: Prisoner Reintegration." *The Society Pages*, April 2, 2013. Accessed: May 8, 2016.
[22] Joan Petersilia. "What Works in Prisoner Reentry? Reviewing and Questioning the Evidence." *Federal Probation*, 68.2 (2004): 4.

that community makes to the individual offenders. This is something that has been widely successful when considering rehabilitation, as can be seen in the use of drug courts. A large part of the communicative aspect of prisoner reintegration is helping families that are affected by imprisonment and incarceration. Later chapters of this book will explore how incarceration has a large negative effect on the lives of children and family members.

There are currently programs at three levels that serve to help incarcerated felons: programs during incarceration, which seek to assist offenders in preparing for their release; programs during release, which try and connect felons with other services that they need; and programs after release that focus on the long-term health of the convict. On all three of these levels, judges can help ex-convicts. By sentencing them into programs that are successful, judges can help reduce recidivism. "Despite the relative lack of highly rigorous research on the effectiveness of some reentry programs, an emerging 'what works' literature suggests that programs focusing on work training and placement, drug and mental health treatment, and housing assistance have proven to be effective."[23] These are examples of practical and very real issues that felons face that go unnoticed but can be helped.

For many prisoners, especially those who have spent extended periods of time behind bars, release comes with both relief and anxiety. One of the goals of the justice system should be to relieve some of that anxiety, but given what human persons need, can we expect government to do this alone? Is government even the best institution to achieve this goal? Communities should be making it as easy as possible for felons to start over and succeed. Ex-offenders often want to start over, but they don't know how. They often need some sort of counseling or outside help but have minute resources. Many do not have the capability to provide for themselves on even the most basic level.

DISCRETION IMPLEMENTED: LEGAL REALITIES

Procedural matters are vital in the effective use of judicial discretion. The ruling of the judge must be able to survive being challenged in appellate court as reasonable. For this reason, in practice, judges have important decisions to make in terms of ensuring that they are doing the right thing in the right way. Ensuring all of the relevant facts are on the record is key for judges so that clearly through evidence presented there will be a clear argument for their decision. judges have found it necessary to spend more time themselves mastering the area of law that corresponds to the case. Relying on memoranda from clerks is too risky because of the scrutiny

[23] Nathan James, "Offender Reentry: Correctional Statistics, Reintegration into the Community, and Recidivism." Washington, DC: Congressional Research Service, Library of Congress, 2009. Congressional Research Service, January 12 2015. Accessed May 15, 2016.

that follows. When Judges successfully apply judicial discretion, they are well rooted in a personal understanding of the area of law in the case.

Rule of law in its application is by definition the absence of individual discretion, in a method that allows for mistakes to be avoided and fixed. The areas where discretion is required are supposed to be upheld by the highest forms of personal integrity of the judges in accordance with what is just. All discretion is not simply in reducing sentencing. In fact, there are a variety of manifestations of judicial discretion, and the flexibility and sometimes creativity of the judge is put to the test in terms of what area of the situation to utilize discretion. Proponents of judicial discretion often rarely consider the legal complexities and realities of its application. There is not a standard process for applying discretion, which often leads to judges not taking action. Discretion was considered, but after careful thought not taking action was determined to be the best course. Although no change was made, discretion was used. If discretion is applied in a way that is significant, the judge must always have a strong and simple argument for right vs. wrong, and why he had to apply his discretionary power in order to ensure the right thing was done and a wrong avoided or mitigated. Judges must employ sharp strategy on the consequences of their decision, both in the lives of the litigants as well as the legal community. Harm must always be avoided. Decisions that utilize judicial discretion are the most time consuming and they place extra emphasis on communicating their decision in a way that translates simply and logically. The proclamation by the judge must be implemented by the criminal justice system so there must be an understandable rationale that can be followed by staff for proper enforcement. In the real world, judges make mistakes. Situations that deserve discretion can still be mishandled. It is important for the public to understand that judges must understand their decisions when they are in error and that they seek to correct mistakes. Beyond doing their best, judges are faced with constant decisions, so once they have made up their mind they move on. By understanding the perspective and experience of judges, advocates for judicial discretion are better empowered to improve the criminal justice system.

CONCLUSION

There are significant strides and advancements to be made in the realms of judicial discretion and rehabilitation. The state and local level are crucial for this reform, as they hold the most incarcerated individuals. It is personalism that calls our attention to the fact that judges need more discretion to consider the consequences of sentencing for the person under the rule of law in every case that comes before the court. Justice administered at the level closest to the offenders will help the offender reintegrate into their community after release.

Although local actions are vital, Congress and federal offices must take strategic initiative to solve the problem because we are not simply talking about law in the abstract but the lives of persons who are profoundly connected to other persons. By reforming the laws at the federal level, Congress can set an example for state and local lawmakers. Ideally, criminal justice reform is something that can take place at each level of government. As we will explore in a later chapter, some states have already taken the step to solving specific criminal justice problems like the lack of judicial discretion, juvenile punishment, and felon reintegration.

Judges are the foundation of the court experience and must be entrusted with the power to make decisions. Discretion involves intelligent judgment, a requirement every citizen trusts a judge with fulfilling with honor. The limitation of judges' powers creates an impersonal system that does not apply common sense solutions to the individual lives of those in the system. Procedures and guidelines cannot accommodate the individual as it is defined in personalism. Unique individual, local circumstances are what bring people into courtrooms, and judges need the ability to apply the law to those particulars. With the ability to use their best judgment, this action will reduce the horrifying mistakes that are made from general guidelines such as mandatory minimums. Even if judges are given more effective discretion by lawmakers, it will not yield better results if defendants are left to the mercy of a public defense system that inadvertently undermines avenues for offenders to receive a fair hearing of their case before a judge. We cannot have good reforms without reforming the ability of public defenders to do their jobs.

4

Disparities in Quality Defense

In 2004, Evans Ray, Jr., arranged a drug sale. He had two prior drug offenses, and the third would cost him the most. During sentencing, the judge told the forty-two-year old barber, husband, and father of four that "[i]t is my desire not to sentence you to life." He added, "I believe that the circumstances justify a sentence shorter than life. I further believe that there is some disproportionality between what you've done and the sentence of life."[1]

Ray had been a middleman in a drug transaction that he was pushed into by a friend, who later turned out to be a government informant, and made no money off of the deal. He got the worse end of the sentencing because of his two priors, and the judge was unable to secure the twenty-seven-year sentence he wanted for Ray because of a prosecutorial appeal. The third-strike law was enacted and the minimum sentence was life in prison. In 2016, President Obama granted Ray clemency. Ray, now 57, spent twelve years in a high-security prison with violent offenders and has now joined forces with the judge who sentenced him to fight against mandatory minimums.[2]

The standard explanation of the mass incarceration problem usually starts with a story like Ray's and ends with a short history of the war on drugs, 1970s politicians campaigning on reducing crime, the rise of intense policing, and using the legal system to fix America's problems. These are contributing factors, but the problem has roots more widespread in American social, economic, and political life.

---

[1] Justin Moyer. "A Drug Dealer Got a Life Sentence and Was Devastated. So Was the Judge Who Sentenced Him." *The Washington Post.* May 06, 2017. Accessed August 01, 2017. www .washingtonpost.com/local/a-drug-dealer-got-a-life-sentence-and-was-devastated-so-was-the-judge-who-sentenced-him/2017/05/04/efb81020-2aa0-11e7-9b05-6c63a274fd4b_story.html?utm_ term=.871f46cd61f0.

[2] James D Walsh. "What It Feels Like When a Life Sentence Is Overturned." *NY Mag.* May 6, 2017. Accessed August 01, 2017. http://nymag.com/vindicated/2016/11/what-it-feels-like-when-a-life-sentence-is-overturned.html.

Our nation has a cultural problem as much as a legal problem, and the "standard story," as John Pfaff calls it, is not the only answer. His book, *Locked In*, describes other causes the standard story fails to tell: the rise in violent crime, public prison unions, rural politicians, prosecutors, and the economic benefits of large penitentiaries.[3] It is time to turn the debate into action to begin to reduce the amount of people who are incarcerated.

Freedom isn't free; justice costs money. Poor people have no money, yet under the Constitution they are guaranteed justice. These simple facts govern the realities surrounding solving the quagmire of indigent defense. The indigent defense system has run into significant problems and is perceived as a system that provides lower quality defense than the services of a private attorney. Across the nation, public defenders are looked at as less than capable lawyers and inadequate defenders for the poor. Lower-income people accused of crimes find their lives at the mercy of overworked public defenders swamped with cases and shockingly often disinterested and unqualified. Research shows that even before incarceration rates accelerated in the 1980s, overburdened systems of indigent defense struggled to meet the Sixth Amendment constitutional mandate. States are unable to fund adequate indigent defense systems or provide sufficient resources for oversight, training, and management of cases. An exchange between a social science researcher an indigent defendant sums up the problem well, "Did you have a lawyer when you went to court? No. I had a public defender."[4] Much of the current research has found that too many public defenders provide a less quality defense that their peers in the private attorney industry. Poor policy and lack of incentives have created poor judicial systems that weaken our nation.

When the right for public defense became common across the United States in the 1960s the goal was to provide the same type of defense across the justice system regardless of wealth or status. The constitutional principle, as it was argued by the Supreme Court, said that equal rights and defense needed to assure that someone did not receive special treatment under the law for their place in society because of the defense they could afford. The quality and competence counsel provided to the poor has diminished for different reasons across the country, from racial bias to funding. The scope of the problem across states indigent defense programs is so large no solution has been comprehensive enough.

The current system of indigent defense across the country does not accomplish its objective. Instead of bringing equitable counsel to a socioeconomic class who cannot afford representation, the system provides defendants with overworked and

---

[3] Matt Ford. "Rethinking Mass Incarceration in America." *The Atlantic*. March 02, 2017. Accessed August 01, 2017. www.theatlantic.com/politics/archive/2017/03/rethinking-mass-incarceration/518229/.

[4] Stephen J. Schulhofer and David D. Friedman. "Reforming Indigent Defense: How Free Market Principles Can Help to Fix a Broken System." Cato Institute. September 1, 2010. Accessed June 29, 2016. http://object.cato.org/sites/cato.org/files/pubs/pdf/pa666.pdf, 7.

underpaid lawyers considered the bottom rung of the legal profession. Large case-loads prevent these individuals from having sufficient time to meet with the defend-ant before court to build a quality defense. This chapter will explore how the indigent defense crisis is one of the contributing factors to the overcriminalization problem in the United States today. The solutions to the problem vary but what is true is that we will not make much progress toward criminal justice reform without also starting with reforming the indigent defense system.

THE CONTEXT FOR INDIGENT DEFENSE AND
THE 6TH AMENDMENT

In 1963 the Supreme Court heard arguments for a landmark case that would shape the approach to justice in the following decades.[5] The defendant, Clarence Earl Gideon, was charged with breaking and entering and intent to commit a misde-meanor, a felony offense in Florida. Gideon could not afford an attorney, and Florida's laws only required court-appointed lawyers in capital offense cases. Gideon represented himself, playing the role of an attorney in every aspect of the trial, but lost the case and was sentenced to five years in prison. Once convicted, Gideon submitted an appeal to the Supreme Court of the United States, and the Court overruled a previous decision regarding appointing a counsel for an indigent defendant. Under the new decision in *Gideon v. Wainwright* (1963), any person on trial cannot be refused a lawyer if he or she cannot afford defense. In his opinion for the majority Justice Black wrote,

> reason and reflection require us to recognize that in our adversary system of criminal justice, any person haled into court, who is too poor to hire a lawyer, cannot be assured a fair trial unless counsel is provided for him.[6]

Before this decision there were several other cases involving the right to a fair trial. In the 1920s and 1930s there were several cases involving the narrow state laws regarding appointed counsel including *Powell v. Alabama* (1932) that set the stage for several important Supreme Court verdicts on indigent defense.[7] In *Powell*, the court held that several black teenagers sentenced to death were underrepresented by attorneys assigned too late in the trial to give them an adequate defense. Justice Sutherland's opinion for the court included arguments for the need for defenders for those who cannot afford one or do not have a knowledge of the law. He wrote about court appointed counsel and said, "Without it, though he be not guilty, he faces the

---

[5] *Gideon v. Wainwright* 372 U.S. 335 (1963)
[6] "*Gideon v. Wainwright.*" United States Courts. Accessed June 08, 2016. www.uscourts.gov/
    educational-resources/educational-activities/facts-and-case-summary-gideon-v-wainwright.
[7] *Powell v. Alabama* 287 U.S. 45 (1932)

danger of conviction because he does not know how to establish his innocence."[8] These words clarify the mindset that allowed for the later *Gideon* decision.

Since this decision, every state has developed a system of public defense. The decision guaranteed that those accused of felony offenses are entitled to a lawyer under the rights outlined in the Sixth Amendment, which include the right to a jury trial, a public trial, and pertaining to *Gideon*, "to have the assistance of counsel for his defence."[9] In the wake of the *Gideon* decision each state was required to develop a system of public defenders to represent those who did not have a legal counsel, and especially those who could not afford a lawyer. There are three basic types of public defense systems across the United States: public defender offices staffed by government attorneys, contractual arrangements between the government and private attorneys to provide services, and a system of private attorneys assigned on a case-by-case basis.[10]

Since inception, indigent defense has had problems that are inherent in providing any attorney services. These issues have plagued states and court systems before overcriminalization became a problem and have helped lead to America's high incidents of incarceration, probation, and parole. When the Supreme Court ruled that there is a constitutional right to representation by an attorney, the court system had to find a way to provide these attorneys. The question of who should pay for the attorney's fees and the quality of attorney that the defendant receives are core concerns of the past fifty years. Often, the problems surrounding indigent defense are separated from overcriminalization, but the two issues are directly linked. Across the United States there are systems that jail poor minorities at higher rates than affluent members of society. There is a link between affluence and quality of defense in courts, and a link between poverty and the chance of spending time in prison. This connection is the problem. Race or income should not determine a fair and just trial. The justice system should convict the guilty and acquit the innocent, but problems in indigent defense grossly distort this standard.[11]

Since 1963, the meaning of "to have the assistance of counsel for his defense," was expanded to mean everyone accused of a crime has a right to a lawyer regardless if they have one or not, or if they can afford to pay a lawyer.[12] When the ruling in *Gideon* expanded the right to counsel to state level courts it opened the floor for all kinds of new questions about dealing with providing counsel to defendants.

---

[8] *"Powell v. Alabama."* LII / Legal Information Institute. Accessed November 02, 2016. www.law .cornell.edu/supremecourt/text/287/45.

[9] "Facts and Case Summary – *Gideon v. Wainwright*." United States Courts.

[10] Stephen J Schulhofer and David D. Friedman. *Reforming Indigent Defense How Free Market Principles Can Help to Fix a Broken System.* Cato Institute. September 1, 2010. Accessed June 29, 2016. http://object.cato.org/sites/cato.org/files/pubs/pdf/pa666.pdf, 2.

[11] William J. Stuntz, *The Collapse of American Criminal Justice* (Cambridge, Mass.: Belknap Press of Harvard University Press, 2011), 209–215.

[12] "Sixth Amendment." LII / Legal Information Institute. Accessed June 08, 2016. www.law .cornell.edu/constitution/sixth_amendment.

After 1963, each state's distinct policies created unique problems which compromise today's justice system. In the 1990s significant research and reporting was done on the growing problems with indigent defense and court-appointed lawyers. As overcriminalization was more apparent, data became even more important. A Bureau of Justice Statistics (BJS) report in 1999 looked at the growing problem in the late 1990s and specifically looked at the state funded indigent criminal defense services of twenty-one states.[13] Eleven of these twenty-one states used 100 percent state funds to support indigent defense, and the other ten used a combination of state, federal, and local money to fund the programs.[14] In 1999 the twenty-one states spent double the amount they did in 1982 on the indigent defense programs to keep up with the increased number of cases and those on trial who could not afford a lawyer.[15] The increases in spending do not always correlate with better representation because they often are in response to an increase in cases as well. As the number of cases began to increase in the 1980s the responses in public defender methods and policies were often slow to respond.

These issues surrounding indigent defense are only made worse by the policing tactics common in poor and minority areas. Arrests are disproportionately felt by poor and minority populations as courts need more people to represent those that cannot afford to pay an attorney. Districts need more funding to pay attorneys, and there are not enough attorneys to keep up with the increasing number of cases. Lack of money to pay public defenders ensures that the best defenders steer clear of careers in indigent defense. The system is on the verge of collapse and is incapable of providing justice for the poor. The system was intended to provide equal justice across socioeconomic barriers, but it fails those it was designed for.

The type of crimes covered by indigent defense and methods of using a public defender have varied since its inception. In 1932, the Supreme Court ruled that indigent defendants facing the death penalty have the right to an assigned attorney.[16] After *Gideon* the types of trials that qualified indigents for defense increased significantly to include felonies, misdemeanors and juvenile trials, as well as some non-criminal proceedings involving parental rights.[17]

---

[13] Carol J. DeFrances. *State-Funded Indigent Defense Services, 1999.* Report. January 10, 2001. Accessed June 8, 2016. www.bjs.gov/content/pub/pdf/sfids99.pdf.

[14] Ibid., 1.

[15] Ibid.

[16] Stevens, Holly R., Colleen E. Sheppard, Robert Spangenberg, Aimee Wickman, and Jon B. Gould. *State, County and Local Expenditures for Indigent Defense Services Fiscal Year 2008.* Report. The Center for Justice, Law and Society at George Mason University, George Mason University. November 2010. Accessed July 7, 2016. www.americanbar.org/content/dam/aba/administrative/legal_aid_indigent_defendants/ls_sclaid_def_expenditures_fy08.authcheck dam.pdf, 1.

[17] Holly R. Stevens, Colleen E. Sheppard, Robert Spangenberg, Aimee Wickman, and Jon B. Gould. *State, County and Local Expenditures*, 1

People most often arrested and put on trial also need indigent defense the most, many are poorly educated and in a cycle of imprisonment. Lawyers in the public defense system make less money and they are overworked compared to their private counterparts. Quality and competency are immediately required in the indigent defense system, and civil society must make it happen.

PROVIDING COMPETENT COUNSEL

The largest problems with the indigent defense is meeting the standards of defendants when public defenders are lower-skill lawyers paid much less than private attorneys. The most experienced lawyers move to private practice for the financial incentives it offers; many of the poorest defendants get the most inexperienced attorneys. The shortage of quality lawyers compounds the problem. The best lawyers in public defense are overwhelmed and up against DA offices with full staffs and comparatively unlimited budgets.

Wealthier areas have more funding for higher-quality indigent defense services. Areas that have less funding have lower quality defenses and more incorrect verdicts. Equal justice does not exist because of these problems. A publication of the *Wisconsin Law Review* said that the breakdown of equal justice occurs when "luck, money, and location primarily determining whether a defendant has meaningful access to justice in this country."[18] How systems are funded creates wealth inequality in the justice system.

Many cases at the federal and state level involve court appointed attorneys. A BJS study found that 82 percent of state defendants and 66 percent of federal defendants in 1996 and 1998 received defense from a publicly appointed attorney.[19] While more received defense from a publicly appointed attorney the problem as it relates to incarceration rates can be seen from the number of guilty verdicts that resulted in imprisonment. The report found that in the late 1990s, more defendants with "guilty" verdicts that were defended by a court-appointed attorney received a sentence of incarceration.[20] In federal courts, 88 percent of defendants with public defenders and 77 percent of those with private attorneys received a sentence with jail or prison time.[21] In State courts, the divide was even wider: 71 percent with public counsel and 54 percent with private counsel were sentenced to incarceration.[22] The type of crimes defended by private attorneys reflect the type of people that can afford

---

[18] Rodney Uphoff. *Convicting the Innocent: Aberration or Systemic Problem.* Report no. 2006–20. School of Law, University of Missouri – Columbia. Wisconsin Law Review. 742. Accessed June 21, 2016. http://papers.ssrn.com/sol3/papers.cfm?abstract_id=912310.

[19] Caroline Wolf Harlow. *Defense Counsel in Criminal Cases.* Rep. Bureau of Justice Statistics, November 2000.

[20] Harlow, *Defense Counsel,* 1.

[21] Ibid., 1.

[22] Ibid.

the better defense available. The report found that the majority of those using private defense were accused of white collar crimes, 43 percent of fraud and 63 percent of regulatory offense which are: "violations of laws pertaining to agriculture, antitrust, food and drug, transportation, civil rights, communications, customs, and postal delivery."[23] Only two in ten of those charged with violent crimes used the services of a private lawyer.[24] The report states that the difference in the incarceration rates can likely be explained by the type of offenses defended by public versus private attorneys. The report found that

> public counsel represented a higher percentage of violent, drug, and public order (excluding regulatory crimes) offenders, who were very likely to receive a sentence to serve time, and private counsel represented a higher percentage of white collar defendants, who are not as likely to receive incarceration sentences.[25]

Those that commit white collar crimes are often those who can afford the high costs of the private attorneys to represent them. The private attorneys are often more experienced and paid more money regardless of what area they are in. The public defenders often do not even have the chance to meet with their clients before representing them, and represent hundreds of cases over the course of a few weeks or months, diluting the possibility of adequate representation.

The BJS report describes that 37 percent of publicly defended state inmates spoke with their attorney within the first week of being arrested. Of those with hired private counsel, 60 percent spoke with their lawyer within the first week. In federal cases, 54 percent with public lawyers and 75 percent with private defense spoke with their lawyer within a week of arrest.[26] The inmates who were privately defended spoke with their lawyers more frequently during their initial imprisonment as well. The ability to be able to speak with an attorney more frequently and earlier on in your trial gives those with private attorneys a different experience than those who cannot afford private counsel. If your counsel is able to hear your case, review the facts, and provide information on release possibilities early on in the process, much of the stress and negative effects of jail after arrest can be avoided. State prison inmates with public counsel were more likely to serve longer sentences than those with private attorneys, and minority inmates were more likely to have publicly appointed defenders than their white counterparts.

For many in minority communities, frequent imprisonment is influenced with the quality of counsel at trials. Public defenders are more likely to encourage those they represent to enter guilty pleas, especially if the verdict of the case does not affect their job, salary, or standing in the public defense community. Thirty years after *Gideon*, the discrimination inherent in the criminal justice system was already

[23] Ibid., 3.
[24] Ibid.
[25] Ibid.
[26] Ibid., 8.

widespread and apparent from both internal and external studies. Over the past decade the problem has reached a breaking point in some states where the crisis of indigent defense is creating injustices against the people the system was intended to help.

When *Gideon* was originally decided the right to counsel was considered fundamental. At the most basic level its goal was to create a system of "fair trials before impartial tribunals in which every defendant stands equal before the law."[27] Over the past five decades since the *Gideon* decision there has been a slow increase in the problems associated with indigent defense, especially at the state level where most cases of public defense take place. Since the fiftieth anniversary of the *Gideon* decision there have been many articles and reports published highlighting the problems in different states.

Caseloads for court-appointed lawyers have been increasing even as funding has decreased. The *Atlantic* published an article by Dylan Walsh about the growing fight in many states for the right to legal counsel. This article focuses on the state of Louisiana and looks specifically the Concordia Parish along the Mississippi river. Like many poor, rural areas of the country, the Concordia Parish suffers from drug problems that flood the local courts with a high volume of cases involving illegal substances. The district's chief public defender's office handles around 3,300 cases per year, three times what the state recommends.[28] This is not a problem unique to Louisiana; most public defender offices operate above recommended levels of cases for their attorneys.

This spiraling problem with public defenders and case numbers is caused by the growing number of cases and the parallel need for more lawyers and more funds to pay them. One example given in the Louisiana case claims that some lawyers were being paid $1000 for 100 cases, or just $10 per case. With this level of income, public defenders in these parishes often need more than one job to cover costs and cannot live on their salary as a lawyer alone. In one parish, the office stopped representing some accused of certain misdemeanors because of financial needs and understaffing. Walsh quotes the Louisiana Public Defender Board (that oversees each district office) which predicted the imminent "systemic failure in the public-defense system."[29] The failure began when the New Orleans Public Defenders office announced it would begin refusing certain cases, even serious felonies involving murder and rape.[30]

---

[27] "*Gideon v. Wainwright.*" LII / Legal Information Institute. Accessed June 14, 2016. www.law .cornell.edu/supremecourt/text/372/335.

[28] Dylan Walsh. "On the Defensive." *The Atlantic*, June 2, 2016. Accessed June 15, 2016. www .theatlantic.com/politics/archive/2016/06/on-the-defensive/485165/.

[29] Ben Myers. "Orleans Public Defender's Office to Begin Refusing Serious Felony Cases Tuesday." NOLA.com. January 11, 2016. Accessed June 15, 2016. www.nola.com/crime/index .ssf/2016/01/orleans_public_defenders_to_be.html?version=meter at 1.

[30] Myers, "Orleans Public Defender's."

Without the funds to pay lawyers, states like Louisiana provide no incentives for those attending law school to become a public defender. It is less a question of serving the community, and more a question of being able to provide for yourself on the incredibly low salaries when compared to other areas of the law. The defendants that need the service of public defenders often have similar traits. To qualify you must be poor, and because of aggressive policing in poor neighborhoods, especially in poor minority neighborhoods, the need for quality public defenders and the funds to pay them is rising. The problem is that even with the court-provided attorneys, the quality of defense is much lower than that received by citizens that can afford their own lawyers. This creates a system where the rich receive better defense than the poor, skewing the justice system against the less fortunate. With the number of cases increasing, and the number of public defenders decreasing, the ability of public defenders to do their job and defend the rights of the poor and marginalized becomes even harder. Louisiana is only one of the many states fighting against these costs, but the deck is increasingly stacked against those who cannot afford a proper defense across the United States.

The competency of a public defense lawyers is something that is questioned in each of these instances, but the standard set for re-trials by the Supreme Court is a high mark to reach. In *Strickland v. Washington* the court held that for a defendant to argue that his or her counsel was ineffective they must prove that the counsel's "conduct so undermined the proper functioning of the adversarial process that the trial cannot be relied on as having produced a just result."[31] To receive a reversal or to set aside of a death sentence the defendant must prove "that counsel's performance was deficient and, second, that the deficient performance prejudiced the defense so as to deprive the defendant of a fair trial."[32]

With the number of cases increasing, and the number of public defenders decreasing, the ability of public defenders to do their job and "defend" the rights of the poor and marginalized becomes even harder. New York, like many other states, does not have a statewide system of indigent defense. In New York, each county provides the resources for indigent defense which results in some of the poorest counties falling far short of providing just trials for defendants. If the quality of defense differs from one county to another the system would seem to be providing adequate defense to some indigents. A 2006 New York State Commission on the Future of Indigent Defense Services report found that "nothing short of major, far-reaching reform can ensure that New York meets its constitutional and statutory obligations to provide quality representation to every indigent person accused of a

[31] "*Strickland v. Washington* 466 U.S. 668 (1984)." Justia Law. Accessed June 15, 2016. https://supreme.justia.com/cases/federal/us/466/668/case.html.
[32] Justia Law, "*Strickland v. Washington.*"

crime or other offense."[33] Without a proper defense and resources to decided cases, many cases in the poorest counties suffer from a higher chance of conviction for innocent defendants and a higher chance of acquittal for those that are actually guilty.

Problems also exist in the relationship between attorneys and their clients. Schulhofer and Friedman argue that a large part of the problem in indigent defense today exists in the public defense attorney client relationship.[34] The authors more affluent defendants know his or her attorney has great incentive to perform well and follow all possible leads to their greatest end to win the case. They will ask the right questions and do their best work possible because their future client base depends on it. They are selling themselves as successful and capable attorneys, and winning cases means more clients and money for themselves or their firm. A publicly defended person does not have the guarantee to this type of defense because his or her lawyer does not have comparable incentives.[35] The Shulhofer and Friedman article classifies the issue into three problems: incentive, information and insurance.[36]

The incentive problem revolves around how public attorneys are paid and how this influences the quality of defense. They are appointed by the court and paid hourly fees that may cause them to cut corners and stall. The lawyer is paid by the state, must satisfy the state, "if he wishes future employment."[37]

The information problem they posit specifically hurts the poor. There is a high likelihood that a poor defendant may not have experience with the criminal justice system and the proper protocols, rights, and other important information that they should know regarding their trial. The poor have the highest likelihood of having been on trial before or knowing someone who has, but even this possible experience does not mitigate from the problems of not having access to private counsel and advice from the earliest moments of their trial. Schulhofer and Friedman argue that while the information problem with regards to choosing an attorney is lower if the court appoints one, but there is still a tension that exists.[38] This tension between the information and incentive problems exists because

---

[33] "New York State Settles Hurrell-Harring Indigent Defense Challenge." *National Association of Criminal Defense Lawyers*. Accessed June 20, 2016. www.nacdl.org/criminaldefense.aspx?id=20192.

[34] Stephen J. Schulhofer and David D. Friedman. "Reforming Indigent Defense: How Free Market Principles Can Help to Fix a Broken System." Cato Institute. September 1, 2010. Accessed June 29, 2016. http://object.cato.org/sites/cato.org/files/pubs/pdf/pa666.pdf, 1.

[35] Ibid., 3–4.

[36] Ibid., 4.

[37] Ibid.

[38] Ibid.

The defendant has the incentive to choose a vigorous, effective advocate but may lack the information to do so. A public official who chooses for the defendant is likely to have better information but a weaker incentive to make the best choice. The official, appraising an attorney's ability from the standpoint of the court system, has incentives to value cooperativeness, a disinclination to work long hours, and other qualities that might not win favor with defendants themselves. Providers may end up being selected according to how well they serve the court system, not how well they serve defendants.[39]

This tension sums up many of the problems that experts find inherent in the indigent defense systems. The incentives for either side are usually against the poorest defendants, and the incentives for their defenders is not always the best for the clients assigned to them.

The insurance problem they argue is best understood through an analogy between healthcare and criminal justice. Unlike the healthcare system where you can buy insurance against the possible risk of sudden sickness or disease, the criminal justice system does not offer any comparable protection, but can consume vast amounts of someone's money. Even affluent citizens can struggle to pay for the ever-increasing costs of a criminal trial. The public defender is in many ways an insurance for those who need defense. More affluent defendants can be made indigent by the high cost of attorneys and may need a public counsel at some point during a long trial. Poor defendants sometimes owe money after their trial, but pay in various other ways, like the loss of income or social status. Schulhofer and Friedman call this economic effect of the criminal justice system an, "insurance policy with a very high deductible."[40]

In fairness, public defenders are motivated to provide the best defense for their clients. The problem is not with the motivation or intent of the defenders themselves, but with the system that they operate in that does not provide a platform for justice. Schulhofer and Friedman argue that the problem exists in the politics of the current system, "Although idealism motivates many public defenders to seek the best outcome for their clients, the system as a whole is driven by political goals that often conflict with that objective."[41]

The indigent defense system revolves around money and the poor. There are real problems with the increasingly common social stigma against public attorneys, inhibiting the proper form of justice in the process. The relationship between how the system is funded and how the poor are treated is important and this chapter explores how the poorest members of society are victimized into becoming the majority of the overpopulated jails and prisons in America.

---

[39] Ibid., 4.
[40] Ibid., 5.
[41] Ibid., 8.

State spending on indigent defense has slowly decreased over time as the number of cases requiring public counsel have increased. The relation of funding to indigent defense has always been a prominent issue and many believe the decrease in funding is primary problem. A 2013 *New York Times* article by Lincoln Caplan published at the fiftieth anniversary of the *Gideon* decision summarized several of current problems in the United States regarding public defense.[42] The article highlighted the problems with meeting the requirements of *Gideon* at the state level where 95 percent of America's criminal trials take place. The article highlights the Miami public defender's office which handle far above the American Bar Association recommendation of 150 cases a year for a public defender. The demand per defender in Miami has reached 500 cases a year, far outpacing the needed funding for proper indigent defense. The important distinction the author makes in this article is that not only is financing public defense an issue, but an increasingly common attitude toward the poor that Caplan describes as "contempt."[43] For Caplan, the growing numbers representing the amount of indigent defendants who arrive in court without a lawyer is not only a policy and funding issue, but it represents a trend in the justice system's attitude toward the poor. If the justice system were committed to providing equal justice across socioeconomic lines the system of public defense would need to change how it handles the most vulnerable when they need defending. The funding mechanism must change.

A BJS report on indigent defense spending found that from 2008 to 2012 the national averages of spending on indigent defense fell by an annual average of 0.2 percent.[44] In 2012, state governments spent an average of $2.3 billion nationally on indigent defense, a number that has shrunk significantly across the nation.[45] While this seems like a significant amount of money once it is broken down into per capita numbers across a state or the nation it seems much less significant. According to a 2008 report by the National Legal Aid and Defender Association (NLADA) the national average of per capita spending on indigent defense was $11.86.[46] Some states, like Michigan, which the report focuses on, spend far less than this national

---

[42] Lincoln Caplan. "The Right to Counsel: Badly Battered at 50." *The New York Times*, March 10, 2013. Accessed June 14, 2016. www.nytimes.com/2013/03/10/opinion/sunday/the-right-to-coun sel-badly-battered-at-50.html.

[43] Caplan, "The Right to Counsel."

[44] Herberman, Erinn, and Tracey Kyckelhahn. *State Government Indigent Defense Expenditures, FY 2008–2012 – Updated.* Report. April 21, 2015. Accessed June 22, 2016. www.bjs.gov/content/ pub/pdf/sgideo812.pdf.

[45] Ibid., 1.

[46] "A Race to the Bottom Speed & Savings Over Due Process: A Constitutional Crisis." Report. June 2008. Accessed June 22, 2016. www.nlada.net/sites/default/files/mi_racetothebottomj serio6-2008_report.pdf. Iii.

average. Michigan ranks forty-fourth out of fifty states coming in at $7.35 per person.[47] The report points out that while there are many negative effects on the indigent defense system from this lack of funding, there are other nonfinancial problems as well. The problem that exists in many of the underfunded counties in Michigan is an inability to meet the American Bar Association's standard for "effective and efficient, high quality, ethical, conflict-free representation to accused persons who cannot afford to hire an attorney."[48] It is almost always the case that low funding and poor quality indigent defense services go hand in hand. There are always ways to allocate monies more efficiently, but some states systems are just underfunded regardless of their other problems and inconsistencies. One of the problems is in determining how successful a high-funded program is or how much funding is necessary because it all depends on a long list of factors unique to each state. There is no clear connection between high funding and success. For example, Alaska sets aside the most money toward indigent defense services, but this is only due to the high cost of transportation and trial because of the size of the state.[49] There are many factors that go onto how much money a state might budget for public defense. The report on Michigan concludes,

> a high cost per capita may not necessarily guarantee that a state is providing adequate representation, a low indigent defense cost per capita certainly is an indicator of a system in trouble.[50]

While more funding sometimes helped, the problems were often diagnosed as more substantial than a budget issue. The study in Michigan came to disturbing conclusions about the negative attitudes of judges and attorneys toward the poor. They found throughout the Michigan indigent defense system there were a myriad of problems including,

> judges handpicking defense attorneys; lawyers appointed to cases for which they are unqualified; defenders meeting clients on the eve of trial and holding non-confidential discussions in public courtroom corridors; attorneys failing to identify obvious conflicts of interest; failure of defenders to properly prepare for trials or sentencings; attorneys violating their ethical canons to zealously advocate for clients; inadequate compensation for those appointed to defend the accused.[51]

While many of the issues are not aided by the underfunded programs, and many of the problems are enhanced because of the lack of funding, the most important issues come down to the mindset of the criminal justice system toward the poor, minorities populations, and failing to provide any administrative oversight, where the systems of

---

[47] "A Race to the Bottom," iii.
[48] Ibid.
[49] Ibid.
[50] Ibid.
[51] Ibid., 1.

indigent defense are delegated to local authorities.[52] The success and quality of indigent defense systems vary from county to county and across states by local municipalities. In this context, 'vary' means that they are worse depending on the socioeconomic levels in the county. This is as much of a financial problem as the funding in indigent defense.

The American Bar Association's (ABA) national standards recommend the use of staffed public defender offices wherever there is the caseload and need for the services of public counsel. In Michigan, most of the indigent defense work is done by assigned counsel and contract attorneys because there are only five public defender offices in the state. The report on Michigan found that, "In Oakland and Macomb counties, both of which are heavily populated portions of the greater Detroit metropolitan area, there is no public defender office at all."[53] Some of the counties and districts in Michigan still paid attorneys and public defenders on hourly rates that had not been reviewed since the late 1970s.[54] It is no surprise that many law students do not want to enter into public defense.

The problem is not only that the current system is experiencing problems and needs reform, but that it has almost always been a problem, and has needed reform for decades. The NLADA report in 2012 was not their first on growing problems. In fact, with funding from the Department of Justice, the NLADA has completed several reports on the problems in Michigan since the implementation of the public defender system after *Gideon*, even completing two in the 1970s. In 1977, the NLADA wrote a warning about Michigan's juvenile justice system,

> Unless serious changes are made in funding to provide adequate staff and facilities, especially social service programs, and unless programs in diversion, remedial schooling, and other approaches are tried, today's juveniles will become alienated and impoverished adults who will flood the jails and infect our entire social existence.[55]

Throughout the next several decades there were efforts to make reforms to the juvenile justice system and especially to the indigent defense system that often was involved in the same cases. Many in the 1990s in Michigan believed that the state should adopt statewide protocols and policies with regards to the court system and indigent defense. In 1995, Chief Justice Brickley of the Michigan Supreme Court said that the state should assume control of many aspects of the judicial system and should specifically oversee, "due process costs including the cost of indigent representation."[56] Various reports at the time acknowledged the problems with the

---

[52] Ibid., 2.
[53] Ibid., 7.
[54] Ibid., 8.
[55] Ibid., 10.
[56] Ibid., 10–11.

judicial system and not all were related to funding, in fact, many of the reports criticized the attitude toward the poor from various levels of the system.

An ABA report from 2005 sums up the problem that had been festering for decades. The report found that "local elected officials are downright indifferent to indigent defense reform at best and opposed at worst."[57] The report also quoted a witness from Michigan during a public hearing regarding the right to counsel,

> I once addressed the Michigan Association of Counties meeting, and a county commissioner raised his hand in the back and said: "Is there any way we could get defendants from the jail to the prison without going to court? Because you would save a lot of money." And that kind of sums up the attitude, especially in the rural counties.[58]

Money is involved at all levels in the indigent defense crisis, but there are also underlying problems at play with attitudes toward the poor and the rights they have with regards to fair and just trials. While money is part of the problem and must obviously part of the solution, saying more funding will fix the problems with the indigent defense system incredibly oversimplifies the problem. While the lack of funding has certainly highlighted the problems going on in Michigan these reports show that problems exist outside of the low per-capita spending and have for decades.

These problems with funding and negative mentalities toward the poor exist outside of Michigan as well. The Michigan example highlights the problems that have become common in the national indigent defense system and were common throughout the history of the system after the *Gideon* decision. The problems of the mentalities toward the poor also affect how pleas are encourage by defenders. There are systematic problems with the advice that poor people receive as part of this right to counsel.

Florida's indigent defense system provides a good example of this attitude that has become normal in public defense. A report published by the National Association of Criminal Defense Lawyers (NACDL) found that "Florida's county courts are consistently sacrificing due process for case-processing speed."[59] They found that 66 percent of defendants in Florida appeared at arraignment without counsel.[60] Many of these defendants were pleading guilty (70 percent), and those who had hired counsel were less likely to be entering pleas of guilty: only 21 percent had been appointed public counsel at their first appearance in court.[61] The defendants were often handed documents that encouraged them to waive their right to counsel and

---

[57] Ibid., 12.
[58] Ibid.
[59] Alisa Smith and Sean Maddan. "Three-Minute Justice: Haste and Waste in Florida's Misdemeanor Courts. Report." July 2011. Accessed June 14, 2016. 15.
[60] Ibid., 22.
[61] Ibid.

enter guilty pleas or no contest. They found that "half of the individuals who appeared at arraignment without counsel wholly waived their right to counsel."[62] Defendants that were in custody were 10 times more likely to waive their right to counsel and those accused of less serious crimes were also more likely to waive this right.[63] In Florida, public defenders are not free, and defendants are often reminded of this before arraignment. One could argue that this "reminder" may help lead to the high rates of defendants refusing counsel. Half of the individuals who appeared at arraignment without counsel pleaded guilty.[64] In some ways the Florida system might actually encourage defendants to plead guilty and forgo their right to counsel. If the system does not provide the environment for poor defendants to learn about their options, to enter the correct plea, or to have a defender if they need one, then it would seem that there was a problem with the standards of the indigent defense system in the state.

Lincoln Caplan mentions in his article for the *New York Times* that poor defendants can sometimes wait a significant amount of time before receiving a trial. This does not reflect the Supreme Court ruling that said they should be entitled to a trial within a reasonable time of arrest.[65] A report that expands on one of the cases he mentions said that in one instance a Mississippi woman waited in jail for eleven months until a lawyer looked at her case, and she plead guilty and was released from jail fourteen months after her arrest.[66] Her crime consisted of shoplifting $72 worth of merchandise from the Walmart and her total time in jail cost taxpayers approximately $12,090.[67] The same report mentions various cases where defendants waited years in jail, unnecessarily costing taxpayers hundreds of thousands of dollars. The report is just one of many from the early 2000s making the case for the problems with the modern indigent defense system. In Mississippi, the 2003 report found that the poor were often incredibly hurt by the way they were represented by public defense. Some counties could hold indigent defendants for up to a year before they even talked to a lawyer, and many of the lawyers would meet their clients just before their critically important hearings. Without the proper funding public lawyers cannot do the proper research or hire experts to do it for them. In many cases it was only possible for a public defender to hire an investigator or psychiatrist in a non–death penalty case if they paid the fees out of pocket. The list of problems throughout the report is lengthy and shows the links between lack of funding, lack of competent defense, and the

[62] Ibid.
[63] Ibid., 15.
[64] Ibid.
[65] Caplan, "The Right to Counsel."
[66] "Assembly Line Justice: Mississippi's Indigent Defense Crisis." Report. Accessed June 15, 2016. www.americanbar.org/content/dam/aba/migrated/legalservices/downloads/sclaid/indigentde fense/ms_assemblylinejustice.authcheckdam.pdf, 3.
[67] "Assembly Line Justice," 3.

burden it places on the poor. Lack of funding and contempt for the poor are compounding problems in almost every state's system.

Funding for indigent defense looks different across the states. An April 2016 *New York Times* article highlighted more weaknesses in the public defense world and odd funding mechanisms in different areas of the country. Forty-three states now require defendants to pay for a public defender, even though the only reason they have a public defender in the first place is because they cannot afford a lawyer.[68] The *Times* article highlights the current policy in South Dakota where a defendant is required to pay $92 dollars an hour regardless of the verdict. The result of this policy is that the defendant might have to pay hundreds of dollars a day to be proven innocent for a crime for which he or she was mistakenly arrested.

The State of Louisiana funds much of its indigent defense through court fees. Dylan Walsh, in his article for *The Atlantic*, found that local revenues from court fees actually fund 70 percent of the public defense system's budget, a majority of which were tickets for traffic violations in the local community.[69] A violation of any law besides a parking violation warrants a $45 court fee which is sent to the district's public defense office. The system relies on the flow of money from criminal activity, basically, the more crime you have in the community the more money flowing to the office's budget. Districts that collect more traffic tickets, specifically districts with heavy interstate traffic, have an advantage over those without a natural place to collect a significant amount of traffic fines. This creates perverse incentives: more crime means more money. Instead of the wealth of a certain county determining the quality of defense, the area with the highest flow of traffic violations and petty crime has the best system.

This Louisiana system works differently than the South Dakota system. Instead of everyone paying court fees, only the guilty pay in Louisiana. The problem with this system is that it leaves lawyers in the morally difficult place where they are paid by the guilt of those they defend. Innocent verdicts mean less money for the district office because only the guilty pay the $45 court fee. This sets the stage for perverse incentives for prosecutors to do whatever is necessary to achieve a guilty verdict.

There are clear common problems in the system: the poorer you are the more likely you are to receive a lower quality defense, the more likely you are to serve time or pay a fine, and the more likely you are to be in a system that is incentivized against you. The poor suffer most from the compounding effects of the requirements surrounding government defenders. The urban minority and lower-class white populations are even more likely than the suburban populations to feel the effects of these policies and perverse incentives. Each of the examples above confirm that

---

[68] John Pfaff. "A Mockery of Justice for the Poor." *The New York Times*, April 29, 2016. Accessed June 15, 2016. www.nytimes.com/2016/04/30/opinion/a-mockery-of-justice-for-the-poor.html?_r=4.

[69] Walsh, Dylan. "On the Defensive."

the problem is diverse and broad, and the solutions are more complicated than many initially think. To have a just and successful indigent defense system in a state, there must be a changes across the board to how people think about the poor and minority populations in their community.

PUBLIC DEFENSE ALTERNATIVES: VOUCHERS, LUMP-SUM PAYMENTS, AND RESTRUCTURING INCENTIVES

There are three main types of defense systems at the state and local level in the United States.[70] The first and most common is a public defender program where the state or county has a public defense office that provides service to indigent defendants. Across the United States, public defender offices account for much of indigent defense as forty-nine states and the District of Columbia have this type of system to some extent.[71] Many of these states use their public defender office as the primary source of indigent defense, while some rely on help from components of the other systems. Centralized systems account for public defender offices in some these states, while others offer more localized offices with county administrations. A second type of public defense is an assigned counsel system. This method involves the court appointing various available private attorneys on a case-by-case basis. In some cases, the lawyer is appointed by a judge, and in others the assignments are made by an administrator in an assigned counsel system.[72] The third type of system is a contract defense system. With contract defense, government officials make a deal with private firms, attorneys, and organizations to provide indigent defense for a certain time period and amount of money.[73]

Many of the solutions posed to solve the problem of indigent defense are based around restructuring the incentives of the defenders and defendants toward their best interest. A just system would offer the same choices to indigent defendants that they would have if they could afford to pay for their own defense. The current system has inherent advantages toward being wealthy, and since most defendants are poor, the majority of defendants are at a disadvantage before they even reach the courtroom. The justice system must provide the same opportunities for acquittal across all racial and socioeconomic lines. There are several solutions posed on various sides of the issue, and many states have already begun to change their systems to help the disadvantaged.

[70] "Bureau of Justice Statistics (BJS)." N.p. Accessed July 19 2016.
[71] Lynn Langton, and Donald Farole, Jr. "State Public Defender Programs, 2007." Rep. Bureau of Justice Statistics, September 2010. Accessed July 18 2016, 1.
[72] Steven K. Smith, and Carol J. DeFrances. "Indigent Defense." Report. February 1996. Accessed July 20, 2016. www.bjs.gov/content/pub/pdf/id.pdf, 1–2.
[73] Ibid., 2.

A report from the ABA published by George Mason University examined each state's system of indigent defense and highlighted the diversity of programs across the country.[74] It found that two-thirds of states have some sort of state commission on indigent defense that oversees standards and creates guidelines for the public defense.[75] These state committees do not necessarily correlate to state funding for indigent defense, as only twenty-three states have state-funded public defense systems.[76] Only one state relies on an entirely county-funded system, Pennsylvania, and eighteen others have systems where the counties provide more than 50 percent of funding. The rest are supported mostly by state funding and rely partially on counties and other sources of funding.[77]

The problems with the United States' current system of indigent defense are apparent in many individual states, but the solutions are not. There are states and counties that are trying many different solutions to properly fund programs, change the mindset and attitude of defenders and policy-makers, and build systems that provide equal justice across socioeconomic and geographic lines. The solutions vary in scope and how they are implemented, but all are looking for ways to improve a system that currently hurts the most vulnerable citizens and fails to provide the justice required by the Constitution.

Jonathan Rapping argues that without a change to the current value system of lawyers in the public defense system there can be no significant or meaningful reforms.[78] Rapping, a former public defender in Washington DC, believed that values were and are partly to blame for the indigent defense crisis. He looked at twenty-four lawyers in Georgia who set out to change the state's system of indigent defense that devalued the poor.

Since the *Gideon* decision, Georgia was one of the many states that was known for the "abysmal quality of representation provided to their poorest citizens in criminal cases."[79] The twenty-four lawyers went to work in the indigent defense system to change this for the sake of the poor who were suffering from the inadequate system. The attitude toward the poor defendants was one set forth by many states after the *Gideon* decision required them to provide defense to indigents, that "poor

---

[74] Holly R. Stevens, Colleen E. Sheppard, Robert Spangenberg, Aimee Wickman, and Jon B. Gould. *State, County and Local Expenditures for Indigent Defense Services Fiscal Year 2008*. Report. The Center for Justice, Law and Society at George Mason University, George Mason University. November 2010. Accessed July 7, 2016. www.americanbar.org/content/dam/aba/administrative/legal_aid_indigent_defendants/ls_sclaid_def_expenditures_fy08.authcheck dam.pdf

[75] Stevens, Sheppard, Spangenberg, Wickman, Gould, *State, County and Local Expenditures*, 5.

[76] Ibid., 5.

[77] Ibid.

[78] Jonathan A. Rapping. "You Can't Build on Shaky Ground: Laying the Foundation for Indigent Defense Reform Through Values-Based Recruitment, Training, and Mentoring." *Harvard Law & Policy Review* 3 (February 17, 2009). Accessed July 21, 2016. http://harvardlpr.com/wp-content/uploads/2013/05/3.1_8_Rapping.pdf.

[79] Ibid., 161.

defendants were not entitled to the time, resources, and commitment the Constitution guarantees."[80] As many articles and reports on the topic found, lawyers did
not provide the same time and effort for indigent defendants as they would for a
more affluent one. Rapping believes that the problem comes down to the values of
the lawyers, and without changes to how lawyers think about the poor one cannot
hope to change the problems in indigent defense. Rapping believes that to fix these
problems there must be a new way to train the new generation of public defense
lawyers with a three pronged method of "values-based recruitment, training, and
mentoring."[81] Instead of spending time trying to change current lawyer's ideas and
methods he argues that a new generation of lawyers needs to be trained with values
instilled in them at the beginning of their legal education. This solution relies on
training and teaching, a process that starts in school and continues into careers with
the hope that when new lawyers interact with the indigent defense system they will
have a different and more positive attitude toward the poor.

This approach is one that relies on reforming the fundamental elements of how
professionals in the criminal justice system view the poor and minority populations
that they interact with. For there to be changes to meet the Constitutional mandate,
the people within the various systems must have the same mindset toward the poor
as they would toward the wealthy, and the same approach to each case regardless of
race, religion, or socioeconomic status. The justice system relies on relationships,
and part of the breakdown in indigent defense is the loss of the attorney client
relationship. If poor defendants receive the same quality defense as a wealthy one,
the instance of incorrect verdicts, pleading guilty innocent, and the vast effects of
these problems will be quickly eliminated across the United States.

A report published by the Brennan Center for Justice at NYU gave three recommendations to help curb the problems happening around the country.[82] They argue
that in order to move our public defense system toward something more functional
and fair we must first reclassify some petty offenses to reduce the number of people
going to jail and the amount of people on trial.[83] This is a move that they argue will
help greatly reduce the workload of public defenders and redirect resources to more
needed places in the criminal justice system. Second, they argue that funding needs
to be increased from a variety of sources.[84] Not only should the federal government
increase grants for state and local indigent defense systems, but private firms should
increase pro bono work in public defense systems. The third solution they suggest is
adding regular training for public defenders as well as increasing the number of

---

[80] Ibid., 162.
[81] Ibid., 175.
[82] Giovanni, Thomas, and Roopal Patel, *"Gideon at 50: Three Reforms to Revive the Right to Counsel."* Report. School of Law, New York University. Accessed July 21, 2016. www.brennan
center.org/sites/default/files/publications/Gideon_Report_040913.pdf.
[83] Ibid., 2.
[84] Ibid., 2.

social workers.[85] They believe state-sponsored attorney training in indigent defense will improve their representation of indigents, and states should fund an increase in social workers to help reintroduce offenders into society and curb recidivism.

Similar solutions were offered by a 2008 report by the Department of Justice and other partner organizations.[86] The report says that the "dizzying array of delivery models and financing structures" that exist in our public defense systems today fail to meet constitutional standards.[87] The report's participants agreed with Jonathan Rapping's ideas about changing the culture surrounding indigent defense and added action steps for change in the system. They proposed solutions that included many similar ideas to the Brennan Center for Justice Report, namely, promoting funding for training for lawyers and others involved with public defense to educate on the current problems as well as ways to make the indigent defense system provide competent and fair defenses. They added a recommendation for more focus groups and national meetings among policymakers and those involved in public defense to help develop a vision for what indigent defense should look like in the future.

Another solution proposed by Schulhofer and Friedman criticizes the many expensive and complicated solutions proposed by governments at all levels.[88] The article proposes a free-market solution to the indigent defense problem, one they say will cure the biggest compounding problem they see with the indigent defense system, that is, the fact that the accused have no say in who will defend them. If the defendant is one of the 80 percent of defendants that are indigent the other plaintiff is the government which appoints the attorney for the defendant, an injustice that the article says would never be tolerated outside of the indigent defense system.[89] The need for more resources and funding for the indigent defense system often overlooks the needs and problems that are inherent in the current system. This proposed solution by Schulhofer and Friedman is one that allows for choice within a free market of indigent defense service much like the one available to more affluent defendants. The contract defense system does not offer a choice of private attorney, thus negating the market benefits of competition. The Schulhofer and Friedman summarized the problem with contract defense saying, "the potential benefits are lost because court officials, rather than clients, control the flow of cases to the attorneys."[90] An assignment counsel system has the same problem; the solution is to eliminate control the court has over which attorneys get specific cases. They argue

---

[85] Ibid.
[86] *Public Defense Reform since Gideon: Improving the Administration of Justice by Building On Our Successes and Learning From Our Failures.* Report. September 2008. Accessed July 21, 2016. www.bja.gov/publications/nlada_pubdefleadership.pdf.
[87] Ibid., 15.
[88] Stephen J. Schulhofer and David D. Friedman. *Reforming Indigent Defense How Free Market Principles Can Help to Fix a Broken System.* Cato Institute. September 1, 2010. Accessed June 29, 2016, http://object.cato.org/sites/cato.org/files/pubs/pdf/pa666.pdf, 1.
[89] Ibid., 19.
[90] Ibid., 9.

that there are incentives built into the private market for attorneys to perform well and by appointing counsel the court takes the natural competition out of the market.[91] Clients in the public area do not choose their lawyer so there is no incentive to work toward being successful and competitive in the public defense arena.

One popular solution is a defense voucher system that would align the interest of the attorney with those of the defendant instead of relying on the incentives built into the market as a solution.[92] For example, the voucher system would make part of the payout conditional on the outcome of the case, providing an incentive for the attorney to perform their absolute best in the case. Schulhofer and Friedman disagree in part with this type of solution. They observe that a problem still arises here, as the goal is not to get attorneys to convince their client to take an easy way out, or to accept a plea deal, but instead convince them to do what is best for them, a hard thing to incentivize through this type of voucher program. Instead, the solution they propose is to give the defendant control over choosing public defenders for themselves as if they could afford to hire counsel out of the private attorney market.[93] Even when the defendant does not have a large amount of information about the attorneys available or the process involved, they will still have an incentive to learn and make a good decision, much like we do for goods and services we buy every day. Under this logic, defendants should always be able to refuse the advice of the court system without being subject to a final decision by the court on their attorney. The system could be paid for with a voucher to be redeemed at a variety of law practices. Firms would be properly incentivized to vigorously defend indigents.

With "consumer sovereignty," the poor acquire an attorney the same way a wealthier defendant would, creating true equality.[94] Implementation in their proposal would include a lump-sum or similar type of voucher. Representation for the poor could improve if defendants were allowed to choose attorneys and the quality of defense would increase if public defense attorneys were part of a competitive market. Schulhofer and Friedman propose one centered on restructuring incentives to provide for justice and give the poor defendants more control over their defense.

Several states have passed or are working on legislation to reform their systems in an effort to provide more fair and equal treatment across the indigent defense system. The New York State legislature approved statewide funding for indigent defense services. With this system, the state will distribute funding more evenly to counties fixing the problems that many of the poorest counties were facing. The county funded system was not working and statewide standards for every indigent case are more equitable.

[91] Ibid., 11.
[92] Ibid. 12.
[93] Ibid., 12.
[94] Ibid., 12.

The current debates in New York began with a 2007 lawsuit by the New York Civil Liberties Union on behalf of several indigent defendants (*Hurrell-Harring et al. v. State of New York*).[95] The Hurrell-Harring case was settled in 2014, but only brought indigent defense reform to five of the fifty-seven counties in New York.[96] In 2016, The New York state senate unanimously approved to extend the reforms statewide.[97] The new measures will take the burden of paying for indigent defense services off counties and place them entirely on the state. The bill has received praise from around the state because it will help many counties provide better services for indigent defense in the future. St. Lawrence County's public defender, Steven G. Ballan, told a local New York paper that "the measure should lead to more equitable indigent defense around the state and provide some fiscal relief for poor counties because the costs will spread over the entire state."[98] The bill will save local taxpayers money and help counties provide the same quality of defense for indigents. The article further quoted Mr. Ballan saying,

> There's a large disparity now between what indigent defense services are offered in wealthy counties compared with poorer counties . . . public defenders in some more affluent counties have lower caseloads and have funds to hire support staff including investigators, social workers, caseworkers and substance abuse counselors.[99]

This problem in New York is the same as it is across the United States; the richer the area, the more likely defendants will receive a better defense. With the new measures approved and taking effect over the next seven years, New York's new system will allow for counties to receive the same funding and provide the same quality of defense for those that need public counsel. This will hopefully provide a more just system for the poor that need defense across the state. While this is one solution among many being proposed across the country, the new system of indigent defense in New York shows that states care about reforming the broken and unjust system. The New York solution is one that many advocates of indigent defense applaud, but it is criticized by many. The solution of providing state control to create consistency of indigent defense is one that is gaining popularity across the United States. Criticism often comes from those who believe that the new system will rob local communities of control over indigent defense, but proponents believe that by removing direct local control there will be a better chance of justice being served to the same effect in each and every county across the state.

95 "New York State Settles Hurrell-Harring Indigent Defense Challenge." *National Association of Criminal Defense Lawyers*. Accessed November 02, 2016. www.nacdl.org/criminaldefense.aspx?id=20192.
96 "New York State Settles Hurrell-Harring Indigent Defense Challenge."
97 Susan Mende. "State Senate Approves Indigent Defense Bill; State Agrees to Pay All Costs." *Watertown Daily Times*, June 17, 2016. Accessed June 29, 2016. www.watertowndailytimes.com/news05/state-senate-approves-indigent-defense-bill-state-agrees-to-pay-all-costs-20160617.
98 Ibid.
99 Ibid.

Michigan made changes to the failing indigent defense system in July 2013. The public defense system in Michigan was considered the worst in the nation. Michigan included the right to counsel in its first state constitution in 1835, but like the rest of the nation, standards set by law were slowly abandoned as the system worsened over time.[100] The report cited a 2008 study by the NLADA that found Michigan, "fails to provide competent representation to those who cannot afford counsel in its criminal courts."[101] Like New York, the Michigan system varied in quality from county to county. None of the states studied in the report met the constitutional requirements for competent counsel. The state's system required county governments to pay for the requirements under *Gideon* without any oversight, causing "financial strains at the county level in Michigan have led many counties to choose low-bid, flat-fee contract systems as a means of controlling costs."[102] Michigan found that their system was causing problems that created an injustice toward the poor, and cited five ways that public defense systems like theirs can hurt the poor and increase incarceration rates. They found that the system pressured defendants to plead guilty, unnecessarily increased pretrial detention, errors in trial verdicts, excessive sentences, and barriers to reentry into communities.[103] Comprehensive statewide reform is required for consistency and uniformity.

The costs of these poor policies and problems across the state were correctly assessed after decades of problems, and the state government is working on reforms to the system. The 2013 legislation created a new system to appoint counsel for indigent criminal defendants. In addition to this the law established a new funding mechanism for public defense.[104] One of the acts requires the court to determine whether or not someone qualifies as indigent, and they established minimum standards for public defense that must be adopted by each county.[105] The legislation ensured all defendants knew their rights, have counsel appointed for them, and that their counsel is fairly compensated for their work. Standardized funding and a system for appointing attorneys that does not vary by county is a crucial foundation for improvement. Much like the New York system, the Michigan system was struggling from lack of standards. Now all counties in Michigan have the same requirements of standards and are responsible to the state for upholding these standards. The next few years will be critical in assessing if the statewide solution is viable and should be considered or recommended for other states.[106]

---

[100] Suzanne Lowe. "Indigent Criminal Defense in Michigan: A New Approach." Report. Accessed July 22, 2016. www.senate.michigan.gov/sfa/publications%5Cnotes%5C2013notes%5Cnotessum13sl.pdf.

[101] Ibid., 2.

[102] Ibid., 5.

[103] Ibid., 3.

[104] Ibid., 5.

[105] Ibid., 6.

[106] Ibid., 7.

A critic of the government solutions, Anthony Thompson argues that these legislative approaches are often inadequate to solve the problem at hand.[107] The legislation and lawsuits that many champion as the solution are not enough, and a change in the mindset toward indigent defense needs to happen across the system. State courts often decree where the problems are and leave it to state legislatures to figure out the details of the solution. The tension this creates is a problem across the country when it comes to finding a solution for the indigent defense crisis. Thompson mentions one example of the conflict between the Florida legislature and the Florida Supreme Court about the solution. The court even threatened to release prisoners if the legislature did not come up with a solution regarding the appeals process at one point. In the case the Supreme Court stated,

> the legislature's failure to adequately fund the public defender's' offices is at the heart of this problem, and the legislature should live up to its responsibilities and appropriate an adequate amount for this purpose, it is not the function of this Court to decide what constitutes adequate funding and then order the legislature to appropriate such an amount. Appropriation of funds for the operation of the government is a legislative function.[108]

This is a unique problem regarding indigent defense that Thompson argues. The solution, because of this common divide, among other reasons, is one that is almost impossible to just legislate or lawsuit into existence. Solutions must come with a change in the indigent defense culture, and sources for funding must come from both private and public accounts to experiment with solutions.[109] For Thompson, both defenders and those funding the defenders need to think differently about their roles. The legislatures need to avoid the "dollars for cases mentality that leads to quick pleas and high recidivism," while also viewing funding as an investment in the communities that the defenders work in.[110] He argues that defenders need to have a different relationship with their work and the people around them. For change to happen, Thompson says that defenders must build "relationships with city and county council members, state representatives, and federal officials in an ongoing effort to bring a more comprehensive understanding to criminal justice policy formation."[111] Without formative relationships with the people and communities, they will not be able to provide fair and just treatment in criminal cases. Being a part of the community and leaving the "confines of their offices and the courtroom" will help them be more successful and transform the attitude in the

---

[107] Anthony C. Thompson. "The Promise of Gideon: Providing High-Quality Public Defense In America." *Quinnipac Law Review.* Accessed July 27, 2016. www.qu.edu/prebuilt/pdf/School Law/LawReviewLibrary/Vol31_Issue4_2013_thompson.pdf.

[108] Ibid., 735.

[109] Ibid., 768.

[110] Ibid., 769.

[111] Ibid.

legal community about indigent defense.[112] Thompson believes that the federal
government needs to have a modernized role as well.

CONCLUSION

Many of the problems, and many of the solutions as well, revolve around the issue of
how much freedom in decision making the public defenders have in the case
brought before them. Personalism demands that public defenders be given all the
resources necessary to properly defend the rights of offending persons. Some argue
that public defenders do not have the best incentives, and they cannot operate with
the interest of their defendants because of lack of funding and procedural weaknesses competing with powerful prosecutors. These attorneys need to be incentivized by the legal system in the same way as private attorneys. The majority of jail
and prison populations are poor minorities. Adequate legal services will reduce the
population by hundreds of thousands across the United States. That influx of justice
will have extraordinarily positive cultural repercussions for decades, demonstrating
the benefits of providing justice for those who deserve it.

The legal profession is one of prestige and status. The modernization of the
indigent defense apparatus could unleash a new era in the glory of practicing law.
High-value attorneys defending the poor citizen against injustice should be something that brings accolades beyond financial compensation. Private attorneys should
be active in the indigent system and be able to collect payment from the court
system, and defendants should not be forced to work with a specific government
attorney. The legal tradition is one where justice is heralded as being blind to
position in society. The capitalist system of the United States has intricately pervaded
the legal system where money is the only tool to unlock the potential for justice. The
legal profession must adopt indigent defense as a segment of modernization where
the best of the industry displays its effectiveness. Even with the right laws, accountable prosecutors, and freer judges, it would be much better if our local communities
were places that did not produce criminal deviance in the first place rather than
assuming that it is a natural given of certain neighborhoods over others, and much of
that has to do with institutions like the family and schools. It is those local contexts
where we must also start serious criminal justice reforms which is the emphasis in
Part II of this book.

---

[112] Ibid., 769.

PART II

5

Ending the School-to-Prison Pipeline

"In these days, it is doubtful that any child may reasonably be expected to succeed in life if he is denied the opportunities of an education. Such an opportunity, where the state has undertaken to provide it, is a right that must be made available on equal terms."[1]
        – Chief Justice Earl Warren, *Brown v. Board of Education* (1954)

The *Washington Post* featured an article in April 2017 about Luanne Haygood and her ten-year-old son John who has autism.[2] Haygood took John to school for standardized testing in 2016, and John spent the following night behind bars in a juvenile detention facility. John had a history of being disruptive at school and had kicked and scratched an educational assistant, resulting in an arrest warrant for battery (a third-degree felony). John and his mother (who drove him in for the testing) had no idea the warrant existed. Two school resource officers handcuffed the struggling ten-year-old while his mother filmed the arrest. John can be heard in the video telling the officers that he: "didn't like being touched," and yelling to his mother, "I don't know what's going on, Mama!"

Disabled students are the most disciplined in states across the country. A Virginia report found that black students with disabilities were nearly thirteen times as likely as nondisabled white students to be punished with short-term suspensions in the 2014–2015 school year.[3] A study on California schools found that "suspensions of African American students occur at rates three to four times higher than the state average for all students." According to that data in 17.8 percent of African American

---

[1] *Brown v. Board of Education of Topeka*, 347 U.S. 483 (1954)
[2] Lindsey Bever. "'I Don't Like to Be Touched': Video Shows 10-Year-Old Autistic Boy Getting Arrested at School." *The Washington Post*. April 21, 2017. Accessed August 01, 2017. www .washingtonpost.com/news/education/wp/2017/04/19/i-dont-like-to-be-touched-video-shows-10-year-old-autistic-boy-getting-arrested-at-school/?tid=a_inl&utm_term=.9fb41b2dc461.
[3] Tom Loveless. "Racial Disparities in School Suspensions." *Brookings*. March 27, 2017. Accessed August 01, 2017. www.brookings.edu/blog/brown-center-chalkboard/2017/03/24/ racial-disparities-in-school-suspensions/.

students were suspended out of every 100 enrolled, while white and Asian students were suspended at less than 5 percent.

John's story is also an example of the extremes of educational discipline. Police involvement takes precedence over parents and educators. This represents a major encroachment of criminal justice and in the lives of young students across the country. The embedded structure of this encroachment is horrifying in its scope and entrenchment in vast regions around the nation. The field of education has developed a symbiotic relationship with the law enforcement apparatus, and entire communities are being destroyed. The citizens of this country must engage in a targeted effort across the states to rescue education. The lives of children are being hijacked through no fault of their own, and the current system makes itself even worse without specific modernizations. The scope of the problem requires direct and sustained action in every state. We will not make criminal justice progress without taking a serious look at the state of our public schools in disadvantaged neighborhoods.

NATIONWIDE SCHOOL-TO-PRISON DATA

Across the United States, a major trend has emerged from emphasis on school safety and juvenile crime. In an effort to end much of the problems with youth misbehavior in schools there has been a convergence between criminal justice system and education. This convergence is often depicted as a school-to-prison pipeline, a metaphor the American Bar Association (ABA) and other academic sources use to describe the current issues in our education system that cause many students to leave school and enter the criminal justice system.[4] There is a direct link between school discipline and the juvenile and adult justice system, many times because of the increased use of "zero tolerance" policies.[5] One report claims that these policies have "had no measureable impact on school safety, but have racially disproportionate effects, increase suspensions and expulsions, elevate the dropout rate, and raise multiple legal issues of due process."[6] The problem is an urgent one. An entire generation of youth, mainly minorities, are losing their lives and becoming a national liability, entering a cycle which leads to prison from these school discipline policies.

---

[4] Sarah E. Redfield, and Jason P. Nance. "School-to-Prison Pipeline Preliminary Report." Report. February 2016. www.americanbar.org/content/dam/aba/administrative/diversity_pipe line/stp_preliminary_report_final.authcheckdam.pdf, 11.

[5] Nancy A. Heitzeg, "Criminalizing Education: Zero Tolerance Policies, Police in the Hallways, and the School to Prison Pipeline." St Catherine University. Accessed August 17, 2016. www .hamline.edu/uploadedFiles/Hamline_WWW/HSE/Documents/criminalizing-education-zero-tolerance-police.pdf.

[6] Heitzeg, "Criminalizing Education."

Discipline policies utilize become criminal law methods for dealing with trouble-some children and teenagers. The inculcation of criminal justice methods instantly impresses these young people who are at the height of their emotional and societal identity development. While children of the middle class enjoy a carefree, inquisitively creative childhood, millions of poor minority students are being exposed to procedures that groom them to be prisoners. Rather than utilize decades of research on discipline, teachers subjectively apply zero tolerance policies toward children and leverage police to enforce discipline. When professional law enforcement is in charge of discipline at schools, common and minor social outbursts create instantly criminal and legal problems. Fighting in the lunchroom becomes a misdemeanor and trip to jail instead of a trip to the principal's office and detention. The NAACP observed that:

> In the last decade, the punitive and overzealous tools and approaches of the modern criminal justice system have seeped into our schools, serving to remove children from mainstream educational environments and funnel them onto a one-way path toward prison … The School-to-Prison Pipeline is one of the most urgent challenges in education today.[7]

The erosion of family structure in poor communities has placed an impossible burden on the educational apparatus in the United States. Schools were not designed to raise children. Emotionally and economically disadvantaged communities have schools where the majority of the young people live troubled lives because of who they were born to. Many troubled children are harder to teach and less disciplined during the eight hours of the school day. School's delegate discipline to law enforcement. Many officers do not have training in how to discipline children, which often escalates confrontation. Law enforcement officers in school treat children as adults, when in fact they are still developing.

Children who are arrested in school are more likely to repeat offenses, be subject to suspension or expulsion, and have a lower likelihood of graduating high school. Once a student is arrested their peers and teachers view and treat them differently. If a student who has been arrested is not kicked out, many drop out because of the social stigma. These young people are treated as criminals, when in a different social class the same behavior would be characterized and responded to as a normal misbehaving teen. Criminal labels on young people in education settings permanently attach themselves to a child's self-identity, and social perception from teachers, staff, and fellow students.[8] Many things considered youthful folly in middle-class communities land young men and women in handcuffs in the hallways in poor communities. These events are leading indicators of future criminal activity for these scarred children. A food fight or speaking out in class leads to a serious

---

7 Ibid.
8 Braithwaite, John. "Shame and Criminal Justice." *Canadian Journal of Criminology* 42, no. 3 (2000): 281–98.

criminal offense as if the child were an adult offender. The stigma and practical liabilities of being labeled a criminal as a youth, or spending time in jail or a juvenile detention center, has lifelong effects. Inner-city schools have been incarceration incubators of teens and young adults.

The pipeline pushes students, mostly African American out of schools at younger ages fueling urban areas as hotbeds of overcriminalization. Record high incarceration rates mirror all-time high school suspension and expulsion rates. Both urban and rural schools are segregated by race and class. One Department of Education review was forced to examine if, "black students are provided an equal opportunity to access and participate in advanced and higher-level learning opportunities."[9] While this task sounds outdated, it pinpoints gaps where there has not been meaningful modernization of school systems through the adoption of best practices for these vulnerable populations.

Grouping of races can indicate academic rigor: "You can ... look in a classroom and know whether it's an upper level class or a lower level class based on the racial composition of the classroom."[10] White middle-class students most often are the majority in the highest performing public schools. The more academically rigorous classes are, the less likely there are to be minority students. The problem is made worse by subjective discrimination; as the same article pointed out, African American students who qualify do not receive the teacher recommendations for higher level courses at the same rate their white classmates do.[11]

Distinctions are not significant just because of class, race is a major variable. In many cases middle-class black students are tracked into lower level courses. One example cited is South Orange Maplewood district, a commutable distance to New York City and a relatively well educated middle-class population, but almost one-fourth of the school qualifies for free or reduced lunches. The total high school population is 38 percent black and 49 percent white, but the white students were much more likely to be placed in honors or advanced classes. In eighth grade at South Orange Maplewood, the class demographic was 44.1 percent white and 47 percent black, but the upper level math course for the grade was 73.2 percent white and 11.6 percent black.[12] In another school district discussed in the article was made up of 38.4 percent white students who were taking almost 70 percent of spots in advanced placement classes.[13]

[9] www.ed.gov/news/press-releases/us-department-education-announces-resolution-south-orange-maplewood-nj-school-di.
[10] Kohli, Somali. "Modern-Day Segregation in Public Schools." *The Atlantic.* November 18, 2014. Accessed August 19, 2016. www.theatlantic.com/education/archive/2014/11/modern-day-segregation-in-public-schools/382846/.
[11] Kohli, "Modern-Day Segregation."
[12] Ibid.
[13] Ibid.

This class segregation, with racial expressions, supplies the pipeline most in places where the schools or school districts are becoming more segregated as a whole according to class as well as race. The segregation of neighborhoods is an important topic as it involves specific policing and the cycle of prison, but the schools in neighborhoods that have high minority populations, specifically high African American populations, are the most active production centers for the pipeline. The schools that have the wealthiest parents often see less arrests and punishment with suspension and expulsion. Parents are perceived as active at home, so school administrators feel the problem can be solved without involving law enforcement. One consultant in New York City said, "It's a fact of urban life that parents with means will go to great lengths to get their children into the best possible programs."[14]

Higher income parents have the means and influence to make sure their children avoid the problems that the poorest students fall victim too, including higher income parents of children of color.[15] The influence of parents plays an important role in the advancement of the child through school. For wealthier families, especially white families in suburban schools, the influence they have over the school's treatment and placement of their children is important, and cannot be ignored. When class placement and educational tracks and opportunities for students are decided subjectively by biased and jaded teachers the child is instantly and unfairly limited in their development.

DISPROPORTIONATE SCHOOL DISCIPLINE AND ITS LASTING EFFECTS

School policing and arrests is one of the most nuanced complexities of overcriminalization. Issues surrounding school discipline and policing attract great media attention and most aggressive policy solutions, yet there is little significant change. New York City Mayor Bill de Blasio announced a ban on suspensions for students in kindergarten through second grade.[16] While Mayor de Blasio's intentions are a step in the right direction, the policy is no solution to a problem broad in scope that plagues urban schools. Mayor de Blasio's proposal will slow the suspension numbers in elementary school in New York City. They will not, however, address the reasons why school districts in the city are suspending kindergarteners in the first place. Solutions for an issue of this scope across the United States need to be more

---

[14] Ibid.
[15] It is important to keep in mind that higher-income African American families tend to not experience the education outcomes with respect to the criminal justice system in the way that disadvantaged African American families do. See Forman, James, Jr. "Racial Critiques of Mass Incarceration: Beyond the New Jim Crow." *New York University Law Review* 87, no. 1 (2012): 21–69.
[16] Rebecca Klein, "Keep Black Kids in School and Out of Jail." July 7, 2016. www.huffingtonpost .com/entry/new-york-city-suspensions_us_57978f5ae4b02d5d5ed2foe8.

substantial than blanket bans or policy changes, but must question the methods for discipline, the reasons for discipline, and the authority of those who decide who to discipline. For the pipeline to be effectively slowed and stopped, the solutions must address the problem. Before any solutions can be considered we must treat children as fully human.

A 2014 study by the Department of Education's Office for Civil Rights compiled much of the current research on the issue.[17] The study found that black students were suspended and expelled at three times the rate of white students: 5 percent of white students were suspended compared to 16 percent of black students.[18] Boys are suspended at higher rates than girls across the board, but black girls are suspended at the highest rates among girls (12 percent), even higher than white boys.[19] Girls in other minority groups (Native American or Native Alaskan communities specifically) are suspended more than white boys. A student with a disability is twice as likely to be suspended as a student without any disabilities. If you combine the two demographics (students with disabilities and minority status) the compounding numbers grow higher.

As it directly relates to the pipeline, students with disabilities represent a quarter of students referred to law enforcement or arrested at school, while they represent only 12 percent of students as a whole. These facts are not just isolated in one area of the country. Only three states (New York, New Jersey, and North Dakota) reported male suspension rates for every racial/ethnic group lower than the national average

The problems surrounding the school-to-prison pipeline and its involvement in the cycle of imprisonment often starts in middle and high school. The report shows the common beliefs that poor and minority students are most likely to be the victims of the school-to-prison pipeline and found various policies and practices that force youths out of school and into the criminal justice and juvenile justice system. Black and Latino youths are the most at risk to being caught in the pipeline, and these policies create a cycle of prison that also heavily affects poor student. Many arrested youths do not finish their education and as a result remain among the poor for much of their lives.

Also highlighted by the report are the debts incurred upon release from prison that keep the poorest prisoners poor. In 1991, 25 percent of inmates owed some sort of court-imposed fee or fine after release. By 2004 the number of inmates that owed money toward these fees and fines increased to 66 percent. Today, the report estimated that 80–85 percent of prisoners leave prison with this debt.[20] These fines and being imprisoned can make you poor even if you are in the minority of prisoners that were not poor before prison. Between the costs of arrest and trial and the

[17] "Civil Rights Data Collection Data Snapshot: School Discipline," Report. March 1, 2014. www2.ed.gov/about/offices/list/ocr/docs/crdc-discipline-snapshot.pdf.
[18] "School Discipline."
[19] Ibid.
[20] Ibid.

struggle to find a job post-imprisonment, many former prisoners become impoverished because of their arrest or time in prison. The report found that those who are
arrested and not convicted may still face the time consuming and costly task of
clearing their criminal record before they can find employment. Other policies the
report cites include the discriminatory use of Civil Asset Forfeiture Laws, and the
criminalization of homelessness. Both have obvious implications for the poor, and
many of the victims of discrimination in these cases have suffered from the other
problems as well. They are often former prisoners and victims of the school-to-prison
pipeline.

For many it all begins with the school-to-prison pipeline, and with the high
likelihood of poor and minority students to be caught in this pipeline they have
increased chances of being poor for the rest of their lives. Without better school
discipline, stronger family structures, and economic sustainability the poorest communities and minority populations are going to continue to be victims of these
vicious cycles of prison and poverty. If we provide the right environment for children
to thrive, and if parents take initiative in disciplining their children instead of relying
on state employees – teachers, social workers, law enforcement officers, and the
like – the cycle of imprisonment and poverty can be stifled early and permanently.
Policy changes can only do so much. The change has to come at the most basic
level – the family – for the pipelines and cycles to be broken. Civil-society institutions are a necessary partner in creating, establishing, and maintaining environments where children and families thrive.

The ABA found in an extensive report on the school-to-prison pipeline found that
teachers view minority students view as "less intelligent and less capable of obtaining
promising career prospects."[21] The discretion of these teachers directly places
vulnerable students at a greater disadvantage to not succeed in school and begin
the path to prison. Labeling and discrimination enable teachers and administrators
to treat some students as if their prospect for education and career success is not
worth the required investment of time and effort.

Those who are imprisoned in their teens have a higher likelihood of spending
time in prison at some point in their lives. The Kirwan Institute at Ohio State
University published an article titled, "The Devastating, Long-Lasting Costs of
Juvenile Incarceration," which examined how incarceration actually affects students
during and after school.[22]

The increased policing of schools is partially to blame with a 30 percent increase
in school resource officers over the past twenty years, making school arrests more
and more common. A twelve-month stay in a juvenile detention center costs

---

[21] Redfield, Nance, "School-to-Prison Pipeline," 19.
[22] Danya Contractor. "The Devastating, Long-Lasting Costs of Juvenile Incarceration." Technical paper. Ohio State University. February 2014. http://kirwaninstitute.osu.edu/wp-content/
uploads/2014/05/ki-implicit-bias-discipline-dc.pdf.

$148,000 a year, while the average cost to educate the same student for a year in public school is only $10,259. The article puts that number in perspective by naming Harvard's tuition cost at $59,959, almost $30,000 less than a year in juvenile detention.

The punishment they receive by way of juvenile detention not only costs taxpayers dearly but also harms their future. Many cannot get jobs or continue their education with criminal records. This leads to high recidivism: 70 to 80 percent of students will be rearrested within two to three years of release. Only 12 percent are incarcerated for violent crimes while the majority are punished for minor offenses. The youth lose social opportunities, experiencing only the debilitating psychological trauma that accompanies incarceration by youth.

While the current debate surrounding overcriminalization and juvenile incarceration is often centered around the male prison population, the debate increasingly forgets to highlight the problems that girls face when caught in the pipeline to juvenile incarceration, which often includes a pattern of sexual abuse. A 2015 report published by Georgetown Law's Center on Poverty and Inequality found that girls in juvenile detention have a high likelihood of being sexual and physical abuse victims.[23] The report summarizes new data on what they call the "abuse to prison pipeline" present in the female juvenile justice system.[24] The report found that there is systemic criminalization of victimized girls, often disproportionately girls from minority populations.

The report highlights the fact that sexual violence against girls is a modern American tragedy, and this sexual abuse is a primary predictor today of a girl's entrance into a juvenile detention center. With juvenile detention and criminal behavior gaining media attention more each year, the sexual abuse pipeline that is a predictor for so many girls is often overlooked as a source for the school to prison pipeline. Girls that were victims of sex trafficking are often arrested on prostitution charges and put in detention centers to be punished instead of being helped to overcome the trauma of the youth sex trafficking industry. Minority girls are increasingly being incarcerated; African American girls make up 14 percent of the national population and 33 percent of girls detained and committed. Native American, African American, and Hispanic girls have the highest likelihood of being incarcerated among young women. One study found that 93 percent of girls in Oregon's juvenile detention centers had experienced some type of abuse; 76 percent had been abused by the age of 13. According the Georgetown report, a California study in 1998 found that 81 percent of incarcerated girls had been physically or sexually abused.

---

[23] Saada Saar, Rebecca Epstein, Lindsay Rosenthal, and Yasmin Vafa. "The Sexual Abuse to Prison Pipeline: The Girls' Story." Report. Georgetown Law. Accessed August 28, 2016. http://rights4girls.org/wp-content/uploads/r4g/2015/02/2015_COP_sexual-abuse_layout_web-1.pdf.

[24] Saada Saar, Epstein, Rosenthal, Vafa, "The Sexual Abuse to Prison Pipeline," 5.

The juvenile justice system is woefully inadequate at providing the support and treatment these girls need, and it exacerbates the trauma because of the harsh conditions and procedures. The report found that the girls become stuck in a cycle: reaction from trauma lands them in detention centers, which leads to trauma from incarceration, then release, and then possible rearrest. Girls that are incarcerated at a young age have a higher chance of mental health problems (80 percent) than boys (67 percent).

The report sheds an important light on an issue that is often overlooked. The sexual trafficking industry and various other sexual and physical abuses have an enormously large influence on young girls' behavior in school. Acting out in school because of sexual abuse triggers the juvenile justice system getting involved by imprisoning victims without providing the needed support. Without finding ways to prevent both the initial abuse, and especially ways to end the common movement of abused girls being placed into the justice system, this will become a lifelong cycle for many girls who have suffered so much before adulthood. For girls stuck in the abuse to prison pipeline and cycle, the same type of factors compound in their lives and leave them without the support of parents, family, teachers, and friends that are required for a stable childhood and success in adulthood.

DISCIPLINARY PROCEDURES

The biggest cause of the school-to-prison pipeline is discipline policies and procedures that lead to the rising number of suspensions and expulsions that involve law enforcement. Zero tolerance policies are used in a subjective, discriminatory, and overly punitive fashion. These policies remove children from school through suspension or expulsion and lead them down the path that ends, for an increasing amount of students, in the juvenile justice system. Zero tolerance policy has no specific definition, but was appropriately described by the ABA as a:

> term [that] became widely adopted in schools in the early 1990s as a philosophy or policy that mandates the application of predetermined consequences, most often severe and punitive in nature, that are intended to be applied regardless of the gravity of behavior, mitigating circumstances, or situational context.[25]

The policies do not just affect high school students but are often applied in preschool and elementary classes. For many students, adults who should be helping children grow and develop are using inappropriate discipline policies by removing them from the classroom. Classroom violations of disciplinary policy are in fact for minor disciplinary infractions. The ABA report found:

[25] "Are Zero Tolerance Policies Effective in the Schools?" Report. December 2008. www.apa.org/pubs/info/reports/zero-tolerance.pdf.

As with referrals to law enforcement and school-based arrests, data also indicate that the majority of these suspensions and expulsions resulted from only trivial infractions of school rules or offenses, not from offenses that endangered the physical well-being of other students.[26]

Instead of teachers doing their job as it relates to understanding and communicating effectively with students, police officers and school resource officers are utilized as enforcers of the strict discipline policies.

The enforcement of zero tolerance policies are often not uniform across public schools, and the data points to these policies as being a leading cause for the increases in school arrests and the school-to-prison pipeline. One paper found that schools often "adopted zero-tolerance policies for a variety of behavioral issues largely directed toward weapons, alcohol/drugs, threatening behavior, and fighting on school premises, and as the name implies, indicate zero-tolerance for any infractions."[27] The same problems exist at white majority suburban schools, but increased police presence "have been most readily adopted and enforced in urban schools with low student to teacher ratios, high percentages of students of color and lower test scores."[28]

These harsh discipline policies at schools across the nation are now regularly under scrutiny from the media. Former Secretary of Education John King has criticized the zero tolerance discipline policies of many charter schools across the country. He claimed that the complicated issues surrounding school discipline were being oversimplified into a binary process at many charter schools that led to a higher number of suspensions.[29] The problem exists across public, private, and charter schools; minor and first-time offenses are ending education for thousands of students every year. The main problem with out-of-school suspension exists in the overabundance of suspension for minor offenses such as "disruption" or "willful defiance." These include other minor offenses such as failure to do homework or not paying attention. Suspension as a punishment for these common acts fails to improve student behavior and increases the likelihood of dropout and delinquency.

A 2014 report from The Civil Rights Project provided excellent examples of how countermeasures to zero tolerance discipline policies in California schools benefited many students and especially minority populations.[30] The report's

---

[26] Redfield, Nance, "School-to-Prison Pipeline," 14.

[27] Heitzeg, "Criminalizing Education," 15.

[28] Ibid. As noted earlier, the challenge with this data is that is does not help us distinguish enough between advantaged and disadvantaged African Americans.

[29] Lauren Camera. "Education Secretary to Charter Schools: Rethink School Discipline." *US News.* June 28, 2016. Accessed August 22, 2016. www.usnews.com/news/articles/2016-06-28/education-secretary-to-charter-schools-rethink-school-discipline.

[30] Daniel J. Losen, Tia E. Martinez, and Valerie Okelola. "Keeping California's Kids in School: Fewer Students of Color Missing School for Minor Misbehavior." Report. UCLA. Accessed August 22, 2016. https://civilrightsproject.ucla.edu/resources/projects/center-for-

findings relied on information from the California Department of Education. The data shows that schools in California are narrowing the racial divide in school discipline and the reliance on out-of-school suspension. In the 2011–2012 and 2012–2013 school years there were decreases in the number of African and Native American students suspended.[31] African American students had the largest decline in suspensions with three less per 100 students than in previous years.[32] In California, 500 school districts reported decreased out-of-school suspension rates while only 245 districts reported increases.[33] One example cited in the report is Baltimore City where decreased suspension rates actually led to increased graduation rates in the district.[34] This example confirms what many experts believe is a direct connection between high suspension rates and low graduation rates.

The results toward racial equality in school discipline is encouraging in California but still requires significant work. Overall, the study found that out-of-school suspension rates out of every 100 students in Los Angeles dropped from 12.1 to 7.1 for Black students; 3.1 to 1.7 for Latino students; and 2.4 to 1.0 for White students.[35] While the racial gap in LA is one of the lowest in the state it still points to the problems inherent in the disciplinary process. With more research coming out each year about the connections between high school suspension, expulsion, delinquency, and the school-to-prison pipeline, these reforms are important steps to take in reducing discriminatory punishment and high numbers of minority youths in juvenile and adult detention centers.

Recent school shootings and violence have prompted many school districts to have law enforcement officers on school grounds to offer protection in emergencies. This practice has led to an increase of student arrests and referrals to law enforcement, a trend some experts are referred to as the "criminalization of school discipline." A November 2015 study by Jason Nance brought to light some of the problems with this approach to safety, school discipline, and the surrounding policies.[36] The number of schools using law enforcement or school resource officers (SROs) as a means of discipline has increased from fewer than a hundred in the 1970s to over 19,000 by the early 2000s.[37] The authority of SROs includes enforcing rules like violent behavior or disturbing the peace. Some states have

civil-rights-remedies/school-to-prison-folder/summary-reports/keeping-californias-kids-in-school/WithChange.pdf.
[31] Losen, Martinez, and Okelola, "Keeping California's Kids in School."
[32] Ibid.
[33] Ibid., 3.
[34] Ibid.
[35] Ibid., 7.
[36] Jason P. Nance. "Students, Police, and the School-to-Prison Pipeline." Technical paper. 2016. Accessed August 31, 2016. http://papers.ssrn.com/sol3/papers.cfm?abstract_id=2577333
[37] Nance, "Students, Police, and the School-to-Prison Pipeline," 946.

even passed laws criminalizing disruption of school activities or talking back to teachers.[38] These laws do not just affect older high school students. In one example, a five-year-old student was arrested for throwing a temper tantrum during a math class, while in another instance a six-year-old girl throwing a tantrum was arrested and handcuffed around her biceps in order to be escorted out of the school.[39] An SRO in every public school would cost an estimated $3.2 billion a year.[40] The study found that while the increases in police officers and SROs is to protect schools from increased juvenile crime and school violence, no data showed it improved school safety.

As officers in schools have increased, there is evidence that school-based referrals to law enforcement have increased. In the Philadelphia Public School District school arrests increased from 1,631 in the 1999–2000 academic year to 2,194 in 2002–2003.[41] Similar to increased suspensions and expulsions, the increase in school arrests were in large part for minor offenses. These policies and actions feed the school to prison pipeline, and in doing so negatively affect minority students who are disproportionately hurt by the phenomenon.

Ultimately the study found that the increased rate of SROs present in schools increased the odds of students being referred to law enforcement, and especially increased the odds of students being referred for offenses that school administrators and teachers should have addressed using other discipline methods. While school safety is of utmost concern, criminal procedures in the classroom prevent the successful education of thousands of students per year and create new criminals. If this problem is not addressed, among the many others proposed here, the crisis in school discipline will still be one of the leading causes of the school-to-prison pipeline over the next decades.

The frequent use of suspension and expulsion for minor offenses has become so commonplace in many schools across the country that Rhode Island passed a law in 2016 aimed at making it harder for schools to suspend students for minor infractions.[42] The law creates stricter guidelines for when students can be sent home from school in order to lower the number of suspensions. It is direct and aggressive actions such as this which are required to end the criminalization of the educational environment in poor, mostly minority communities. When schools lighten policies on discipline, criminality decreases in the juvenile population.

---

[38] Ibid., 948.
[39] Ibid., 946.
[40] Ibid., 947.
[41] Ibid., 953.
[42] "Raimondo Signs Law Limiting School Suspensions." *Associated Press* WJAR. July 3, 2016. Accessed September 14, 2016. http://turnto10.com/news/local/raimondo-signs-law-limiting-school-suspensions.

HIGH SCHOOL DROPOUT RATES AND JUVENILE DELINQUENCY

An ABA report found that when students received any type of exclusionary discipline (suspension or expulsion) they were 23.5 percent more likely to drop out of school entirely.[43] Juvenile justice did not successfully rehabilitate students to the point where they were able to readjust and becomes successful high school students again. Instead, the policies often increased delinquency rates and increased a student's chance of being involved with juvenile justice in the future. Recidivism with juveniles works the same way as with adults: juveniles, especially young teens, are impressionable. Without positive discipline and adult figures in their lives, many will end up leaving the education system and never returning. This problem can lead to a lifetime of poverty and crime. One study cited by the Justice Policy Institute found that in Texas, "31 percent of students who were suspended or expelled repeated a grade."[44] The Texas study still found that "students who had been suspended or expelled were twice as likely to drop out compared to students with similar characteristics at similar schools who had not been suspended."[45] Students who struggle academically and are expelled or suspended have a much higher chance of giving up on their education.

The number of high school dropouts in the nation is growing and the problem is heavily weighted toward minority populations. In 2007, the 6.2 million high school dropouts were made up of a majority of men (60.1 percent) of which the largest percentages were Hispanic (18.8 percent) and black (30.1 percent).[46] With the problem slowly becoming one of race as well as socioeconomic status, reports like these are becoming more common. The subjective nature of many of the zero tolerance policies are leading the dropout crisis to become a crisis of race and poverty where the most vulnerable teens are pushed away from a chance at education. A growing portion of the population is made up of high school dropouts: 16 percent of persons between age16 and 24 did not finish high school.[47]

In many cases, the high rates of juvenile incarceration and dropouts are caused by these factors and are something that can be changed and reformed by communities that care about the vulnerable populations of students at schools. Schools need to make discipline policies that help build character in young men and women, encouraging them to overcome peer pressure and outside influences to finish their education. Without the proper support that young men and women could be

---

[43] Redfield, Nance, "School-to-Prison Pipeline," 23.
[44] Nelson, Libby, and Dara Lind. "The School to Prison Pipeline, Explained." Justice Policy Institute. February 24, 2014. Accessed October 17, 2016. www.justicepolicy.org/news/8775.
[45] Nelson, Lind, "The School to Prison Pipeline."
[46] "Left Behind in America: The Nation's Dropout Crisis." Report. May 5, 2009. Accessed May 11, 2016. http://hdl.handle.net/2047/d20000598, 2.
[47] "Left Behind in America," 2.

receiving in mentors and teachers they resort to other influences outside of school. For many teens, the dropout crisis leads them to the prison pipeline.

One promising project by local Rotary clubs was featured in a Memphis newspaper to help reduce juvenile delinquency.[48] The goal of the Rotary Club program was to reduce delinquency by 50 percent in their community. This would be a major accomplishment that a local juvenile court judge said could have a "big impact" on the adolescent population. The leaders of Rotary clubs in the area are meeting with law enforcement, city and county officials, and forming a nonprofit to raise money and awareness about juvenile delinquency. They realize that the dysfunction of homes and relationships is often the cause of delinquency, and providing mentorship and support is a step toward helping these young men and women away from these negative trajectories. One mentor of a 17-year-old offender said, "Relationships are what get children into trouble, and relationships are what will help them stay out of trouble."[49] The research on this topic increasingly proves this statement true. A report released in January 2015 showed that often the relationships around youths can be the cause of delinquency and recidivism later in life.[50]

The study found that juveniles aged sixteen to eighteen were most likely to commit crimes, and risk factors for delinquency include low educational attainment, low aspirations, and low attachment to school.[51] Without education as a priority and motivation, it is easy for high school students to drift toward peer pressured crime. Socioeconomic status often played a large role in predicting future delinquency and was often cited by teens as a reason for the crimes they committed. One theory cited by the report claims that poverty makes it less likely for youths to be able to achieve goals valued by society by a legitimate means, making them more likely to turn to crime to achieve a status they could not before. An unstable economic background was found to be a significant predictor of youth crime rates.

Relationships are incredibly important to fixing the problems in delinquency. The report found that one of the largest reasons for juvenile crime was negative influences from peers. A lack of positive role models often pushed youth into negative relationships that encourage criminal behavior. Many of the respondents to the research reported spending a majority of their time with friends, many of

---

[48] David Waters. "Rotary Defeated Polio, Why Not Juvenile Crime?" July 6, 2016. Accessed October 14, 2016. http://archive.commercialappeal.com/columnists/david-waters/rotary-defeated-polio-why-not-juvenile-crime-epidemic-36837aeb-f3ba-7199-e053-0100007f1685-385749751.html.

[49] Waters, "Rotary Defeated Polio."

[50] Muhammad, Nisar, Shakir Ullah, Madad Ali, and Sadiq Alam. "Juvenile Delinquency: The Influence of Family, Peer and Economic Factors on Juvenile Delinquents." Report. January 20, 2015. http://pscipub.com/Journals/Data/JList/Scientia Agriculturae/2015/Volume 9/Issue 1/6.pdf.

[51] Muhammad, Ullah, Ali, Alam, "Juvenile Delinquency," 41.

whom had a negative impact on their lives.[52] Family structure has one of the largest influences on a child's likelihood of delinquency. Single parenthood, especially the absence of a father in the home, is a sure predictor of juvenile deviance and criminal activity. Without the positive influence of a parent teens often look to peers instead of other positive role models (like a teacher or mentor). Instead of relationships that encourage and build teens toward career and educational goals many turned to friendships that could have a negative influence on their development.

FAILED PROGRAMS: SCARED STRAIGHT, CURFEW LAWS

There have been several prominent programs over the past several decades that have failed to help deter youth from a life of crime. Two of the biggest attempts were Scared Straight programs and juvenile curfews. Scared Straight programs have been deemed unsuccessful from almost every outlet. These programs are part of a larger group of solutions sometimes called juvenile awareness programs. The programs are discouraged by the Department of Justice because of the risks and varied results the programs receive.[53] When the programs began in the 1970s their goal was to discourage youth crime by visits to prison, talks by prisoners or wardens, and other presentations meant to actually scare the misbehaving youths "straight."[54] In short they "are designed to deter participants from future offending by providing first-hand observations of prison life and interaction with adult inmates."[55] Various studies cited by the Justice Department found that in some cases recidivism actually went up among youths in the program.[56] Another said that crime increased 28 percent in the group receiving the "Scared Straight" treatment over the group that did not participate. One report given in 1997 to Congress actually listed it on the "does not work" category among crime prevention policies.

One of the studies concluded that the program was "likely to have a harmful effect and increase delinquency relative to doing nothing at all to the same youths."[57] The students who participated were usually not discouraged by the program, and some were actually harmed by the experiences. The original program in the 1970s boasted that it had a 94 percent success rate, or as a fraction of its focus group, sixteen out of seventeen students avoided crime. The goal of

[52] Ibid., 40.
[53] "Justice Department Discourages the Use of 'Scared Straight' Programs." Department of Justice. Accessed November 2, 2016. www.ncjrs.gov/html/ojjdp/news_at_glance/234084/topstory.html.
[54] Justice Department Discourages the Use of "Scared Straight"
[55] Anthony Petrosino, Carolyn Turpin-Petrosino, Meghan E. Hollis-Peel, and Julia G. Lavenberg. *Scared Straight and Other Juvenile Awareness Programs for Preventing Juvenile Delinquency: A Systematic Review*. Report.
[56] Justice Department Discourages the Use of "Scared Straight"
[57] Petrosino, Turpin-Petrosino, Hollis-Peel, Lavenberg, *Scared Straight*, 7.

the program is deterrence, and the hope is that the shocking images and experiences will be enough to turn at-risk students away from crime. Programs offer inmates a chance to teach students how not to follow their path and are inexpensive while following the modern narrative of the "get tough" mentality. Modern programs exist around the world, identifying at-risk students and providing them prison tours or showing videos on the subject. The biggest problem, according to this report, is the policy does not seem to follow the evidence. The report used research complied with diverse groups of students over several decades and found that overall the programs actually increased recidivism and crime among the groups studied. The programs that use fear as awareness are not the solution for the school-to-prison pipeline. They oversimplify the issue without dealing with the causes or sources of the problem. Solutions have to be multifaceted and target discipline, family issues, and discrimination to treat the underlying problems.

Another failed program to fight these issues are juvenile curfews enacted to help reduce crime. The problems are abundant, but they are most often criticized for being paternalistic or even unconstitutional. One law journal article makes the case for both of these options.[58] The author argued that the foundation of the law is paternalism as a policy to fight juvenile crime, and an invasion of privacy.[59] In one court case, the argument was made that the rule of law exists to take care of those who do offend it, but that there laws created a sort of military law in the town. The legislation was for the protection of minors and the community, to protect the streets at night. The criticism of paternalism is obvious from this sort of language, but the goal seems logical, preventing crime by not allowing youths on the street. This type of curfew is a blanket curfew, a nonemergency law to prevent crime under normal circumstances. The curfew had limitations and allowances. If a minor had work, or was attending a civic event, they were perfectly allowed to do so. The problem that the author points out is that even with the curfew exceptions there are still limitations on an innocent minor's movements at certain times. This, to the author, seems to be an unwarranted limitation on free movement that could not survive a constitutional challenge no matter how many exceptions were added. While the laws have a compelling upside, the possibility of reducing crime, they are considered by many to be a restriction of liberty. The journal article sums up the common problems with these one-policy fixes to juvenile crime: they do not help troubled youth, they fail to address underlying family problems, and they restrict liberty in the process. Criminalizing being a teenager from a disadvantaged community will never deter juvenile delinquency.

[58] Tona Trollinger. "The Juvenile Curfew: Unconstitutional Imprisonment." *William & Mary Bill of Rights Journal* 4, no. 3 (1996). Accessed November 2, 2016. http://scholarship.law.wm .edu/cgi/viewcontent.cgi?article=1478&context=wmborj.
[59] Trollinger, "The Juvenile Curfew," 949.

CONCLUSION

Solutions to the school-to-prison pipeline will need to address the issues and causes of how children end up in the pipeline in the first place. Because the relationship between education and offending, personalism points us to the fact that caring about education reform is a necessary part of ending overcriminalization and mass incarceration as we care about the whole person. Many of those problems and solutions fall far outside of the scope of government policy because children need affectional connection and reinforcement from adults who are committed to their thriving. Real relationship, in person, because children are persons who require particular attributes and skills in order to flourish and make contributions to the common good. Without a holistic approach to reform and support, the school system, and surrounding external factors, will continue to initiate and control the cycle of crime at a young age for many youths. The effects that will continue for generations start in education, and systematic discrimination is alive in too many classrooms. The solutions cannot be blanket policies but must come from the person up, across communities, beginning with how to compensate for lack of family support that send many youths toward a life in and out of prison. The pipeline must be permanently dismantled, not simply tampered with. To start, law enforcement officers do not belong inside of schools. What is also true is that many of the children who find themselves in the juvenile justice system experience collateral damage for the breakdowns in employment opportunities and family nurturing.

6

The Social, Moral, and Economic Costs of Overcriminalization

An article in the *Atlantic* highlighted the story of DeShawn Smith, who, when her partner was imprisoned, moved her two children into public housing in a poor neighborhood. After losing the income from her partner, everything was too expensive.[1] In the poor neighborhood, her second-grade daughter was the only person in the new school who could read, and her teacher admitted that she only showed up for the paycheck. A report cited in the article claims that when someone goes to prison nearly 65 percent of families are suddenly unable to pay for food and housing. Up to 70 percent of those families are caring for kids under the age of 18, "Poverty, in particular, perpetuates the cycle of incarceration, while incarceration itself leads to greater poverty."

The criminal justice system punishes many more than just offenders who are incarcerated. Of the many people affected by mass incarceration, often the most hurt are the spouses, children, parents, and siblings that an inmate leaves behind when they enter prison, especially children. Crimes relating to property show a financial desperation; these dependents become even more vulnerable after they lose any economic support the incarcerated were providing prior to their arrest. The immediate surrounding community is damaged as the more people that are in jail the weaker the economy becomes. These factors corrode the foundation of the entire community and trap new generations of children.

Compounding this is the most powerful force in the mathematical world; every citizen must understand that the problems of crime and poverty get proportionally worse with every new person behind bars. The startling statistics in every area of criminal justice are simply measurements of the devastation that are results of continually putting people in jail. We are creating our own problems, which seep

[1] Alana Semuels, "What Incarceration Costs American Families." *The Atlantic.* September 15, 2015. Accessed August 01, 2017. www.theatlantic.com/business/archive/2015/09/the-true-costs-of-mass-incarceration/405412/.

into each aspect of society. For a nation to reach its full potential, every citizen must be empowered to engage in community-enhancing activities. In the United States, the growth of the prison population is destroying the potential for major segments of our society, holding the entire nation back from what could be accomplished. By extension, criminal justice will not succeed if we do not focus our attention on the types of civil society institutions that contribute to well-being and human flourishing like marriage, the family, and the marketplace.

THE SOCIAL COSTS OF OVERCRIMINALIZATION

Social Networks: Marriage, Family, and Their Importance for Human Flourishing

Overcriminalization attacks the central social structure of society: the family. With each incarceration a network of people on the outside are left weakened, often losing their main income earner. Prisons are full of sons, daughters, mothers, and fathers each leaving a social circle that is damaged by their absence in the community, lasting generations.[2] Single parent homes, unstable financial situations, and various lasting psychological effects plague those communities affected by imprisonment and those around them.

Marriage, family, and poverty are connected. People across racial lines living in low-income areas tend to have lower rates of marriage. The tendency to marry less causes a strain on family relationships, especially children. Conservatives have highlighted these intersections for decades. For example, in a study on the relationship between marriage and child poverty, the Heritage Foundation reported findings by a 2009 US Census Bureau report that discovered 37.1 percent of single parent families were poor, compared to just 6.8 percent of married families.[3] Overall, single parent families were six times more likely to be poor than their married counterparts. Marriage between a child's parents reduces the chance of that child being raised in poverty by 82 percent. This is important to consider from the other side of the data as well. The study goes on to explain why the majority of poor families in the United States are not married. Children with unmarried parents have a greater likelihood of being impoverished, and poor families are the most likely to not be married. In all, 71 percent of poor families with children are unmarried couples. The study also found that education of parents also has an important impact of family life and flourishing.

[2] John F. Pfaff, *Locked In: The True Causes of Mass Incarceration – and How to Achieve Real Reform* (New York: Basic Books, 2017), 1–18.

[3] Robert Rector, "Marriage: America's Greatest Weapon against Child Poverty." The Heritage Foundation. September 16, 2010. www.heritage.org/research/reports/2010/09/marriage-america-s-greatest-weapon-against-child-poverty.

Single mothers have the highest likelihood of being poor from the lack of income caused by the father's absence, and single mothers have lower average education than fathers. Births outside marriage have a more lasting effect on the mother and this factor reduces their ability to finish their education and get jobs that can lift them out of poverty. Across the United States, 65.2 percent of children born to female high school dropouts are born outside of marriage, but among college graduates only 8.1 percent.[4]

When children are raised in these environments they are more likely to follow a similar path to their parents because many of these factors have a high chance of being symbolically hereditary. Family systems and patterned behavior matter and the growing trend for couples to have children outside of marriage only increases the chance of poverty.[5] The bottom economic third of the population has the highest likelihood of being imprisoned, making the chances of the negative effects of prison on the family high among unmarried couples with children.[6] All of these factors are compounding. The highest likelihood of poverty occurs when all or most of these factors are found within one family, or in a community, or in a city. When these trends appear, poverty appears, and both are a factor in the growing criminalization that we see in communities across the United States. The links between marriage and poverty are becoming more obvious as larger segments of the population have children out of wedlock, consistently. The connection between imprisonment, poverty, and unmarried parents is a reminder of the importance of marriage to stable financial situations and in raising children without the risk of having a parent in prison.

Marriage, and especially the marriage of a child's parents, gives them a higher chance of growing up outside of poverty, and gives them greater chances through education and location not afforded to those who might be impoverished because of a single parent or an imprisoned parent. Marriage provides a crucial structure to raising children in emotionally and financially stable homes. With married parents at home, children are more likely to complete their education and have a productive career.

Single-Parent Families and Incarceration

Across the United States, especially in poor rural and urban communities, there are many children that have incarcerated parents, mostly fathers. This leads to a higher chance of imprisonment for these children later in life and a higher chance that they will grow up in poverty. Millions of women raise children with their child's

---

[4] Ibid.
[5] Ibid.
[6] Bernadette Rabuy and Daniel Kopf, "Prisons of Poverty: Uncovering the Pre-incarceration Incomes of the Imprisoned." Prisons Policy Initiative. July 9, 2015. www.prisonpolicy.org/reports/income.html.

father behind bars, and these children grow up with their only experience of their fathers being imprisoned. Growing up without a father has negative effects on children, felt both when their father was always behind bars, or when a father is taken away to prison at critical points in their development. If a child loses their father early in life these effects are felt even more. There are direct links between single parenting, educational achievement, and the chance of future imprisonment. According to new research, the loss of a father due to death, divorce, or jail is associated with children having shorter caps on the ends of their chromosomes, known as telemores, which shrink as a result of stress.[7] Biological consequences to cultural problems should be a clear sign that our civil society must end these serious problems immediately.

It has primarily been conservatives who make the point that marriage is the structure for nurturing children. The presence of two parents contribute toward psychosocial stability, which have socioeconomic consequences later in life.[8] Married parents work toward financial goals and supporting their family and providing opportunities and privileges for the children. A study conducted using data from the US Census Bureau found that some 37 percent of single-parent families lack self-sufficiency, rendering them officially poor.[9] When compared to the number of married couple families, just 7 percent are considered poor. A Heritage Foundation study states,

> Children raised by single parents are more likely to have emotional and behavioral problems; be physically abused; smoke, drink, use drugs; be aggressive; engage in violent, delinquent, and criminal behavior; have poor school performance; be expelled from school; and dropout of high school.[10]

Many of these attributes are commonly found with children raised by single mothers, pointing to the benefits of having a father in the home. The number of children born outside of marriage is growing and has been for decades. In 1964, 93 percent of children were born to married parents. By 2007, the number had dropped to 57 percent. Children born out of wedlock and raised by single parents make up the majority of poor children in the United States, and these single-parent families make up one third of families with children.[11]

---

[7] See Colter Mitchell, Sara Mclanahan, Lisa Schneper, Irv Garfinkel, Jeanne Brooks-Gunn, and Daniel Notterman. "Father Loss and Child Telomere Length." *Pediatrics* 140, no. 2 (2017).

[8] P. S. Blair, R. Drewett, P. Emmett, A. Ness, and A. Emond. "Family, Socioeconomic and Prenatal Factors Associated with Failure to Thrive in the Avon Longitudinal Study of Parents and Children (ALSPAC)." *International Journal of Epidemiology* 33, no. 4 (2004): 839–47.

[9] Robert Rector, "How Welfare Undermines Marriage and What to Do About It." The Heritage Foundation. November 14, 2014. Accessed April 30, 2016. www.heritage.org/research/reports/2014/11/how-welfare-undermines-marriage-and-what-to-do-about-it.

[10] Rector, "How Welfare Undermines Marriage."

[11] Ibid.

While it is no surprise that education brings families out of the risk for poverty, it is less known that marriage tends to do the same. According to data cited in the Heritage study from the US Census Bureau, the poverty rate for a single mother with a high school diploma or equivalent is 31.7 percent, while the poverty rate for a married couple headed by one member with a high school diploma is 5.6 percent. Marriage in this situation drops the chances of being poor by 80 percent. The rate of births out of wedlock differs greatly by race and ethnicity as well. In 2008, the percentage of white children born out of wedlock was 28.6 percent, the percentage of Hispanic births out of wedlock was 52.5 percent, and for black births the statistic was highest, 72.3 percent.[12] These numbers have grown significantly since the mid-twentieth century where only 2 percent of white children and 14 percent of black children were born out of wedlock.[13]

These factors point not only toward a decline in what was the normal family structure, but also in the increase that children will not receive the benefits they have when parents were married. The financial and educational stability that comes with marriage is something once taken for granted, but in many cases now the influence by necessity comes from other family members, teachers, and peers. The less involved their parents are the more likely that a child will be influenced negatively from peers or other sources that damage their chances of success. For many children, this leads toward the school to prison pipeline, and others, toward a life very similar to their parents.

Over the course of the last fifty years, the state of marriage and the once normal family structure has diminished greatly. In 1965, the Moynihan Report provided data regarding the disparities between education, living standards, and income. Assistant Secretary of Labor Daniel Patrick Moynihan, who also served as a Senator from New York, introduced the report, and concluded that marriage was the problem causing the current economic disparities. He found that "[t]he fundamental problem ... is that of family structure." This is important today as well because the trends in families have only continued to follow the same patterns. Another report compared the data from the Moynihan Report to the data from 2014, almost 50 years after the report was published. The study found that over the course of the five decades since the report was published, the degradation of the family structure across racial lines got worse.[14] Whether one considers oneself a conservative or not, it seems hard to argue against the fact that children thrive the best in loving, stable, affectionate, supportive homes where they learn and experience the type of prosocial

---

[12] Ibid.
[13] Ibid.
[14] Martin D. Brown and Rachel Sheffield, "The Moynihan Report 50 Years Later: Why Marriage More Than Ever Promotes Opportunity for All." The Heritage Foundation. March 26, 2015. Accessed May 09, 2016. www.heritage.org/research/reports/2015/03/the-moynihan-report-50-years-later-why-marriage-more-than-ever-promotes-opportunity-for-all#_ftn1.

norms that resist deviance from the parents. As such, keeping families together should be a priority in the criminal justice system as well.

According to the CDC's 2013 birth information cited in the report, "More than 40 percent of children in the United States are born outside marriage. About 29 percent of white children, 72 percent of black children, and over half of Hispanic children were born to single mothers in 2014."[15] The problem with this, as the article states, is that children born into single parent homes are more likely to live in poverty, less likely to graduate from high school or go to college, more likely to become teen parents, and more likely to engage in criminal activity and be incarcerated.[16] The family structure is important, and in its current state breeds a cycle of delinquency, poor education, and poverty that perpetuates itself for generations. Children that are raised in these situations have a higher likelihood of remaining in them for their lifetimes and repeating the cycle with their own children. The increase in problems from the time the Moynihan Report until now show the repetitive nature of single-parent homes, poor education, imprisonment, and poverty becoming generational and getting worse.

When incarceration creates single parent families and the parents remain in a cycle of prison sentences, it has lasting psychological effects on children. According to a Department of Justice study, "more than 4 in 10 mothers in state prison who had minor children were living in single-parent households in the month before arrest."[17] This means there is a percentage of the population that has seen their only physically present parent taken always to prison. These children are then raised outside of their parent's care and they lose the required parental nurturing. For these children, deviance becomes an acceptable way to live because they have been exposed to so much dysfunction. When children see this way of living as normal, dysfunction can cycle throughout successive generations.

Christopher Wildeman argues that, "mass imprisonment may contribute to a system of stratification in which crime and incarceration are passed down from fathers to sons."[18] Wildeman says that his research "[s]uggests that the financial effects of paternal incarceration are long lasting and large. Because incarceration elevates risks of divorce and separation, children's family structure may change as a result of paternal incarceration."[19] He goes on to argue that because most imprisoned parents are fathers, the mother is likely to find a new partner, further

[15] "National Center for Health Statistics/Births: Final Data for 2013," Report no. 1. January 15, 2015. www.cdc.gov/nchs/data/nvsr/nvsr64/nvsr64_01.pdf.
[16] Brown and Sheffield, "The Moynihan Report."
[17] Lauren E. Glaze, and Laura M. Maruschak, "Parents in Prison and Their Minor Children." Report. Bureau of Justice Statistics, 2008. August 2008. www.bjs.gov/content/pub/pdf/pptmc .pdf, 5.
[18] Christopher Wildeman. "Paternal Incarceration and Children's Physically Aggressive Behaviors: Evidence from the Fragile Families and Child Wellbeing Study." *Social Forces* 89.1 (2010): 285–309.
[19] Ibid.

changing the children's family structure. The stigma of having a father in prison also affects children, and Wildeman says that research shows "partners of incarcerated men often withdraw from social networks, thereby diminishing the number of ties children can draw upon."[20]

For many children, they try and avoid this social stigma by withdrawing from circles that look differently on them because they have an incarcerated parent. Children with parents caught in the cycle of imprisonment are affected in the long and short run. While it might seem like once a father returns to the family things can return to normal, research shows that the effects can continue. Young boys especially feel the pressure of having a father in prison, and it tends to affect them as they externalize the pressure through physical aggression. Even when or if their father returns from prison while a child is at home, the effects of their absence still can have an impact on the children.

There is data that not only suggests that many inmates have children, but also that many inmates have minor children or even young children still at home. According to a Department of Justice (DOJ) study on inmates, "An estimated 809,800 prisoners of the 1,518,535 held in the nation's prisons at midyear 2007 were parents of minor children, or children under age 18."[21] These 1,706,600 minor children account for 2.3 percent of the US population under 18.[22] The number of incarcerated parents and children with incarcerated parents has increased especially over the past thirty years with the biggest increases in both demographics coming in the 1990s and early 2000s. From 1991 to mid-year 2007, the number of parents held in state and federal prisons increased 79 percent and children with incarcerated parents increase 80 percent; the fastest growth occurred in the 1990s (44 percent), but the growth continued into the 2000s at 25 percent.[23] One of the most interesting statistics from the DOJ study is that the number of incarcerated mothers with a child under eighteen increased by 131 percent from 1991 to 2007.[24] Not only are the number of children with a father increasing as the prison populations increase, but the number of children being raised without a mother is as well. This opens up all different kinds of questions as to how this could have lasting effects on children. Across racial boundaries, black children were seven times more likely and Hispanic children two and a half time times more likely to have a parent in prison than their white counterparts.[25] The Department of Justice conducted a survey of prison inmates and found that one in four state and federal prisoners had a minor child.[26] For both

---

[20] Ibid.
[21] Glaze and Maruschak, "Parents in Prison and Their Minor Children," 1.
[22] Ibid., 1.
[23] Ibid., 2.
[24] Ibid., 2.
[25] Ibid., 2.
[26] Ibid., 2.

state and federal prisoners more than half of their children were age nine and younger.[27] Those serving sentences for drug and public order offences were more likely to have children than those serving for violent crimes.[28] Most inmates referred to the other parent as the primary caregiver of their child while they were in prison (84 percent), followed by the child's grandparents (15 percent). Prior to incarceration, 52 percent of mothers, and 54 percent of fathers, reported being the primary provider of financial support.[29] This means that half of the children with incarcerated parents lost the parent that provided the primary source of income for their family when they were arrested, more than likely for a nonviolent offense. Mothers are more likely than fathers to be receiving government support if they are the primary financial provider of their children.

Further proving the generational cycle of poverty and imprisonment, 40 percent of parents in prison reported growing up in a home that received public assistance.[30] Half of the parents in prison studied reported to having a family member incarcerated before them, with the most commonly reported being a brother (34 percent) or a father (19 percent).[31] The data suggests that many people who are imprisoned today had family imprisoned as well, especially the relationship between father and sons. When there is a generational trend for imprisoned fathers it is a hard trend to break because the problems compound with each new family and generation. A jailed father, poverty, and low educational attainment all end up compounding many young men's lives and they are increasingly likely to follow a similar path.

Overall, this research suggests that incarcerated parents are likely to have come from single parent homes, poverty-stricken homes, and homes that saw previous incarcerations. Once a family member is incarcerated there is a higher likelihood of another family member, especially a child, being sent to prison in the future. The patterns of poverty, single parent homes, and family member imprisonment lead to more instances of imprisonment in communities. Once the cycle begins it is hard for children to break out of these situations.

The Effects of Marriage on Community and Social Cohesion in Inner-Cities

Overcriminalization has direct results on families and communities because of the breakdown of the family. Since there are higher numbers of imprisoned parents than ever before, and especially higher numbers of incarcerated fathers, the effects on children are increasingly important. Fathers, and especially the absence of a father, have a direct effect on the behavior and life paths of their children. Absentee fatherhood, especially when those fathers are imprisoned, leads to higher risks of

[27] Ibid., 3.
[28] Ibid., 3.
[29] Ibid., 3.
[30] Ibid., 5.
[31] Ibid., 7.

children being entered into the juvenile justice system and eventually into prison as adults. This repeated cycle of prison breaks down families and communities. Once imprisoned or released back into communities these prisoners are prevented from enjoying the freedoms that many citizens do, and the things that allow communities and individuals to flourish.

The number of children that are raised with a father in prison is growing. According to a report published by the US Department of Health and Human Services, 92 percent of state and federal prisoners who had minor children in 2004 were men.[32] The data from this study is at times overwhelming, but only captures a small part of the problems. Each page of statistics reveals the growing number of young children, especially in minority or poor populations, who grow up or spend significant time without their fathers. Growing up without a father can have a number of significant negative effects on a child's development as well as their potential for success. Communities and families that see this happening at a significant rate experience the problems amplified and the complications manifest on a broader scale in everyday community life.

When a child is raised in a family structure with a single parent, and especially without a father figure in the home, it can have negative effects on the long-term lifestyle of the child. Young boys raised without a father figure are more likely to be imprisoned at some point in their life and follow the same path as their father, whether that is abusive or violent behavior, abusing drugs and alcohol, or dropping out of school. Demuth and Brown observe that the likelihood of youths committing crimes dropped when they were a part of intact two-parent families, and this was a result of the supervision and instruction of their families.[33] Children raised in single-parent homes are more likely to participate in neighborhood violence, leading to a direct correlation between single-family homes and neighborhood safety and violence. In many places this leads to a trend of neighborhoods with high minority populations that are especially prone to raised levels of neighbor violence among youths. According to study on the US Census Bureau's data from 2014, 24 percent of children in the United States were living in a single-mother household, double the amount that were living with a single mother in 1965.[34]

With the data pointing to single-mother households raising children with more likelihood of committing neighborhood violence, the likelihood of minority children being raised in violent neighborhoods increases significantly, leading to

---

[32] "Incarceration & the Family: A Review of Research & Promising Approaches for Serving Fathers & Families: Characteristics of Incarcerated Fathers." ASPE. 2015. Accessed May 11, 2016. https://aspe.hhs.gov/legacy-page/incarceration-family-review-research-promising-approaches-serving-fathers-families-characteristics-incarcerated-fathers-146361.

[33] Stephen Demuth and Susan L. Brown, "Family Structure, Family Processes, and Adolescent Delinquency: The Significance of Parental Absence versus Parental Gender," *Journal of Research in Crime and Delinquency* 41, no. 1 (February 2004): 58–81.

[34] Sheffield and Brown, "The Moynihan Report."

increased targeting by law enforcement, and an increased influence on youths to join in the cycle of violence. According to research done by the Patrick Fagan, "Adolescents who live in an intact married family are least likely to get into a fight."[35] Fighting at school and other similar metrics of youth violence were found to have increased among children living in single-parent or divorced homes. Chris Knoester and Dana Haynie, referenced in the same report, found that neighborhood violence is linked to single parent homes as well. It found that "the proportion of single-parent families in the neighborhood [is] positively associated with an adolescent's risk of committing violence."[36] The facts point to the absence of a father in a child's life leading to greater risk of them being incarcerated at some point in their life as well. An article published by the American College of Pediatrics on the benefits of fatherhood said that

> Even after controlling for income, youths in father-absent households still had significantly higher odds of incarceration than those in mother-father families. Youths who never had a father in the household experienced the highest odds.[37]

The study also noted that the evidence suggests higher drug and alcohol use among youth who do not live with their parents, and that family structure can be a significant predictor of delinquency. The article references another study done by the *Journal of Family Psychology* where researchers found that father–child interaction was connected with better academic functioning and socio-emotional interaction. The results of the study found that children with involved fathers experienced far fewer behavioral issues and scored higher on reading tests. This points to the fact that family structure is important for opportunity, especially for educational opportunity.

POLITICAL PARTICIPATION, CIVIC ISOLATION, AND THE IMPORTANCE OF CIVIL PARTICIPATION

Civil society institutions are essential to the success of a community, and to the flourishing of individuals within a community. Participation in the important and influential civil society institutions around the United States leads to better foundations for a community through inclusive programs and environments which accommodate specific needs of the population. Churches, schools, sports, charities, and various men's and women's organizations help better communities and involve community members in activities that help develop individual skills while serving

[35] Patrick F. Fagan. "Family Structure and Fighting." Accessed May 11, 2016. http://marri.us/fighting-family.
[36] Chris Knoester and Dana L. Haynie, "Community Context, Social Integration into Family, and Youth Violence," *Journal of Marriage and Family* 67 (2005): 767–780.
[37] "Fatherhood." American College of Pediatricians. 2015. Accessed May 11, 2016. www.acpeds.org/family-cycle/fatherhood.

others. One of the most important aspects of social citizenship is political participation, the idea that an individual can shape and influence government and similar institutions within a community.

For current prisoners, and many who have a criminal record, the ability to participate in civil society is limited. Most ex-offenders are prohibited from participating in society in many ways or are ostracized to the point that they are not willing to participate. The social stigma that comes with a criminal record leads people to not finish their education, not participate in churches and other social circles, and draw away from the type of places that should help them integrate back into community successfully. There is a certain amount of isolation a person receives when he or she is imprisoned, and the effect compounds once they are released.

The problem of overcriminalization affects the civic isolation a person might feel once he or she is labeled an ex-convict or felon. A significant number of American citizens live under this negative influence because of their time incarcerated. A report by the American Bar Association and Yale Law School states,

> [R]each of the criminal justice system extends even further. For every person in prison, America has two more people on parole, probation, or some related form of control by the criminal justice system. In actual numbers, that means we have a total of over 7 million people behind bars or subject to some kind of control that can land them behind bars.[38]

In all, the problems of prison life follow millions of Americans outside of the walls of their cells. Once outside they find it even harder to participate in life than before being sent to prison. A study from the Center for Economic and Policy Research and the Bureau for Justice Statistics found that in the United States there were between 12 and 14 million ex-offenders of working age in 2008.[39] The problem "isn't just that we have the highest incarceration rate in the world, we have created a situation over the last 30 years where about one in eight men is an ex-offender," causing economic effects on the country as well as political effects from civic isolation.[40] Since so many men of working age are unable to participate in life as they were before prison, a significant economic and political weight is growing on the communities that are most affected by imprisonment.

---

[38] Hope Metcalf and Sia Sanneh. "Overcriminalization and Excessive Punishment: Uncoupling Pipelines to Prison." Technical paper. July 2012. Accessed May 11, 2016. www.americanbar.org/content/dam/aba/administrative/litigation/overcriminalization_conference_report.authcheck dam.pdf.

[39] John Schmitt and Kris Warner. "Ex-Offenders and the Labor Market." The Center for Economic and Policy Research. November 2010. Accessed May 11, 2016. http://cepr.net/publications/reports/ex-offenders-and-the-labor-market.

[40] "Growth of Ex-Offender Population in United States Is a Dramatic Drag on Economy." CEPR. November 15, 2010. Accessed May 11, 2016. http://cepr.net/press-center/press-releases/growth-of-ex-offender-population-in-united-states-is-a-dramatic-drag-on-economy.

In 2008, one in thirty-three working-age adults was an ex-prisoner, and about one in fifteen working-age adults was an ex-felon.[41] The statistics among working age men are even more shocking: one in seventeen was an ex-prisoner and one in eight was an ex-felon. These numbers have an important impact on civic life in the United States. This translates into millions of men and women who cannot vote, and who cannot participate in activities in the same way as their peers, even after they have served a full sentence for their crimes. According to the Sentencing Project, there are 5.85 million Americans who are disenfranchised because of a felony.[42] Only two states, Maine and Vermont, allow prisoners to vote in elections, while thirty-five states prohibit parolees from voting, thirty-one of which prohibit voting while on probation as well.[43] Four states completely disenfranchise ex-cons who have completed their sentences and eight others disenfranchise certain categories of ex offenders.[44] When you look at the numbers of Americans that have been isolated by voting laws, the numbers are staggering, especially when it comes to disenfranchised black men. This is a significant nonvoting population. In all, one in forty adults do not currently have voting rights, and many will never have them again.[45] The number of disenfranchised voters among African Americans is 2.2 million, or 7.7 percent of black adults.[46] The number of disenfranchised voters among the non–African American adult population is 1.8 percent, but when one looks at the current incarceration rates in the United States, around three out of every ten black men may lose their right to vote at some point in their lifetime.[47] The number of disenfranchised persons that have completed their sentences totals over 2.2 million former prisoners, 45 percent of the disenfranchised population.[48] In many cases the confusion about the laws, and the misapplication of other, disenfranchise many more Americans. For many, an experience with arrest or imprisonment has left them without the ability to participate in the political community. With millions of Americans stripped of their right to political participation, the effects of overcriminalization can be felt at the polls and in an ex-convict or ex-felon's civic life by never having the civic input of citizens that have fulfilled their obligation of punishment from society.

---

[41] Ibid. See also Brian Schaefer and Peter B. Kraska. "Felon Disenfranchisement." *Race and Justice* 2, no. 4 (2012): 304–21.

[42] Christopher Uggen, Sarah Shannon, and Jeffery Manza. "State-Level Estimates of Felon Disenfranchisement in the United States, 2010." Report. July 2012. http://sentencingproject .org/wp-content/uploads/2016/01/State-Level-Estimates-of-Felon-Disenfranchisement-in-the-United-States-2010.pdf, 1.

[43] Uggen, Shannon, and Manza. "*Felon Disenfranchisement*," 2.

[44] Ibid., 1.

[45] Ibid.

[46] Ibid., 1–2.

[47] Ibid., 2.

[48] Ibid., 1.

THE IMPORTANCE OF PARTICIPATION IN CIVIL
SOCIETY INSTITUTIONS

The importance of civic participation goes beyond political participation and into other types of civil institutions. There is a vital importance to the welfare of a society that comes from its mediating institutions. Schools, churches, community organizations, and other associations people bring people together in communities over common bonds and challenges. Whether it is church youth groups, the Boy Scouts, or the local baseball team, the role of social networks plays a large part in how our communities develop and maintain their vitality.

The church is one part of civil society that has historically brought men and women out of poverty, crime, and affliction, surrounding them with community. As President Obama acknowledged in 2014, "And by almost every measure, the group that is facing some of the most severe challenges in the 21st century in this country are boys and young men of color."[49] The conversation about why more black men struggle than other demographics often glosses over the fact that most African American men are involved in their communities and mediating institutions.

In one article, W. Bradford Wilcox and Nicholas H. Wolfinger addressed one possible solution to the question of why some black men do not flourish while others do.[50] The answer they suggest is the power of faith. In a General Society Survey, researchers found that African American men attend church at rates higher than the national averages: 37 percent of black men between the ages of eighteen and sixty attend church several times a month or more, while only 30 percent of nonblack demographics attend as regularly.[51] The research done by Wilcox and Wolfinger suggests that these 6 million men are more likely "to be working, avoid crime and incarceration, and get married."[52] The participation of men in the black church gives them "a sense of dignity, purpose, and inspiration."[53] In a community like the church, faith defines the culture. In sports, teamwork and camaraderie are taught to young men and women. These and other positive community organizations of the community help maintain a high level of desired culture. A Bureau of Labor Statistics study cited by Wilcox and Wolfinger found that 20 percent of black men aged twenty-two to twenty-six who attended church regularly reported to committing

---

[49] Barack Obama, "Remarks by the President on 'My Brother's Keeper' Initiative." The White House. 2014. Accessed May 11, 2016. www.whitehouse.gov/the-press-office/2014/02/27/remarks-president-my-brothers-keeper-initiative.

[50] Bradford W. Wilcox, and Nicholas H. Wolfinger, "How the Church Helps Black Men Flourish in America." *The Atlantic*. February 28, 2016. Accessed May 11, 2016. www.theatlantic.com/politics/archive/2016/02/soul-mates-black-church-marriage/470760/?utm_source=SFTwitter.

[51] Wilcox and Wolfinger, "How the Church Helps Black Men Flourish in America."

[52] Ibid.

[53] Ibid.

a crime, while 24 percent of their nonchurch attending peers reported to committing a crime.[54] This means that church attending young black men are one third less likely to incarcerated than men who do not attend church regularly. Institutions like the church are not just helping men stay out of prison, but the faith they have gained helped them end the cycle of imprisonment in communities through marriage and employment. The Bureau of Labor Statistics study also points to higher rates of employment, enrolment in education, and marriage by the age of 35 in men who regularly attended church.[55]

The church is not the only institution that has played a part in community formation in the United States. Community organizations such as the Boy Scouts, Girl Scouts, or Little League Sports encourage communal bonds and build character among young people in a community. These positive social networks build bonds between young people so they understand the importance of community and apply the lessons they learn into their adult life. These types of organizations exist in order to strengthen youths and give them skills to bring into their future work and family. The rising number of former inmates in communities around the United States means that it can be increasingly hard for organizations to help those who have been outside of a healthy community for so long. Without successful reintegration and active community participation of acceptance, many people released from prison fall back into a life of crime.

For many, the retreat of the modern citizen from mediating institutions marks the turn toward government intervention. William M. Klimon said that mediating institutions are "One of the most vital insights of modern social thought [for a] free society."[56] Alexis de Tocqueville observed that mediating institutions are a "bulwark of freedom against the encroaching power of the state."[57] These institutions provide an outlet for creativity and for community. They are where young men and women can channel their efforts toward goals that better communities, forge relationships, and create innovation. Without them, the growth of inefficient government involvement in many of these areas of life is inevitable. Tocqueville also wrote that, "[Americans]carried to the highest perfection the art of pursuing in common the object of their common desires."[58] Without this passion to drive the further community of mediating institutions problems like overcriminalization will only continue to hold back the full potential of community life which defines the majestic concept of freedom in the United States.

---

[54] Ibid.
[55] Ibid.
[56] William M. Kilmon, "Mediating Institutions," Acton Institute. Accessed October 28, 2016. www.acton.org/pub/religion-liberty/volume-2-number-3/mediating-institutions.
[57] Kilmon, "Mediating Institutions."
[58] Ibid.

Recidivism is one of the most basic and consistent problems in criminal justice, referring to the relapse of a person into criminal behavior. Usually, recidivism is measured by criminal actions that resulted in rearrest, reconviction, or reincarceration within a three year period following a prisoner's release.[59] The Bureau of Justice Statistics (BJS) released a report following the patterns of prisoners released from prison in 2005.[60] The report followed them for five years from 2005 to 2010 and found that overall, 67.8 percent of the prisoner's release from state's prisons were arrested within three years of their release.[61] The problem of recidivism is at the center of the cycle of imprisonment. The cycle of imprisonment and how it affects families, communities, and the broader body politic. These statistics on recidivism show how this problem is one that compounds and gets worse over time and over generations. Without mediating institutions, job opportunities, and ways for ex-prisoners to be reintegrated successfully back into society, the problem of recidivism will continue to feed overcriminalization at an alarmingly increasing rate.

A side effect of the high crime rates among poorer communities referenced earlier in this chapter is the excessive targeting of low-income neighborhoods and people of color by law enforcement. In neighborhoods with high rates of youth delinquency the policing of these areas tends to be stricter and more punitive than in the suburbs or in wealthier areas.[62] This system feeds the problem of overcriminalization because of the prohibitively high costs of quality lawyers and the prevalence of drug trafficking in low income neighborhoods. The problem of drugs is a key factor in the targeting of crime in specific communities. A report by the Human Rights Watch that was published in the *Stanford Law Review* pointed to the problem of law enforcement targeting people of color and the poor.[63] One finding that points to the problem is that black Americans are especially targeted for drug crimes and are disproportionally arrested compared to other races. With the introduction and prominence of drugs like crack cocaine in the mid 1980s, the number of arrests for drug use and distribution went up, especially in poor neighborhoods. The use of

[59] "Recidivism." National Institute of Justice. June 17, 2014. Accessed May 11, 2016. www.nij.gov/topics/corrections/recidivism/pages/welcome.aspx.
[60] Matthew R. Durose, Alexia D. Cooper, and Howard N. Snyder. *Recidivism of Prisoners Released in 30 States in 2005: Patterns from 2005 to 2010.* Report. April 2014. Accessed May 11, 2016. www.bjs.gov/content/pub/pdf/rprts05p0510.pdf.
[61] Durose, Cooper, and Snyder. *Recidivism of Prisoners Released in 30 States in 2005*
[62] Stuntz, 30–36.
[63] Jamie Fellner, "Race, Drugs, and Law Enforcement in the United States." Human Rights Watch. 2009. Accessed May 11, 2016. www.hrw.org/news/2009/06/19/race-drugs-and-law-enforcement-united-states#_ftnref2.

these drugs was not only in poor areas but pervaded all levels of income and wealth. In fact, drug use in the suburbs and wealthier communities often rivals that of urban areas. Legislation and law enforcement emphasize the drug problem as linked specifically to poor areas and minority communities in cities. The report cited a study conducted by the 2006 federal Substance Abuse and Mental Health Administration that found 49 percent of whites Americans and 42.9 percent of black Americans twelve and older had used illegal drugs in their lifetime.[64] Because of the significantly larger number of the white population in the United States, these percentages show how significantly larger the number of the drug-using white population is. It is uncommon for many white Americans to be prosecuted for drug use because of how law enforcement targets neighborhoods. Racial targeting in poor neighborhoods is significant, and much easier to police than the suburbs. For law enforcement, the easiest way to enforce drug laws is to target poor minority neighborhoods. A former New York City Police Commissioner said that:

> Conspicuous drug use is generally in your low-income neighborhoods that generally turn out to be your minority neighborhoods . . . It's easier for police to make an arrest when you have people selling drugs on the street corner than those who are [selling or buying drugs] in the suburbs or in office buildings. The end result is that more blacks are arrested than whites because of the relative ease in making those arrests.[65]

Because of this type of policing and targeting of minority neighborhood there are significantly more black than white arrests for drug crimes. According to the FBI, the most common arrest in 2008 was drug arrests, and in 2007, 77 percent of drug arrests occurred in cities.[66] The Human Rights Watch Study found that among people sentenced to prison for drug crimes,

> the black rate (256.2 per 100,000 black adults) is ten times greater than the white rate (25.3 per 100,000 white adults). Disaggregating these rates by gender reveals that black men were sent to prison on drug charges at 11.8 times the rate of white men and black women are sent to prison on drug charges at 4.8 times the rate of white women.[67]

The result of the specific targeting of poor disadvantaged neighborhoods contributed largely to the overcriminalization problem. For justice to be applied fairly, there must be a different approach to how policing works and how police officers

---

[64] *Results from the 2006 National Survey on Drug Use and Health: National Findings.* Report. Department of Health and Human Services, 2007. Accessed May 11, 2016. www.asipp.org/documents/2006NSDUH.pdf, 238.
[65] *Results from the 2006 National Survey on Drug Use and Health: National Findings.*
[66] "Arrests." Crime in the United States 2008. Accessed May 11, 2016. www2.fbi.gov/ucr/cius2008/arrests/.
[67] Ibid.

relate to neighborhoods. Without a change, the richest whitest suburbs will always be the epicenter of the most under prosecuted drug use in the United States.

MASS IMPRISONMENT DISTORTS SOCIAL NORMS: HOW PRISON CHANGES VALUES AND ASPIRATIONS

The emotional trauma from time spent incarcerated warps individual personal values and aspirations. There is a mentality that is cultivated by the environment and culture of American prisons that creates future criminals. The identity required to mentally and physically survive in prison directly conflicts with the life of a productive citizen. Leaving a cell does not deactivate the mindset of the released prisoner. The psychological effects of prison are individually unique, and corroding the minds of the millions of citizens in the United States released from prison each year. A report written by the US Department of Health found the physiological effects of imprisonment are, "extraordinarily prolonged and intense."[68] The physiological effects that prisoners face create enormously difficult transitions into the free world after their sentences are fulfilled.

The United States incarcerates more people than any other nation in the world, sometimes five times as many as other free Western nations.[69] The sheer number of prisoners being introduced to the system means that living conditions have fallen over the course of the last several decades, which "adversely affected living conditions in many prisons, jeopardized prisoner safety, compromised prison management, and greatly limited prisoner access to meaningful programming."[70] In the 1990s, two of the states with the largest prison overcrowding problem, Texas and California, lost several federal lawsuits over unconstitutional means of confinement. The courts found that the "prison systems had failed to provide adequate treatment services for those prisoners who suffered the most extreme psychological effects of confinement in deteriorated and overcrowded conditions."[71] The ideological movement in the prison system in the late twentieth century seems to have shifted from prisons existing to incarcerate and, in some cases, rehabilitate offenders to holding facilities to keep them away from the rest of society.

There is evidence that people suffer psychological harm in prison, the more harsh the confinement, the greater the potential of psychological distress and neurosis leading to more subtle emotional and psychological punishment.[72] Research

---

[68] Craig Haney, "The Psychological Impact of Incarceration: Implications for Post-Prison Adjustment." ASPE. 2015. Accessed May 11, 2016. https://aspe.hhs.gov/basic-report/psychological-impact-incarceration-implications-post-prison-adjustment.

[69] "States of Incarceration: The Global Context." Prison Policy Initiative. Accessed May 13, 2016. www.prisonpolicy.org/global/.

[70] Haney, "Psychological Impact of Incarceration."

[71] Ibid.

[72] Mika'il DeVeaux, "The Trauma of the Incarceration Experience." Review. *Harvard Civil Rights-Civil Liberties Law Review* 48.

suggests that "these forms of punishment result from deprivations caused by a loss of liberty, material impoverishment, personal inadequacy, loss of heterosexual relationships, loss of autonomy, and loss of personal security."[73] These however are not the only physiological effects that prison can have on a person's mind. A US Health and Human Services (HHS) report includes many of the possible psychological effects that can be brought on in prison. The first is a dependence on the institutional structure. Over time, a person may lose their independence and self-initiative and start to rely on the structure of the institution they live in. As young offenders serve long prison sentences, an inmate can fail to develop the necessary internal organization and personal limits that someone outside of the prison walls would naturally develop over time. While some might become dependent, the danger in prisons can lead prisoners to become highly suspicious and distrustful of other people. More obvious forms of alienation and psychological distancing can influence some prisoners, and this can be especially dangerous for some especially after leaving prison. The HHS report observes,

> Prisoners who labor at both an emotional and behavioral level to develop a "prison mask" that is unrevealing and impenetrable risk alienation from themselves and others, may develop emotional flatness that becomes chronic and debilitating in social interaction and relationships, and find that they have created a permanent and unbridgeable distance between themselves and other people.[74]

Some prisoners experience this in terms of social withdrawal and isolation, retreating within themselves, and losing trust in other people. One psychologist cited in the report wrote that a long-term prisoner, "shows a flatness of response which resembles slow, automatic behavior of a very limited kind, and he is humorless and lethargic."[75]

Since a high number of the incarcerated population are released after serving their sentences, these increasing numbers of prisoners reentering society make it an important social issue which must be addressed immediately. In 2009, 1,998 prisoners were released from state and federal prisons each day, and as a whole, 95 percent of all prisoners in state prisons are released after serving their sentences.[76] Most prisoners do not serve long sentences, but even a short time in prison can have a negative effect on a person's psychological well-being.

Once a prisoner is released, the effects of his or her incarceration can cause problems adjusting back to life in society. The newly free citizens must now adjust to working life, family, and the responsibilities that come along with the full role of responsible citizen. There is a significant problem posed by parents returning after

[73] DeVeaux, "The Trauma of the Incarceration Experience."
[74] Haney, "Psychological Impact of Incarceration."
[75] A. J. W. Taylor, "Social Isolation and Imprisonment." *Psychiatry: Interpersonal and Biological Processes* 24, no. 4 (1961): 373. Accessed May 11, 2016.
[76] DeVeaux, "Trauma."

serving time in prison. For many parents, returning to the role of providing for dependents is a hard adjustment after a time of little to no responsibility inside the prison. The HHS report stated the problem,

> Parents who return from periods of incarceration still dependent on institutional structures and routines cannot be expected to effectively organize the lives of their children or exercise the initiative and autonomous decision making that parenting requires. Those who still suffer the negative effects of a distrusting and hypervigilant adaptation to prison life will find it difficult to promote trust and authenticity within their children. Those who remain emotionally over-controlled and alienated from others will experience problems being psychologically available and nurturant.[77]

Once home from imprisonment, the parents will have a hard time adjusting to the role they will now play in their children's lives and will oftentimes be split from their children again as the likelihood of them returning to prison rises with recidivism.

A report published by the Urban Institute looked at the challenges that face prisoners and their families as they return home. The report observed: "More prisoners are returning home, having spent longer terms behind bars, less prepared for life on the outside, with less assistance in their reintegration"[78] The prisoners are onset with different problems ranging from physical and mental health to violence and alcohol and drug abuse. This period of release is hard on the families of prisoners returning home, especially as many of them will be returning to prison within five years.[79] There are extremely high social costs to prisoner reentry linked to these high recidivism rates.

There are two challenges that are concomitant with releasing prisoners back to the public. The first is public safety, and the second is how to transition someone back to being a productive member of society.[80] In regards to public safety, a large number of the released prison population reoffend with the same types of crimes that resulted in their incarceration. The second challenge must be met by education and the need for training to integrate former prisoners successfully back into employment and family life. A report of parolees in California in the late 1990's found that "about 85 percent of the state's parole population are chronic drug or alcohol abusers; 70–90 percent are unemployed; 50 percent are functionally illiterate; 18 percent have psychiatric problems; and 10 percent are homeless."[81] Many of these problems existed with the prisoners before prison, and upon release the data

---

[77] Haney, "Psychological Impact of Incarceration."
[78] Jeremy Travis, Amy L. Solomon, and Michelle Waul, "From Prison to Home: The Dimensions and Consequences of Prisoner Reentry." Urban Institute Justice Policy Center. June 2001. Accessed May 11, 2016. http://research.urban.org/UploadedPDF/from_prison_to_home.pdf.
[79] Durose, Cooper, and Snyder. "Recidivism of Prisoners."
[80] Travis, Solomon, and Waul, "From Prison to Home."
[81] California Department of Corrections, "Preventing Parolee Failure Program: An Evaluation." Sacramento: California Department of Corrections. 1997.

shows that they easily relapse. These problems among the recently released fuel the high rates of recidivism in the United States.

The protocol of the release process is not conducive for successful reintegration back into civic society. Research done by the Vera Institute on the first month after release show those who had strong networks of family and friends were often rehired by former employers and offered a place to stay.[82] Those who were not returning to strong family networks often even lacked the proper identification to find employment and would end up in shelters where they were three times as likely to violate parole.[83] Overall, the study found that those with family and friends to return too were more likely to find a job and return to a life similar than when they went to prison. Those without a family or friend network often relapsed into old habits, and even if they did return to the same friend groups many returned to old habits. Many just do not understand the requirements that they must fulfill once leaving prison. Some states do not provide any reporting instructions or documentation upon release from prison. Without proper identification, strong family structure outside of prison, and aid from the facility on how to assimilate back into culture, many inmates are set up to fall back into crime and return within a few months to the prison system. The Urban Report claims that since more funds are being diverted to accommodate for larger prison populations, less are being allocated toward preparing prisoners for life outside of the prison walls.[84] With less preparation for life outside of prison the cycle of imprisonment continues for many former prisoners, continually devastating families and communities.

POST-TRAUMATIC STRESS AND MENTAL HEALTH AFTER PRISON

Once outside of the prison walls many prisoners suffer from physical and mental health issues. Leaving the structure of the prison environment and joining society can have extreme effects on those prone to mental illness. For over twenty-five years we have data demonstrating that the experience in prison especially has negative effect on those with preexisting psychological disorders. An HHS report estimated that 20 percent of prisoners suffer from some sort of disability or disorder, and one expert cited said that "The lack of mental health care for the seriously mentally ill who end up in segregation units has worsened the condition of many prisoners incapable of understanding their condition."[85] He goes on to say that this becomes a vicious cycle of increasing mental disease and violence which can become a

---

[82] Marta Nelson, Perry Deess, and Charlotte Allen, "The First Month Out Post-Incarceration Experiences in New York City." Report. Vera Institute of Justice, 1999. Accessed May 11, 2016. www.vera.org/sites/default/files/resources/downloads/first_month_out.pdf.
[83] Nelson, Deess, and Allen, "The First Month Out."
[84] Travis, Solomon, and Waul, "From Prison to Home," 21.
[85] Streeter, P., "Incarceration of the Mentally Ill: Treatment or Warehousing?" *Michigan Bar Journal* 77(1998): 166–167.

repetitive cycle over a prison sentence.[86] Because of overcrowding and the large numbers of prisoners with these preexisting conditions and lack of treatment, this is becoming a larger problem.

A report from the BJS found that many prisoners were prone to physical and mental illness while in prison.[87] Around 40 percent of prisoners in 2011–2012 reported to having a chronic medical condition and were found more likely than the general public to have a chronic condition or an infectious disease.[88] Twenty-one percent of prisoners were reported to have had Tuberculosis, Hepatitis B or C, or other non–HIV/AIDs related STDs.[89] The majority of prisoners (74 percent) could be categorized as either overweight, obese, or morbidly obese.[90] About a quarter of prisoners (27 percent) did not report having a condition when admitted, but were told since admission that they had the condition since admission.[91] The report also found that between 2004 and 2012 the rate of prisoners with diabetes almost doubled, and the rate of prisoners with high blood pressure rose 1.5 times.[92]

Prisoners are also prone to mental illness and can be subject to greater risks of mental illness even after they leave prison. An HHS report of the effects of prison said that,

> Clearly, the residual effects of the post-traumatic stress of imprisonment and the retraumatization experiences that the nature of prison life may incur can jeopardize the mental health of persons attempting to reintegrate back into the freeworld communities from which they came.[93]

Once out of prison many former inmates have trouble assimilating with society because of the way prison life has shaped their habits and lifestyle. For many inmates, the return to the "real world" outside of prison can result in posttraumatic stress because of the traumatic stress they encountered in their time behind bars. Many of them have experienced other sorts of trauma even before they went to prison such as child abuse, violence, negligence, victimization, and the stresses of prison life can bring what an HHS report calls "re-traumatization."[94] This re-traumatization means that some prisoners find the explosive, violent, and discipline heavy prison lifestyle similar to what they experience in childhood or

---

[86] Ibid.
[87] Laura M. Maruschak, Laura M., Marcus Berzofsky, and Jennifer Unangst. "Medical Problems of State and Federal Prisoners and Jail Inmates, 2011–12." Report. February 2015. Accessed May 11, 2016. www.bjs.gov/content/pub/pdf/mpsfpji1112.pdf.
[88] Maruschak, Berzofsky, and Unangst. "Medical Problems of State and Federal Prisoners and Jail Inmates," 1
[89] Ibid., 1.
[90] Ibid.
[91] Ibid., 10.
[92] Ibid., 6–7.
[93] Haney, "Psychological Impact of Incarceration."
[94] Ibid.

at another time in life. The report says that, "time spent in prison may rekindle not only the memories but the disabling psychological reactions and consequences of these earlier damaging experiences."[95]

One of the dangers of Post-Traumatic Stress Disorder (PTSD) resulting from prison sentences is that the minimum structures that surround inmates after they return to society often cause them to internalize their feelings, something they learned while institutionalized, and manifests itself in internal stress and chaos.[96] Many former inmates mask their feelings of stress and chaos that are a result of returning to life after prison with a facade of normalcy. Without family and friends to help their transition this attempt at normalcy can deteriorate quickly leading to recidivism and other symptoms of PTSD, returning to various dysfunctional and destructive lifestyles.[97]

Without programs to encourage healthy transitions to society, the problems will only grow along with prison populations, contributing to overcriminalization and the prison cycle. Ex-offenders need to become functioning members of society in every capacity for there to be flourishing among the millions released each year. Without it, there will always be problems of this nature in the communities most affected by overcriminalization, communities who are often poor and urban.

THE ECONOMIC COSTS OF OVERCRIMINALIZATION: ECONOMIC CONSEQUENCES OF BEING A FELON OR ON PAROLE

There are significant economic and political hardships that accompany felons and parolees. Once someone has a criminal record, has served time in prison, or is out of prison on parole, the chances of emerging to economic and financial success are low, leaving many former prisoners out of work and not able to provide for themselves. Many prisoners held stable jobs before incarceration, and want stable jobs again once outside of prison walls. The inability to provide for themselves financially leading to depression and recidivism. The economic consequences of a criminal record are debilitating, incentivizing many to return to a life of crime.

A report done by *Justice Quarterly* found that prisoners said finding stable employment after imprisonment is the chief element in their reintegration into society and transition successfully into life outside of prison.[98] Research compiled by an Urban Institute study found that many prisoners lack the education needed to find jobs, or have been convicted for crimes that prohibit them from working in

---

[95] Ibid., 10.
[96] Ibid., 6–7.
[97] Haney, "Psychological Impact of Incarceration."
[98] Christy A. Visher, Sara A. Debus-Sherrill, and Jennifer Yahner, "Employment after Prison: A Longitudinal Study of Former Prisoners," *Justice Quarterly*, 28:5, (2011): 698–718.

certain environments.[99] In the first eight months after release, 65 percent of the respondents to the study had been employed at some point, but only 45 percent were currently employed.[100] The financial burden of many inmates falls on family and friends, leaving these relationships strained and becoming more of a burden as they cannot find employment. Many of the respondents found work through connections of friends and family, and once they started earning higher wages were less likely to return to prison. Those who were a part of job-training programs in prison had better chances of finding work after incarceration, and many who could not participate in work-training programs after prison cited the top reason as they were "unaware" of the program's existence.[101] The main problem for securing employment is the difficulty in finding a job with a criminal record. Of the Urban Institute's survey respondents, only 4 percent were not searching for a job because they did not want to work, some could not work because of prior disabilities or illness, but the majority began seeking employment immediately after leaving prison.[102]

For those able to secure employment, the majority earn less than those without a criminal record, many times because their education, skills, and work experience is below the average of the general population.[103] The most common types of employment held were general manual labor or construction (24 percent), food service (12 percent), and maintenance (10 percent).[104] Those who were employed for the most part enjoyed their work (90 percent), got along with their coworkers, and were confident that their current job would lead them to better opportunities in the future.[105] The ability to find work that paid enough money to support themselves and any dependents is hard for almost all newly released citizens. Many cannot find work in the first few months of being free, and once they do find work it is often in industries and positions that do not pay enough or train them with skills that allow upward mobility within the field.

A study done by the University of Michigan and the Population Studies Center looked at the ways that ex-offenders make ends meet after they return from a prison sentence.[106] The study followed several prisoners for years after their release and

---

[99] Christy Visher, Sara Debus, and Jennifer Yahner. "Employment after Prison: A Longitudinal Study of Releasees in Three States." Issue brief. October 2008. www.urban.org/sites/default/files/alfresco/publication-pdfs/411778-Employment-after-Prison-A-Longitudinal-Study-of-Releasees-in-Three-States.PDF.

[100] Visher, Debus, Yahner. "Employment after Prison," 4.

[101] Visher, Debus-Sherrill, and Yahner, "Former Prisoners," 1.

[102] Ibid., 3.

[103] Ibid., 1.

[104] Visher, Debus, Yahner, "Employment after Prison: A Longitudinal Study of Releases in Three States," 4.

[105] Ibid., 5.

[106] David J. Harding, Jessica J. B. Wise, Cheyney Dobson, and Jeffrey D. Morenoff. "Making Ends Meet after Prison: How Former Prisoners Use Employment Social Support, Public Benefits, and Crime to Meet Their Basic Material Needs." Report no. 11–748. December 2011. www.psc.isr.umich.edu/pubs/pdf/rr11-748.pdf. 2.

looked at their economic stability after prison. The study found that the inmates struggled to meet even their basic needs without help from family, friends, and other social support. Most of the ex-offenders rarely achieved economic independence and stability without social support and long-term public benefits, but a few were able to find economic independence and upward mobility through proper leveraging of social relationships and material support.[107] The report found that because of the barriers to the job market that prisoners face (e.g., social stigma, poor education, low skills), "few prisoners leave prison with jobs or other necessary resources waiting for them on the outside."[108] High rates of recidivism alone show us that many are not adjusting to life after prison in an economic sense, and many are returning to crime in the absence of stable employment and income. The report's findings,

> reveal a sobering portrait of the challenges of meeting even one's basic needs for food and shelter after prison, as many subjects struggled with economic security while navigating the labor market with a felony record and low human capital, attempting to stay away from drugs and alcohol, and re-establishing social ties.[109]

The prisoners who found a balance of steady employment, public benefits (SSI or housing assistance), and social service and support, were able to break the temptations of recidivism and move upwards economically. However, this number only represents a small portion of ex-offenders, and most find it impossible to escape poverty and the temptations of alcohol, drugs, and crime.

There are high rates of homelessness among former prisoners because of their inability to find work after prison. Many must rely on family and friends, and others need halfway housing and public aid in order to find shelter. Research cited by this report found that in many ex-offenders the need for housing assistance lasts long after release. One report on 147 prisoners release in Baltimore found that one year after release, 19 percent of ex-offenders lived in their own home, 69 percent live in someone else's home, and 10 percent lived in a residential treatment center.[110] Some states ban ex-prisoners from receiving federal aid like food stamps and housing vouchers after incarceration. These restrictions mostly apply to drug-related offenses which constitute the majority of crimes committed by women.[111] These restrictions lead to higher rates of homelessness and inability to find the means to climb the economic ladder out of poverty.

---

[107] Harding, Wise, Dobson, and Morenoff. "Making Ends Meet after Prison," 2.
[108] Ibid., 3.
[109] Ibid., 4.
[110] Ibid., 5.
[111] Ibid., 6.

THE ECONOMIC COSTS OF OVERCRIMINALIZATION: PERILS OF THE LOW-SKILLED LABOR MARKET

Nearly one-third of Americans have a criminal record, and this record keeps many from holding steady jobs and avoiding recidivism.[112] A criminal record keeps many from a job, and the problem is, a job will keep many from reoffending and continuing in the cycle of imprisonment. Once someone has served a prison sentence their ability to find a job that pays more than minimum wage is significantly deterred. Minimum wage jobs held by low-skilled workers do not offer upward mobility or skill training for higher-paying jobs and escape from poverty.

Inner cities do not have thriving industries which allow for diversification of available living wage jobs. The economic depression that exists in these areas make the private employment landscape dominated by retail and fast food establishments. Many people released from prison are placed into these low income, economically stagnant environments. The lack of familiarity with areas with dynamic job prospects traps these individuals in poverty.

Many have a hard time securing a minimum wage job in the first place, and when they do, it does not allow them to work their way out of poverty or out of the economic situation they were in upon release.

Some industries, especially higher skill or higher paying industries, have both direct and indirect barriers to hiring those with a criminal record. Indirect barriers could include laws at federal, state, county, or even local level that might preclude ex-offenders from certain professions based on their conviction. Some laws bar ex-convicts no matter what type of crime they were imprisoned for. A Justice Quarterly study on Employment after prison found that in addition to this:

> employers may be unwilling to risk liability for hiring individuals with criminal records into jobs requiring interaction with the public, the handling of cash, or the direct supervision of children. These "collateral consequences" of incarceration negatively affect the employment and earnings of former prisoners.[113]

These factors make finding a job difficult, let alone finding a position that pays enough to live above the poverty line or to match what they could have made before having a criminal record. Prisoners are more likely than the general population to have educational and experiential deficits that make it more difficult for them to find work. Employers are most likely to hire ex-convicts for positions "that require few skills or limited customer contact."[114] Discrimination based on age and race often make it harder for older felons and minority populations to find high-paying jobs after incarceration. The *Justice Quarterly* study found that many of the

---

[112] Amy L. Solomon, "In Search of a Job: Criminal Records as Barriers to Employment." National Institute of Justice. June 2012. www.nij.gov/journals/270/pages/criminal-records.aspx#note1.
[113] Visher, Debus-Sherrill, Yahner, "Former Prisoners," 700.
[114] Ibid., 701.

respondents were working multiple jobs and sometimes more than forty hours a week, others reported doing "informal work," and still others received some sort of financial assistance from friends or family.[115] Around half of the respondents (47 percent) reported doing some sort of informal work such as carpentry, automotive repairs, or lawn maintenance, all jobs that paid low hourly wages.[116] Among these men who reported having found work after being released from prison, "most men could not be characterized as having found a steady job with sufficient income to support themselves and any dependent family members."[117] The median income reported by respondents was just $700 a month, and the study concluded that "the relationship between employment and recidivism in this sample indicate that individuals who had higher wages in the early months after release were more likely to avoid a return to prison."[118] Within two months of release those unemployed were three times (23 percent) more likely to return to prison than those making more than $10 an hour.[119] One can conclude from the evidence found in this study that it is not just employment alone that reduces recidivism in the ex-offender population, but also how much that person is compensated for their work. A salary that is not enough to support oneself or and dependents can lead back to criminal behavior.[120]

One of the results of the number of prisoners in the United States is a growing population of citizens with criminal records. These ex-offenders suffer from all of the negative consequences of having served a prison sentence including the inability to work and earn what they did before being sent to prison, or what they might have earned if they had never gone to prison in the first place. In 2011, 61 percent of people serving prison sentences were under the age of thirty-nine.[121] Since most prisoners are in their twenties and thirties they are missing the prime working years of their adult life. An article from New York University's Brennan Center for Justice argued that since mass incarceration removes these able-bodied men and women from the workforce they face damage to their employment and educational opportunities, as well as a daunting unemployment rate for ex-offenders.[122] The Center for Economic and Policy Research observed,

> Because a prison record or felony conviction greatly lowers ex-offenders' prospects in the labor market, we estimate that this large population lowered the total male

[115] Ibid., 708.
[116] Ibid., 709.
[117] Ibid.
[118] Ibid.
[119] Ibid.
[120] Ibid., 713.
[121] Ann E. Carson and William J. Sabol. *Prisoners in 2011.* Report. December 2012. www.bjs.gov/content/pub/pdf/p11.pdf, 7.
[122] Julia Bowling, "Mass Incarceration Gets Attention as an Economic Issue (Finally) | Brennan Center for Justice." Mass Incarceration Gets Attention as an Economic Issue (Finally) | Brennan Center for Justice. September 13, 2013. www.brennancenter.org/blog/mass-incarceration-gets-attention-economic-issue-finally.

employment rate that year by 1.5–1.7 percentage points. In GDP terms, these reductions in employment cost the US economy between $57 and $65 billion in lost output.[123]

There are hundreds of thousands of prisoners released each year, all of whom contribute to a lower employment rate and lower earnings across the board. The economic effects of overcriminalization become more and more apparent each year.

One of the biggest problems facing ex-convicts as they search for jobs is the job sprawl over large areas, or the idea of spatial mismatch. This concept in the job market looks at how the best jobs are several miles away from inner-cities and the people in the lowest income bracket have to travel several hours or several miles a day for even a minimum wage job. Most of the jobs that would have the ability to pull those in poverty out of their income bracket are too far away for them to access. This especially affects minority population in the inner-city, and in turn ends up affecting many who have served time in prison. A study by the Brookings Institute in 2000 looked at spatial mismatch between in cities across the United States, especially in relation to minority populations. The report found that job decentralization from the inner city in places like Detroit hurt minority population the most, and especially the black population in those cities. The gap is largest in the Midwest, and in small to medium sized cities, especially places where the city is sprawling instead of centralized.[124] In many cities, the best jobs are in the suburbs, and for those with the lowest income levels these jobs can be impossible to travel to. Without adequate transportation or the ability to get high paying jobs, many ex-convicts in poor minority communities are unable to work their way out of poverty.

CONCLUSION

The social and economic costs of overcriminalization are what unite all citizens in needing to respond to the crisis and the type of holistic issues that personalism brings to the forefront of ending overcriminalization and mass incarceration. The problems, which are common, growing, and have negative effects, are very undesirable components of our country and identity. It is with an understanding of the social and economic implications that we must fully engage our civic institutions to orchestrate positive interaction with those who pass through the criminal justice system. Every community that experiences a scourge of citizens in prison faces negative economic consequences, which compound themselves into multigenerational social problems. These communities then become cultural deserts, limiting the amount of

---

[123] Warner Schmitt, "Ex-Offenders and the Labor Market."
[124] Michael Stoll, "Job Sprawl and the Spatial Mismatch between Blacks and Jobs." The Brookings Institution. February 01, 2005. www.brookings.edu/research/reports/2005/02/metropolitan policy-stoll.

value they can provide other communities and regions. Every incarceration makes the problem worse. It is with this realization that positive outcomes must be engineered with the individual persons who are in need of rehabilitation. Since the imprisoned can have such a powerfully negative impact on the system and community, they have the potential to have an enormously positive impact as well. It is through the data proven and vigorous application of best practices in each of these communities that steady improvement will be made.

7

Toward Structural Solutions at the State Level

In 2010, a young man wrote into an "Ask Annie" column with an increasingly familiar problem in the job market.[1] He had a degree in computer science and was laid off from his Uncle's IT company in the recession. The job hunt was hard because of a drug-related arrest he had in college. The arrest left him without callbacks or interviews and no way to prove himself to employers because he had to check the box on every application that asks about ever being convicted of a felony. At the state level, programs are being initiated to help curb some of the economic loss from the population with criminal records (America has just about as many people with college degrees as people with a criminal record.)[2] Rather than restricting them from the workforce, legislation and programs are aiming toward banning the felony checkbox from job applications, a box that often just discourages those with a record from applying.

Nearly 90 percent of all America's prisoners are in-state prisons. Laws vary by state, meaning there is not just one criminal justice system, there are over 50. The states are the key battlegrounds for criminal justice reformers. John Pfaff adds, "when focusing on states, however, we still can't tell a single story. Punishment in highly localized in the United States, and state and county officials have tremendous discretion over who gets punished and how severely."[3]

For many states, the problem seems almost unsolvable, and the benefits of any policy change seem so far away. While any solution will take decades, the changes

[1] Anne Fisher. "After a Drug Conviction, Can You Ever Get Hired?" August 30, 2010. Accessed August 01, 2017. http://archive.fortune.com/2010/08/27/news/economy/drug_conviction.for tune/index.htm.
[2] Matthew Friedman. "Just Facts: As Many Americans Have Criminal Records as College Diplomas." Brennan Center. November 17, 2015. Accessed August 01, 2017. www.brennancen ter.org/blog/just-facts-many-americans-have-criminal-records-college-diplomas.
[3] John F. Pfaff, *Locked In: The True Causes of Mass Incarceration – and How to Achieve Real Reform* (New York, NY: Basic Books, 2017), 14.

are necessary to restore communities and states that have felt the negative effects of mass incarceration. The proposed solutions change by state, but many of them have shown great promise. This chapter highlights the problems in specific states and the solutions they are working toward to alleviate some of the problems. It also focuses on a few American states that are making real progress. The work being completed in these states shows the recurring nature of the problems and trends across the nation.

Utah is now making it easier for former prisoners to expunge their record, and some states are trying to make it easier for those with a record to get licenses they might need for a career and limiting court fees from hurting the poor. Louisiana policymakers are working to divert prisoners to programs outside the walls, shorten sentences to help with the overcrowding, and to bring down the high recidivism rates. Louisiana state Rep. Walt Leger said article: "One of the biggest challenges we have is successful re-entry,"[4] a problem that they are not alone in fighting. Arkansas, Kentucky, and Louisiana all have similar legislation to help lower recidivism and keep people out of jail and at work. The state-level legislation represents a solution that can help restructure the prison culture in local communities to help those with records get and keep employment which will start to slow the effects of mass incarceration. Because criminal justice reform is a local issue, reform must start within individual states if incarceration rates are going to change nationally. This chapter highlights a few American states that are making real progress – the type of progress that needs to duplicated and expanded across the country in many ways.

GEORGIA

In 2010, Georgia was the ninth-most populous state in the nation, and had the fourth highest incarceration rate.[5] Georgia incarcerated every seventieth adult of its 9.7 million residents, and there was no inclination that its pace would slow down in the coming years.[6] After Georgia's adult prison population and spending on corrections more than doubled in twenty years, the outlook was bleak on any potential decline. Georgia faced decreasing revenues, a continuously expansive budget, increasing probation population, and a lack provision for services such as mental health.

---

4 Beitsch, Stateline Rebecca. "How States Are Working to Reduce Recidivism among Ex-Offenders." PBS. July 27, 2017. Accessed August 01, 2017. www.pbs.org/newshour/rundown/states-working-reduce-recidivism-among-ex-offenders/.

5 "QuickFacts: Georgia." U.S. Census Bureau Quick Facts. Accessed September 09, 2017. www.census.gov/quickfacts/fact/table/GA,US/PST045216.

6 Boggs, Michael P., and W. Thomas Worthy, comps. "Report of the Georgia Council on Criminal Justice Reform 2016." Report. Accessed September 9, 2017. https://gov.georgia.gov/sites/gov.georgia.gov/files/related_files/document/GA%20Council%20on%20Criminal%20Justice%20Reform_2016%20Report_Final.pdf., 3.

At the time, the estimate was that there would be an 8 percent increase over the next five years in incarcerated persons – an additional 4,480 Georgians.[7] Georgia being a "tough on crime" state resulted in the recidivism rate of former inmates hovering around 30 percent, a rate with no notable change over the past decade.[8] Crime rates were not decreasing despite a continuous year-over-year rise in the number of convictions and the total number of individuals incarcerated. The public safety mission laid out by the Georgia Department of Corrections was stagnant with a vast probation network, nearly triple the size of the prison population. Over 2.6 million have a criminal record on file in Georgia, meaning that close to one quarter of the state's population could be discriminated against by employers who use the public record to deny employment.[9]

This discrimination only made the problem worse, and as a response the legislature proposed some reforms. The Georgia General Assembly passed HB 265 to create the "Special Council on Criminal Justice Reform for Georgians" with three mandates in mind: Address the size, scope, cost, and effectiveness of Georgia's correctional system; reinvest savings from the Department of Corrections into strategies to decrease recidivism and crime; and strengthen community-based supervision. The first-year results of the Special Council brought about HB 1176, policies for reforming both sentencing reforming as well as correctional facilities and practices, which passed in May 2012. That bill was quickly followed by HB 242, an initiative to rewrite the juvenile justice system's penal code. One year later, the General Assembly voted to extend the Special Council's timeframe for five years, to increase the amount of investment in policy recommendations to achieve the three original mandates.[10]

The results were apparent after only a few years: from 2012 to 2015, rather than follow the predicted trend toward an 8 percent increase, Georgia's prison population dropped by 5.6 percent.[11] More importantly, the number of annual commitments to prison in Georgia were the lowest since 2002. Reforms in the sentencing methods used by Georgia's courts resulted in 18,139 commitments in 2015, down from 21,655 in 2009.[12] As of 2016, Georgia's 60 total prisons employ some 10,500 employees.[13] In 2010, Georgia's Department of Corrections employed a total of 13,000.[14] The decrease over six years coincides with the increasingly lower total adult prison

---

[7] "Report of the Georgia Council on Criminal Justice Reform 2016," 3.
[8] Ibid., 14.
[9] The State of Corrections Fact Sheet. Report. Accessed September 9, 2017. http://georgiaopportunity.org/assets/2014/10/GCO-prisoner-reentry-fact-sheet-2014.pdf, 2.
[10] "Report of the Georgia Council," 3.
[11] "Report of the Georgia Council," 5.
[12] Ibid., 5.
[13] Georgia Department of Corrections, "2016 Facilities Fact Sheet."
[14] Carrie Teegardin. *The Atlanta Journal-Constitution.* "Georgia Prison Population, Costs on Rise." April 7, 2010. Accessed September 09, 2017. www.ajc.com/news/news/local/georgia-prison-population-costs-on-rise/nQdsN/.

population, noted previously. As less nonviolent convicts are incarcerated, both the recidivism rate and the crime rate are decreasing. All of these decreases are helping the state overcome the problems created in the last few decades, and these reforms are just the beginning.

Recidivism was and continues to be a main focus of Georgia's Special Committee. One of the major tenets of Georgia's penal code was the "second chance law," or the 1968 First Offender Act, which was created to help first-time offenders keep their record clean after serving their sentence. If utilized, the Act made it possible for those first-time offenders to expunge the conviction and public record after completing their sentence. Yet the Act became a bygone opportunity for defendants. The Special Council worked to restore awareness of the First Offender Act through HB 310, which informed all eligible Georgians of the opportunity to earn a clean slate. A second state-wide effort from the Special Council was the expanded usage of accountability courts to provide a method of sentencing nonviolent offenders. The result was a greater proportion of inmates in state prison serving violent or sexual sentences, representing an increase from 58 percent of the total prison population in 2009 to 67 percent in 2016.[15]

Corruption, however, plagues the Georgia Department of Corrections. In February 2016, the Department of Justice indicted 49 current and former Georgia Department of Corrections officers for seven federal incidents of accepting bribes and smuggling contraband in exchange for drug deal protection.[16] A federal undercover investigation, led by Atlanta's Federal Bureau of Investigation Field Office, uncovered corruption activities within eleven of Georgia's thirty-five Department of Corrections facilities.[17] The indictments represent one of the continuing frustrations to reform: the myriad issues that come with the bloated bureaucracy of mass incarceration in the status quo, both in Georgia and in many states across America.

Flawed systems are not devoid of possibility for reform. One of the most meaningful reforms presented by Georgia's Special Council came about in January 2014. With HB 242, Georgia's juvenile courts began the new year with a new mandate: strengthening family relationships to boost juvenile safety and long-term security.[18] As a result, the number of youth in Georgia's secure confinement reduced by 17 percent from 2013 to 2016.[19] And, similar to the decreasing number of adult commitments in Georgia's correctional system, juvenile commitments decreased 33 percent in the same three-year period.[20] By refocusing its juvenile system to

[15] "Report of the Georgia Council," 6.
[16] "Further Corruption Involving Georgia Department of Corrections Guards Exposed." The United States Department of Justice. February 11, 2016. Accessed September 10, 2017. www.justice.gov/usao-ndga/pr/further-corruption-involving-georgia-department-corrections-guards-exposed.
[17] "Further Corruption Involving Georgia Department of Corrections Guards Exposed."
[18] "Report of the Georgia Council," 33.
[19] Ibid., 33.
[20] Ibid., 34.

prioritize the family and community in the development of juveniles character, rather than continuing its policy of putting them behind bars at detention centers, the Special Counsel found a rapid decrease in recidivism and the need for juvenile detention facilities.

Georgia's work is far from over. The most recent February 2016 report from Georgia's Special Counsel stated a breathtaking number of recommendations on more than a dozen topics. The entire criminal justice process is being placed under careful analytical scrutiny from the time a person is charged: the penal code, the accountability courts, the correctional facilities, the reentrance communities, and the processes of support and monitoring after release. By not ignoring the failures of the past twenty years and more, Georgia is already leading the nation in criminal justice reform. The last report from the Special Counsel understood the need for states to implement their own innovation: "It is often said that the states are our laboratories of democracy. With criminal justice reform, this is undeniably true."[21]

ALABAMA

Alabama's incarceration population is not that the system is just over its capacity; it is holding nearly twice as many inmates as intended. In 2014, Alabama's state prisons operated at over 195 percent capacity, some of the most crowded in the nation.[22] The state's current, crippling situation is the outcome of a soaring prison population due to changes in criminal statutes, beginning in 1977. The 1990s saw Alabama's tough on crime mindset reach new heights with the reintroduction of chain gangs. In 2016, four decades later, Alabama's prison population had risen 840 percent.[23]

Governor Robert Bentley in 2014 stated that "82 percent of the offenders with the highest risk of reoffending, including property and drug offenders, reached the end of their sentence while in DOC custody, with no supervision to guide re-entry."[24] As a result, Governor Bentley signed into law legislation SB 67 in May 2015, with the intended goal of reducing the state prison population by 4,200 inmates within five years.[25] SB 67 came about through the work by the Justice Reinvestment Initiative

[21] "2016 Recommendations from the Criminal Justice Reform Council." Georgia Public Policy Foundation. February 05, 2016. Accessed September 10, 2017. www.georgiapolicy.org/2016/02/2016-recommendations-from-the-criminal-justice-reform-council/.

[22] State of Alabama. Office of the Governor. "Statement of the Honorable Robert Bentley, Governor of Alabama Before the House Oversight and Government Reform Committee on 'Criminal Justice Reform'". July 14, 2014. Accessed September 10, 2017. https://oversight.house.gov/wp-content/uploads/2015/07/Governor-Bentley-Alabama-Statement-7-14-Criminal-Justice.pdf.

[23] Josh Siegel. "Why Alabama Is Working to Free Convicted Felons." *The Daily Signal*. August 10, 2015. Accessed September 19, 2017. http://dailysignal.com/2015/07/31/breaking-point-how-overcrowding-has-forced-alabama-to-confront-its-prison-problem/.

[24] "Statement of the Honorable Robert Bentley."

[25] "Alabama's Justice Reinvestment Approach." Publication. Accessed September 19, 2017. https://csgjusticecenter.org/wp-content/uploads/2015/05/AlabamasJusticeReinvestmentApproach.pdf.

(JRI), which Governor Bentley formed in June 2014 to study the horrific status quo environment of prisons fraught with investigations into sexual assault, homicide, and the smuggling of prohibited items. The JRI's Prison Reform Task Force produced multiple reports, which led to the creation and goals of SB 67.

In March 2015, the JRI published its exhaustive "Analysis and Policy Framework" report, which began with the statement that "Alabama's correctional system is in crisis."[26] Alabama's status quo will mean the state must "spend hundreds of millions of dollars to increase capacity."[27] Yet that would still leave the underlying system, and growth of inmates, in place. The report recommends the state adopts policies "to avert significant costs and reduce recidivism."[28] Aside from sentencing reform and probation caseload redistribution, the report recommends the further establishment of Community Corrections Programs (CCPs).

These CCPs work as an option that is more intensive than a normal probation program especially for those who fall within Alabama's least serious Class C offense class. Going beyond the supervision aspect of probation (in a similar manner to Illinois' Adult Transition Centers [ATCs]), the CCPs provide educational, vocational, cognitive behavioral, and substance abuse treatment services. They are operated and maintained by counties, not the state, however not every Alabama county has a CCP or access to another county's program. This method of sentencing can be both an alternative to prison as well as a part of a split sentence. The JRI recommended expanding the program in both the amount of locations and the scope of their usage as an alternative to prison. As of 2014, thirty-five CCPs serve forty-five counties in Alabama – twenty-two counties either have no facilities of their own or no options available to use an adjacent county's CCP program.[29]

Two fundamental missing elements of the CCPs also place a limit on their current effectiveness. First, there are no state requirements that the programs must measure the result of their programs, such as how well the program adheres to evidence-based rehabilitation practices or antirecidivism education or release methods. Second, the programs must have no mechanism of accountability for how CCP funding is appropriated to deliver treatment or bolster services for those within its programming.

Beyond CCPs is the failing probation and parole supervision branch of the Alabama Department of Corrections (ADOC). In 2013 more than 40 percent of those admitted to state prison were for violation of conditions of probation or parole, but the more revealing statistic is the 47 percent rise in the number of people on felony probation revoked to prison between 2009 and 2013.[30] The bill, SB 67, places

[26] "Alabama's Justice Reinvestment Approach," 1.
[27] Ibid., 1.
[28] "Justice Reinvestment in Alabama." Report. Accessed September 24, 2017. http://ali.state.al.us/documents/AlabamaJusticeReinvestmentfinalreport.pdf.
[29] "Justice Reinvestment in Alabama," 13.
[30] Ibid., 16.

a specific emphasis on reforming parole and parole supervisors to divert more people from going to prison and others from going back. The average parole officer in Alabama supervises a caseload of 200 parolees, a daunting if not unimaginable task.[31] Even with the minimal contact and care that parole officers could provide with equal attention paid to all cases, it is unrealistic to believe that the ADOC's parole system can provide an effective method of transitioning felons back into their community.

The framework of JRI's research found that the most significant reductions in the recidivism rates came from concentrating the resources on the highest risk individuals. What may sound obvious is far from the practice in Alabama. In the ADOC there is no increase of concentration based on risk; all offenders receive the same level of attention. This is highly counterproductive, as it often increases the recidivism rates of low-risk individuals as well as has little to no effect upon high-risk individuals.

The Prison Reform Task Force is focused on more than the incarceration side of Alabama's crisis. Sentencing reform is also a major priority, as SB 67 creates "a new class of the least serious nonviolent felony offenses" and updates "felony thresholds for certain property and drug offenses."[32] The new category, Class D, would be for lower-level property and drug offenses with a sentencing range of over one year to five years.

The addition of Class D would be most useful in the classification of burglary. Currently, all categories of burglary in Alabama are classified as violent crimes in three degrees of seriousness. Currently, 10 percent of annual prison admissions are for the lowest level of burglary, third-degree, "wherein no person is encountered while the crime is being committed."[33] Third-degree burglary is also the most common property offense of Alabama inmates and ranks second among all types of offenses by inmates.

Beyond the failure of Alabama's standards for lower-level sentencing is the way inmates within that category are treated and released. Most importantly, 69 percent of inmates released without supervision are property and drug offenders, therefore falling within that class of lower level sentencing.[34] Yet those who spend time in state prisons (rather than county jails, CCPs, or in parole programs) for lower-level sentences have some of the highest recidivism rates. While Alabama does not have state specific data for its lower level sentencing recidivism rates, the Prison Reform Task Force found the recidivism rate for state inmates across the nation was 81 percent for property offenses and 76 percent for drug offenses.[35] The tough on

---

[31]   Ibid., 3.
[32]   Ibid., 3.
[33]   Ibid., 19.
[34]   Ibid., 27.
[35]   Ibid.

crime practice of "straight sentencing" tends to have a heightened probability of those inmates committing a second crime within three years of release.

Alabama is facing hundreds of millions of dollars in added costs across the next six years. The reforms of SB 67 aim to stabilize the influx of inmates year-over-year and steadily decrease the total incarcerated population to avoid the oncoming hundreds of millions of added costs beyond the already bloated ADOC budget.

ILLINOIS

The State of Illinois created the "Illinois State Commission on Criminal Justice and Sentencing Reform" to address its systemic mass incarceration problem. As of December 2015, Illinois Department of Corrections (IDOC) was operation at around 150 percent of design capacity. In Fiscal Year 2015, the IDOC housed 42,278 inmates, with the majority serving time for nonviolent offenses. Similar to the efforts in Georgia, in February 2015 Illinois Governor Bruce Rauner created the aforementioned Commission "to review the State's current criminal justice and sentencing structure, sentencing practices, community supervision, and the use of alternatives to incarceration, and to make recommendations for amendments to state law that will reduce the State's current prison population by 25 percent by 2025."[36]

The incarceration rate in Illinois, adjusted for population growth, reveals a 500 percent increase over the past 40 years: by 1975, the state had 66 inmates imprisoned for every 100,000 citizens and by 2014, that number risen to 380 inmates per every 100,000 citizens.[37] Recidivism, like in most other states, was a major problem and a problem the state tried to combat with ATCs, which allowed inmates to spend the final six to twenty-four months of their sentence in a community-based, work-release setting with subsidized housing. It was a good start to fighting the problem, but the total number of operational ATCs in Illinois peaked in 1986 with fifteen. Today only four are still in operation.[38]

In a 2008 IDOC recidivism study, the rate of recidivism after three years was 52.3 percent for inmates released by IDOC and 18 percent for inmates released from an ATC. Even the highest recidivism rate reported by an ATC, the Crossroads facility in Chicago's west side, was 33 percent. The ATCs reduce inmate recidivism through a dedicated, five-level work program at each facility. Inmates have the opportunity to also work to earn educational certificates.

A second focus of the 2015 Commission is that of treatment of offenders through community support. Admitting to an overuse of prisons, the Commission found that

---

[36] "Illinois State Commission on Criminal Justice and Sentencing Reform." Report. Parts I & II. Commission on Criminal Justice and Sentencing Reform, 2016. Accessed September 24, 2017.

[37] Illinois State Commission on Criminal Justice and Sentencing Reform, 6.

[38] "2014 Monitoring Visit to Crossroads Adult Transitional Center." The John Howard Association of Illinois, 2014, Accessed September 24, 2017, 2.

the mass incarceration practices "stymied the development of a systemic ability to sanction, supervise, and treat offenders in the community."[39] Moreover, the 2015 Commission found that a disproportionate, "overwhelming majority" of people from Cook County sent to prison are from "impoverished, mostly African American neighbors on Chicago's south and west sides." Residents of those neighborhoods, as a result, have extreme distrust for the legitimacy of the corrections system. The lack of perceived authority not only increases the crime rate but also decreases the likelihood of those neighborhoods' residents to report crimes and cooperate with police. Put curtly, the 2015 Commission "found that high levels of legal cynicism are associated with high rates of crime."[40]

In December 2014, a bill was introduced to the Illinois General Assembly that would have amended the Criminal Identification Act to allow nonviolent felony offenders to protect their criminal records from potential employers. The proposal was to allow court-ordered sealing of some records if the offender earned an educational certification of a high school diploma or higher while as an inmate or on mandatory supervised release. Had the bill passed, eligible offenders would be able to petition the courts to have their record sealed, with a judge deciding if the petition would be granted or not. While this effort never gained any traction, other bills in the state are, including one to remove the barriers for obtaining professional licenses. The 2015 Commission recommendation provides an opportunity to take a second look at the right of offenders to protect themselves from undue discrimination by job recruiters. Education remains a primary barrier to decreasing recidivism in inmates in Illinois. Less than half of inmates have a partial or complete high school education, with the vast majority reading at a less-than sixth grade proficiency. Additionally, around half of inmates were assessed as urgently needing substance abuse treatment.

Two of the 2015 Commission recommendations are worth noting for their specific efforts to reform the severity of prison sentencing. Recommendation #5 is to "prevent the use of prison for felons with short lengths of stay," with short lengths meaning less than twelve months.[41] The IDOC estimates that "more than 10,000 offenders" per year are sentenced to prison yet serve less than twelve months of time. Put simply, "using prison to house short-time inmates is wasteful at best and counterproductive at worst."[42] State prisons, compared to local jails, are expensive and time-intensive. Most importantly, inmates who "stay in prison for only a few months do not have time to participate in programming in that will assist with rehabilitation."[43] The short-term use of state prisons is wasteful for IDOC and harmful to the present and future of offenders. Recommendation #7 requires "that

---

[39] "2014 Monitoring Visit to Crossroads Adult Transitional Center," 10.
[40] Ibid., 13.
[41] "Illinois State Commission on Criminal Justice and Sentencing Reform," 21.
[42] Ibid., 13.
[43] Ibid., 38.

a judge explain at sentencing why incarceration is an appropriate sentence" when an offender has no prior violent crime convictions or probation sentences.[44] The goal is to provide a public argument and rationalization for why incarceration is necessary in the specific instance. The alternatives of a mandatory supervised release or rehabilitation program provide a less costly and harsh sentence. In Fiscal Year 2015, the IDOC estimates that around 30 percent of inmates had no prior probation sentence and 58 percent had no prior convictions for violent crimes.[45] The added articulation is intended to "reveal cases where imprisonment is unnecessary."[46]

The reforms that are happening in Illinois are important to strengthen the perceived legitimacy of the corrections program and in restoring trust in the populace that the system will do its work and root out injustices. As with most other states, recidivism remains a problem, but many of the reforms take necessary steps toward reducing the problem. The changes that affect the long-term legislative and enforcement mindset of those making policy are most important, and hopefully more of the Commission's recommendations have an effect on the legislation coming out of the state over the next several years. It is a promising start, and the state is ahead of many of its peers in reform, but the changes need to happen at the legislative level to see the fruit of the proposals.

UTAH

Utah ranks well below the national average in its total prison population but has a major problem common in the age of mass incarceration: growing prison populations coinciding with falling crime rates. In 2013, Utah incarcerated 244 people for every 100,000 citizens, more than 43 percent below the national average rate of 428 per 100,000 citizens.[47] Utah's crime rate is falling – between 2004 and 2013 the violent crime rate fell 4 percent and the property crime rate fell by 27 percent. Yet, while Utah's rate of imprisonment is low relative to other states, it is still growing even as crime slows. Utah legislators are beginning to focus on reversing Utah's continually growing prison population. Utah's prison population has grown by 18 percent over the past decade, six times the national growth rate.[48]

Even more critical is the impending prison population growth rate: a recent Pew Charitable Trusts report found that, with Utah's current sentencing policies and rehabilitation programs, the state's inmate population would grow by 37 percent over the next twenty years.[49] The estimated 2,700 additional inmates would cost

[44] Ibid., 3.
[45] Ibid., 44.
[46] Ibid.
[47] "Justice Reinvestment Report. Report. Utah Commission on Criminal and Juvenile Justice," 2014, 4.
[48] "Justice Reinvestment Report," 1.
[49] "Utah's 2015 Criminal Justice Reforms," The PEW Charitable Trusts, June 18, 2015.

Utah more than $500 million in revenue, $25 million more per year.[50] This staggering total is the result of incremental year over year increases in Utah's tough on crime attitude over the past several decades.

Much like Alabama, Utah partnered with the JRI as well as the Pew Charitable Trusts. The goal of the partnership was to analyze the situation and propose legislation to reverse the influx of inmates to the state. Legislation HB 348, proposed in February 2015 and signed into law March 2015, came about as a direct result of Utah's commissioned research, known as the Utah Commission on Criminal and Juvenile Justice. The Commission developed eighteen policies that aim to improve the use of state prisons for more serious and violent offenders and strengthen existing communities and rehabilitation programs by expanding and improving reentry and treatment services.

One critical aspect of HB 348 the Commission focused on was the downgrading of both first- and second-time drug possession convictions from felonies to misdemeanors. The Commission recommended another 241 misdemeanors be downgraded to citations to no longer allow for arrest or jail sentencing. The downgrades are an attempt to funnel less offenders toward arrest and prison and more toward community-based treatment. The Commission's executive director, Ron Gordon, believes this exhaustive overhaul must be given a few years to show results. Appropriately, the Commission will continue to survey the state of the Utah Department of Corrections (UDOC) and the sentencing practices of state court judges. The intention of HB 348 is to shift the focus of UDOC to reentry. The focus is now on what they are going to do on the outside of the cell walls.

Although Utah's status quo is far from as dismal as Alabama's or Illinois', the state still faces the challenge of improving treatment for mental and substance abuse disorders. The Commission's Gordon also highlighted the focus on treatment in HB 348, especially when it comes to the oversight and workload of parole and probation officers. The underlying problem is Utah's high recidivism rate, as more than 46 percent of Utah's inmates released from state prison return within three years.[51] By decreasing many felonies to misdemeanors and redirecting much UDOC funding to parole and adult treatment programs, HB 348 aims to lower that recidivism rate.

The decrease in Utah's overall crime is a point of hope but should not overshadow the need for immediate and drastic improvement for those already in the system. Utah's high rate of imprisonment per citizen is most troubling. Offenders on probation or parole are failing at the highest rates in a decade. Despite the low number of violent offenders, nonviolent offenders continue to make up the majority

---

[50] Ibid.
[51] "Utah's 2015 Criminal Justice Reforms."

of state inmates. Parole violators accounted for 67 percent of state prison admissions in 2013, revealing a massive flaw in the treatment of those currently in the system.[52]

With nonviolent offenders making up 62 percent of new criminal conviction sentences in 2013, HB 348 is working to redress probation and parole.[53] The vast majority of those who returned to state prison for violating probation or parole had committed at least one previous nonviolent offense. That is to say, those who were on probation or parole for nonviolent offenses and violated the conditions of their release did so via a new nonviolent offense. UDOC's parole system is unsuccessful at an enormous level, with a lack of effective transitional services making it likely that current inmates will return as new inmates are added. It is a growing cycle that needs to be broken for Utah to avoid the forecasted increases in the prison population. The Utah Commission on Criminal and Juvenile Justice will continue to monitor the results of HB 348 over the next several years. The Commission's priority is to continue to provide data and policy suggestions to Utah's legislature to improve the state's criminal justice system.

Utah's deliberate actions to mitigate over criminalization discourage recidivism through transitional programs and consistent reform of the penal code. It is a promising picture of what many states could accomplish in the next decade with comparatively aggressive practices.

NEBRASKA

Nebraska rivals Alabama when it comes to overcrowding, with facilities operating at 159 percent capacity in Fiscal Year 2014, with 5,221 people.[54] In the previous decade, Nebraska saw spending on corrections rise more than 20 percent from $131 million to $157 million as the state inmate population grew.[55] The bleak outlook requires immediate action. Under current projections from the Nebraska Department of Correctional Services (NDCS), the prison population will increase by 7 percent by Fiscal Year 2020.[56] This would push the 159 percent overcrowded population to 170 percent of capacity.[57] In an attempt to solve this crisis, the Nebraska legislature proposed in October 2014 that the NDCS add 1,100 beds to the existing prison systems at an estimated cost of $262 million.[58] This proposal represented the traditional solution of allocating money in an attempt to solve a problem, which is ineffective.

---

[52] Ibid.
[53] Ibid.
[54] "Nebraska's Justice Reinvestment Approach." The Council of State Governments Justice Center. Publication. Accessed September 19, 2017, 2.
[55] "Nebraska's Justice Reinvestment Approach," 2.
[56] Ibid., 2.
[57] Ibid.
[58] Ibid.

Four months later, in January 2015, the Nebraska legislature introduced another proposal: LB 605. The aims of LB 605 were to decrease the overall state inmate population while prioritizing prison space for those convicted of violent crimes through diverting funds and inmates to treatment and reentry programs. The legislation amended probation for greater use for those convicted of low-level offenses, ensures moderate supervision for those released, and improved funding to parole supervision needs. LB 605 passed unanimously and Nebraska Governor Pete Ricketts signed the bill into law on May 29, 2015.[59]

The pragmatic goal of LB 605, according to primary sponsor Senator Heath Mello, is a decrease from 159 percent capacity to 140 percent capacity within five years, a drawdown of 624 inmates to a new total of 4,597. This would also help avoid an onslaught of possible federal lawsuits and more than $300 million in new prison construction. The Council of State Governments Justice Center has led the creation of LB 605 and will continue to help assess its initial results and further amendments.[60]

The June 2014 report on Nebraska from the Council of State Governments Justice Center outlined the scary outlook Nebraska was facing without LB 605.[61] Measuring a decade period, from 2002 to 2012, the report laid out statistical problems facing the state. While Nebraska's resident population rose by 7.5 percent, the number of reported index crimes decreased 24 percent and arrests decreased 17 percent, putting Nebraska's property and violent crime rates below the national average.[62] Despite having the twenty-fourth lowest index crime rates in the United States, Nebraska had felony district court case filing increases. Criminal felony case filings increased by 10 percent, and by 2012 Nebraska had the twelfth lowest probation rate in the United States as the probation population had fallen 27 percent.[63] At the same time, with population rising but reported crimes and probation rates falling, Nebraska's prison population still rose 20 percent.[64]

As court filings piled up and the prison population continued to rise, state spending rose for the Nebraska Department of Correctional Service. Across that decade, Nebraska's spending on corrections rose 34 percent to $157 million and the number of prison admissions began to surpass the number of releases at an increasingly higher rate each year. Prison admissions increased 22 percent to 3,351 inmates

---

59 "Nebraska's Justice Reinvestment Approach," 1.
60 Bureau, Paul Hammel / World-Herald. "3 prison reform bills aimed at easing overcrowding win 1st-round approval." Omaha.com. April 15, 2015. Accessed September 26, 2017. www .omaha.com/news/legislature/prison-reform-bills-aimed-at-easing-overcrowding-win-st-round/ article_95f34706-8d6d-5592-9fcc-5292e2c69296.html.
61 "Justice Reinvestment in Nebraska," The Council of State Governments Justice Center. Publication. Accessed September 19, 2017, 2. https://csgjusticecenter.org/wp-content/uploads/ 2014/06/JR_Nebraska-Overview.pdf.
62 "Justice Reinvestment in Nebraska," 2.
63 Ibid., 2.
64 Ibid.

per year while releases increased 18 percent to 3,113. New sentences (which excludes those sentenced for revoking their probation) rose 34 percent to account for more than three quarters of admissions. Even more importantly, while the average time served by inmates remained stable across that decade, the number of people completing sentences of six months or less increased 5 percent. Additionally, by fiscal year 2013 more than one-third of those released by NDCS had no supervision.[65] From 1995 to 2005 the state inmate population also grew by 34 percent and overcrowding in NDCS dates back to the 1980s, with no prison operating at less than 100 percent.[66] When the NDCS built more correctional facilities in 2006 to alleviate the problem, the new facilities simply filled up and the problem continued.

The early 2000s represented a further shift away from community supervision alternative programs in the NDCS. Incarceration was used more and alternatives used less for low-risk offenders, and the lengths of sentences increased. The Platte Institute published a February 2015 report which found that "a presumptive sentencing policy is important" to resolve Nebraska's high admission rate of low-risk offenders.[67] There is "a role for elected lawmakers to provide guidance that channels the exercise of [judicial] discretion through creating a presumptive sentence that can help prioritize prison space for violent and dangerous offenders."[68] LB 605, almost in response to these findings and those of CSGJC, will in part attempt to accomplish just that.

Rehabilitation is the flip-side to sentencing and Nebraska, both before and after LB 605, invests millions of dollars each year to fund rehabilitation programs. Working in conjunction with the NDCS, CSGJC assessed "institutional programs to identify how the department can modify its investments to maximize recidivism reduction."[69]The CSGJC published a June 2016 report, just over a year after the passage of LB 605, and found that NDCS programs are both "state-of-the-art" and underutilized. The report found that those "who need these programs face clear and persistent barriers to accessing them."[70] While the treatment of the programs themselves is above average, inefficient bureaucracy destroys any potential benefit: "One-third of people within a year of their parole eligibility date are denied a parole hearing due to a lack of programming, leading to numerous people [exiting state

---

[65] "Justice Reinvestment in Nebraska," 3.

[66] Levin, Marc, and Vikrant Reddy. "Controlling Costs and Protecting Public Safety in the Cornhusker State." Report. February 2011. Accessed September 25, 2017. http://rightoncrime .com/wp-content/uploads/2011/04/Controlling-Costs-in-the-Cornhusker-State.pdf.

[67] Levin, Marc. "Securing Nebraska: Correctional Policy Improvements in the Cornhusker State." Report. February 2015. Accessed September 25, 2017. www.platteinstitute.org/library/ docLib/Securing-Nebraska-Correctional-Policy-Improvements-in-the-Cornhusker-State.pdf.

[68] "Securing Nebraska: Correctional Policy Improvements in the Cornhusker State," 9.

[69] Bree Derrick, Sara Friedman, and Jennifer Kisela. "Findings of the Justice Program Assessment of Nebraska's Prisons." Report. Accessed September 26, 2017, 2. http://nebraskalegislature.gov/ pdf/reports/committee/select_special/lr34_2015/lr34_appendixC-13b.pdf.

[70] "Findings of the Justice Program Assessment of Nebraska's Prisons," 2.

prison] without supervision."[71] The NDCS existing programs "do not fully use the many assessment results available in an inmate's pre-sentence investigation and often duplicates assessments unnecessarily" despite the NDCS having very accurate risk assessment tools.[72] The NDCS is able to group inmates according to the likelihood of recidivism in three segments – low-risk (9 percent likelihood of reoffending), moderate-risk (34 percent likelihood of reoffending), and high-risk (59 percent likelihood of reoffending) – yet incomplete programming eliminates hope of treatment for 33 percent of these inmates.[73]

Beyond treatment as a whole is the participation in juvenile reentry programs. In 2013, with the passage of LB 561, the Nebraska legislature established the "Community-based Juvenile Services Aid Program."[74] This was one of the first efforts, just before LB 605, to reassess community treatment and reentry of state inmates. Year after year since its passage the CJSA Program has received increased funding, from an initial $3 million to its most recent $7 million for 2015. An underlying principle of the CJSA Program makes it stand out from previous efforts for juvenile correctional treatment: "It is essential that communities have programs to prevent youth from becoming unnecessarily involved in the juvenile justice system."[75] Through individual comprehensive community teams, the CJSA Program is a system of careful planning to assess existing programs while implementing "preventative measures to keep youth from entering the juvenile justice system, pinpoint duplication and gaps in services to youth," while focusing on evidence-based treatment strategies.[76] Current community plans represents seventy-two counties and two federally recognized Indian tribes. The Juvenile Justice Institute assesses the effectiveness of the program and found, after surveying 130 programs, that "the strongest positive impact on recidivism to four general characteristics: 1) treatment modality; 2) amount of services; 3) quality of service; and 4) the risk level of the juveniles served." In an analysis of six respondents, five of the six programs "reported that the quasi-experimentally designed study found their program to be effective."[77]

Nebraska represents a unique opportunity to implement prison population reduction policies in a state that already has a decreasing overall crime rate. It is clear that Nebraska's long history of overcrowding has reached an emergency crisis point requiring an immediate and new approach. This last attempt (LB 605) appears to be an adequate first attempt to remedy the problem, as it is addressing both the

[71] Ibid., 2.
[72] Ibid., 12.
[73] Ibid., 9.
[74] Darrell Fisher, "Nebraska Commission on Law Enforcement and Criminal Justice Community-Based Juvenile Services Aid Program." Report. Compiled by Cynthia Kennedy. Accessed September 26, 2017. www.nebraskalegislature.gov/FloorDocs/104/PDF/Agencies/Crime_Commission/565_20160126-144645.pdf.
[75] "Nebraska Commission on Law Enforcement and Criminal Justice," 2.
[76] Ibid., 1.
[77] Ibid.

source of the problem (through reforming the prioritization of violent crime offenders and access to parole programs for low-risk offenders) and the treatment inmates need to receive before reentering their communities.

TEXAS

Texas has more people behind bars than any other state in the nation. It is a problem that has plagued their justice system for decades, but has not gone without significant effort toward reform and change. In 2007, the Texas prison population was at 150,000 and was projected to grow by more than 17,000 over the five following years. To compensate for the growth, the state was planning an additional three prisons to be constructed at a cost of $530 million. Instead of spending the money, a member of the House of Representatives and the chair of the Senate criminal justice committee came up with an idea: invest that money into the inmates at most risk to be repeat offenders to curb the flow of recidivism. With success, there would be less need for adding prison beds as fewer released prisoners would be returning.[78]

The state devoted $270 million to this idea, researching the strongest areas requiring investment to break the recidivism cycle, and gained bipartisan support due to the cost savings of nearly half of the money set aside to build new prisons. These new initiatives also "improved addiction treatment, boosted education opportunities and rebuilt the juvenile justice system where chronic sexual abuse was rife."[79] New programs, money, and personnel led to results which were huge: "parole went from 22,000 a year with 11,000 revocations to 29,000 with 6000 revocations. Improved efficiencies resulted in the wait for parole dropping from one year to 90 days, which saved $20 million in prisoner costs."[80]

Overall the reforms not only stopped the projected growth of 17,000 prisoners, they actually reduced the prison population by 3000 and the state began actually closing prisons.[81] The results went even further than the prison system as the crime and arrest rate dropped as well. The type of people imprisoned are different, to put it lightly, "the prison mix has changed with more dangerous offenders (those we fear) in custody and less of the knuckleheads (that make us mad)."[82] One of the elected officials sponsoring the bill calmed the irrational fears that some have with prison reductions by saying, "We weren't soft on crime we just were smart on crime."[83] It is a method that is starting to work, and other states are noticing the success.

---

[78] John Silvester. "Lock 'Em Up Lunacy: How We Turn Small Fry Crooks into Dangerous Sharks." *The Age*. September 02, 2016. Accessed September 26, 2017.
[79] "Lock 'Em Up Lunacy."
[80] Ibid.
[81] Ibid.
[82] Ibid.
[83] Ibid.

Also in 2007 there were a series of changes at various levels of government and the criminal justice in the state. Alongside the previously mentioned legislation was a significant reduction in the state's juvenile justice system. While the changes to the prohibition system capped the growth and help lower recidivism, there needed to be other ways to continue to curb recidivism and slow the number of people entering prisons for nonviolent offenses. Currently, numerous bills are being debated and enacted, from changing property theft thresholds to sentences for low-level drug crimes, which are projected to save the state hundreds of millions of dollars to put toward treatment not available in prisons.[84]

There were also several abuse scandals involving the Texas Youth Commission in 2007 that forced the state to investigate the juvenile justice system. When the scandal broke, the Texas Youth Prison system held 4,200 young men and women. Today it holds 1,000 inmates, a 76 percent reduction.[85] The juvenile crime rate has dropped, not because of a complicated reform bill, but rather because of a realization that "[t]here wasn't a public safety justification for locking up so many youth, and the Legislature last session moved to divert even more youthful offenders from state lockups to community based corrections."[86] Reforms were implemented that aided in the reduction: "The legislature passed reforms aimed at banning the commitment of juveniles to secure state facilities for misdemeanor offenses, reducing the maximum age in which juveniles would be permitted in those facilities, and redirecting certain offenders toward evidence based community programs instead of jailing them."[87] Each of these reforms show a posture toward juvenile justice that is working to end the prison pipeline and source of mass incarceration. That reduction in juvenile crime also saves the state money to put toward other juvenile programs: once source cited in 2016 said the state had already saved $200 million.[88]

Much is being done with the juvenile justice system in Texas, and there are still major problems to overcome. One of these problems is receiving little attention but is an injustice that many are trying to fight every year: Texas teenagers are considered adults once they turn seventeen, although federal law states they are not adults until eighteen. This discrepancy places younger teens in adult prisons where there is "a serious risk of abuse of young inmates by older ones and puts most county jails out of compliance with the federal Prison Rape Elimination Act, which treats

---

[84] "Raising the Bars for Texas Criminal Justice Reform." *The Texas Observer.* February 28, 2017. Accessed September 27, 2017. www.texasobserver.org/raising-the-bars-criminal-justice-reform/.
[85] Ibid.
[86] Ibid.
[87] Ken Cuccinelli. "Texas Shows How to Reduce Both Incarceration and Crime." *National Review.* May 18, 2015. Accessed September 27, 2017. www.nationalreview.com/article/418510/texas-shows-how-reduce-both-incarceration-and-crime-ken-cuccinelli.
[88] "Juvenile Justice: State Sees Decrease in Incarcerated Youth." Amarillo.com. December 29, 2012. Accessed September 27, 2017. http://amarillo.com/news/local-news/2012-12-28/fewer-texas-youth-incarcerated.

17 year olds as juveniles."[89] This means adult jails do not meet juvenile jail standards and the cost is too much to change them, and is a reason according to the Texas Observer that Texas Sheriffs' Association came out as a large supporter of the "Raise the Age" legislation.[90]

Some of the most recent changes to the Texas system came in 2013, adding to the 2007 changes that earned the state acclaim because of its stereotype as being "tough on crime."[91] The Texas legislature cut $97 million from the budget of the Texas Department of Criminal Justice to make it clear that "their intent was to reduce [the capacity of prisons]."[92] In 2011, they had already proved that it was possible by closing three youth facilities (590 beds), a feat that was possible after several years of declines.[93] Today there are half as many youth facilities as there were in 2006 in Texas, and the state is beginning to enact the same policies with adult prisons. Time will tell if the Texas method will become a popular one for other states to adopt.

MINNESOTA

Minnesota has historically had a criminal justice and penal system known for its low prison population and for pushing rehabilitation as a philosophy of punishment. According to a 2015 essay by Andy Mannix, the 1980s and 1990s helped solidify this picture of the state, especially when the prison populations in places like California were quickly growing.[94] His essay asks a simple but provocative question in the title, "Minnesota crime is at a 50-year low. So why are we imprisoning more people than ever?"[95]

By 1990 the prison population was growing but far slower than the national averages. By 2000 that number had nearly doubled, and is still lingering at those numbers by the time of Mannix's essay in 2015. A report from 1999 quoted the former corrections officer, as other states moved to more "punitive-minded" punishment tactics, that Minnesota "never really deviated from its early hope that the operation of prisons would result in a safer society by making prisoners better people."

Minnesota was among the first states to battle the problem and worked to get ahead of the mass incarceration issue before it got out of control – implementing

[89] "Raising the Bars for Texas Criminal Justice Reform."
[90] Ibid.
[91] "State Criminal Justice Advocacy in a Conservative Environment." Report. Accessed September 26, 2017. http://sentencingproject.org/wp-content/uploads/2015/09/inc_Conservative_State_Advocacy.pdf.
[92] "State Criminal Justice Advocacy," 6.
[93] Ibid., 6.
[94] Andy Mannix, "Minnesota Crime Is at a 50-Year Low. So Why Are We Imprisoning More People than Ever?" *MinnPost*. Accessed September 27, 2017. www.minnpost.com/politics-policy/2015/06/minnesota-crime-50-year-low-so-why-are-we-imprisoning-more-people-ever.
[95] "Minnesota Crime Is at a 50-Year Low."

guidelines for punishment to ensure that punishments fit the crimes being punished. They even had a task force in place to make sure that prisons did not become overcrowded. By the early 2000s the population was growing faster than ever – the system was threatened with overcrowding, and the growth seemed to stay steady without any policy changes or pushes for reform. "I'm not seeing anywhere near the same reform spirit that we had 30 to 40 years ago," said David Schultz, a political science professor at Hamline University, in the essay, "I think we're making it easier for people to get in prison."[96]

What caused the change in mindset? One Minnesota justice said that the rise can be explained by the sheer number of criminal statutes in the laws of the state: the criminal code was 65 pages long in 1965 and 228 pages in 2013. The justice commented, "if the code continues to grow at that pace, it will hit 1,770 pages 50 years from now."[97] The problem is a common one. The legal director for the local ACLU chapter said, "I can't remember a legislative session where the Legislature didn't create new crimes and enhanced penalties ... So when you have longer sentences, you're going to have more people in prison."[98]

The bump in sentencing is due to a number of factors: enhanced sentencing policy on drugs and DUI's account for many of the new arrests, and many other types of crime received increased penalties. Mannix pointed out the jump in drug sentencing almost doubled the number of people incarcerated for substances: "from 2000 to 2005, the number of Minnesotans in prison for drug offenses more than doubled to 2,178. To put it in perspective, that's more than the state's entire prison population circa 1981."[99] There is some hope, however, because that number fell to 1,633 by 2013. Many of the drug-related arrests are not for low level substance, and half of those in prison are there for a methamphetamine-related crime. Recidivism is high in Minnesota as well, with about 60 percent of prison sentences going to probation and supervised release violations.[100]

While many think that reform will be hard to implement, the state legislature worked hard to pass a new reform bill in 2016 aimed at bringing some change to the current trend.[101] The bill, which passed unanimously, is one of the most significant reforms of criminal justice in decades for the state. It changes several key elements of the system and importantly demonstrates the legislature is committed to efforts to change their philosophical approach toward punishment. The bill was proposed as a way to reduce sentences in some cases, raise the bar for high-level charges, and free

[96] Ibid.
[97] Ibid.
[98] Ibid.
[99] Ibid.
[100] Ibid.
[101] "2016 Drug Reform Act." Minnesota.gov. September 18, 2017. Accessed September 27, 2017. https://mn.gov/sentencing-guidelines/assistance/drug-modifications-2016/2016-drug-reform-act/; www.startribune.com/minnesota-house-unanimously-approves-drug-sentencing-reforms/ 380369111/.

up prison beds by using rehab as an alternative to jail cells. The bill's Senate sponsor Sen. Ron Latz quantified the objectives, estimating that by diverting some into treatment, the measure would free up more than 600 prison beds over time.

Overall, the bill looks to more effectively sentence those with drug-related crimes and to work on employing the money to better use in rehabilitation and treatment, and is a step in reducing both the prison population and the number of new prisoners being admitted. The bill suggests another focus on how drug problems can be dealt with, a focus on rehabilitation instead of incarceration.

A more drastic approach came in 2014 when the state sent a message that it cared about the problem on a broader scale. Minnesota rid the state's criminal code of 1,175 obsolete laws making the process simpler, and lessening the burden of the law on the people of the state.[102] The laws included everything from tax-related issues to permits, representing a wish to reduce the code to help stop the flow of people both entering the courtroom and the jail cell.

MICHIGAN

Michigan has spent years working on ways to curb recidivism and successfully reintegrate former inmates into society. The effects of recidivism are multifaceted – affecting economic, social, and cultural life – and places like Michigan have been hard hit by the prison cycle it causes. The Michigan Prisoner Reentry Initiative (MPRI) started in 2005 under the Michigan Department of Corrections to help reduce recidivism by investing the ways to stop future criminal activity through education. In Michigan, like many other states, a large part of the overcriminalization problem is connected to recidivism. Many states cannot figure out how to slow recidivism, and their prison populations stay stagnant.

The mission of the MPRI program, as one article in the Michigan Policy Network put it, is "to educate prisoners on how to adjust back into the public sphere by the time their minimum term of imprisonment has been completed."[103] It is a simple formula of assistance: when an inmate's release time is near they are provided resources that will help them find housing, new jobs, and healthcare, including a variety of substance abuse and mental health treatments. When the article was published in 2015 the prison population in Michigan had dropped 15 percent from its 2007 high – something many believe is a result of the MPRI program. The main focus of the program is on investing in the areas that will ensure someone will not return to prison or commit the same crimes once outside the cell. The article

---

[102] Bill Salisbury, "Minnesota 'Unsession' Dumps 1,175 Obsolete, Silly Laws." *Twin Cities.* November 03, 2015. Accessed September 27, 2017. www.twincities.com/2014/05/26/minnesota-unsession-dumps-1175-obsolete-silly-laws/.

[103] Vincent Szczerowski. "Policy Briefs Michigan Prisoner Reentry Initiative." Michigan Policy Network. Accessed September 27, 2017. http://michiganpolicy.com/index.php/agriculture-back ground-2/policy-briefs-11/1497-michigan-prisoner-reentry-initiative.

highlighted some positive changes coming with the new parts of the program including a partnership with colleges, "to provide post-secondary schooling options, along with instituting options to offer education on skilled trades."[104] An American Bar Association (ABA) study quoted by the Michigan Policy Network also said that the program contributed to "reducing the prison population in Michigan by 7,500."[105] The article concluded that: "out of the 22,000 participants in the program, the rate of returning to prison for a new crime is at its lowest number since 1995."[106]

The program is still currently undergoing many improvements, and is not immune to critics, many of whom believe that the program is too costly, and the benefits and inmate reduction is coming from other sources. The program overall has not lessened the costs of the corrections department, and many have questioned the management of the program as one that can have long-term sustainability. However, it is hard to argue with the numbers that the MPRI has behind its work: 33 percent fewer returns to prison for violating parole of committing a new crime, a prison population that has dropped from 51,554 to under 46,000, and three prisons closed in 2010, all at a savings of $118 million.[107] According to the ABA, it seems that the concerns over cost are less worrisome than some think: if you compare the money spent on the program to the amount it takes to house an inmate for a year ($34,000), the $56 million a year seems small when one considers the 25,000 inmates who participated in the program.[108]

Another article in Michigan policy network highlighted a different solution to Michigan's incarceration problem. Between 1980 and 2010 Michigan's prison population was growing twenty-nine times faster than the general population, and the average time served was well above the national average of 2.6 years at more than six years.[109] A report cited in the article, titled "Denying Parole at First Eligibility: How Much Public Safety Does It Actually Buy?," by the Citizens Alliance on Prisons and Public Spending (CAPPS) found that problems with the rate of parole approvals was leading to a large proportion of inmates being held longer than might have been necessary.[110] Problems like the one the CAPPS report suggested are the ones that programs like MPRI set out to fix – making sure that inmates could succeed outside of the prison walls as soon as possible, and hopefully not have to return.

---

[104] "Policy Briefs Michigan Prisoner Reentry Initiative."
[105] Ibid.
[106] Ibid.
[107] State Policy Implementation Project. Report. Accessed September 26, 2017, 2. www.american bar.org/content/dam/aba/administrative/criminal_justice/spip_reentry.authcheckdam.pdf.
[108] Ibid., 5.
[109] Mike Sayre. "Efforts to Reduce Michigan's Prison Population through Sentencing and Parole Reform." Michigan Policy Network. Accessed September 27, 2017. http://michiganpolicy.com/index.php/agriculture-background-2/policy-briefs-11/1447-efforts-to-reduce-michigans-prison-population-through-sentencing-and-parole-reform.
[110] "Efforts to Reduce Michigan's Prison Population."

Perhaps the biggest change and provides the most hope for Michigan's over-criminalization problem is one that has to do with criminal intent or *mens rea* on the part of the accused. It is an issue that is just starting to be discussed in many states, but one Michigan has worked toward reforming over the last couple years. A study conducted in 2014 by the Manhattan Institute and the Mackinac Center for Public Policy found that the state had 3,102 statutory crimes that lay outside the penal code, and that for 26 percent of the felonies and more than 59 percent of the misdemeanors the state did not have to show *mens rea* on the part of the accused.[111] A reform to this practice appeared in 2015 when the Governor signed a bill establishing a default criminal-intent standard for Michigan.[112] This reform ensured that, "the state had to show that a defendant acted with intent, knowledge, or recklessness to convict him of a crime unless the state legislature clearly specified a lower level of mental culpability in the criminal statute."[113] The new bill is not perfect, and has gained some scrutiny for not having enough scope in what parts of the penal code it affects, but it is an important step in the direction of reducing injustices in the system and unnecessary penal codes from the books. Perhaps most importantly, it shows an openness and a prioritization for criminal justice reform by the state's leadership. The type of reforms happening in Michigan have a chance for permanence – not only to reduce prison populations but to also change an entire system.

CONCLUSION

For those truly seeking to advocate for criminal justice reform, Washington, DC, should not be the focus. Personalist criminal justice reform directs our attention to the local sources of overcriminalization and mass incarceration – viz., the states. The focus for criminal justice reform must be with state legislatures and county/city officials. It is at the local level that change is going to come. Federal drugs laws, and the sentencing therein, most certainly must be reformed. However, the majority of criminal justice reform progress will come at the local level. This will require a new generation of reformers who work at the state levels and can conceptualize new localized paradigms to combat overcriminalization.

Many national problems are slow to be solved because of the sheer size of the challenge and logistical problems with implementation across the country. The need for criminal justice reform is acknowledged by most major segments of society, and it can reasonably and realistically be implemented because local actions are ground zero. With a multitude of successful examples, each state can create a

[111] James R. Copland, Isaac Gorodetski, and Michael J. Reitz, "Overcriminalizing the Wolverine State: A Primer and Possible Reforms for Michigan," Issue Brief 31, October 28, 2014.
[112] James R. Copland and Rafael A. Mangual. "Michigan Overcriminalization Update 2017." Report. Accessed September 27, 2017.
[113] "Michigan Overcriminalization Update 2017."

tailored approach to reducing their population of the incarcerated. It is this liberation of these citizens which will unleash the potential and productivity of local communities. Many areas of the nation are suffering because they lack a home grown and engaged blue collar workforce. Each of our cities and major regional corridors require hundreds of billions of restoration and maintenance work. There is an abundance of talent that can be unlocked through immediate and direct actions to reduce the populations of state prisons. Methods have been proven effective, and the major requirement is a collective moral reasoning that criminal justice reform is a national priority and the tools at the disposal of states need to be unleashed aggressively.

8

Toward Civil Society Solutions

Gerald Alvarez said that he "almost felt more secure in prison" after leaving the structured environment of incarceration for life in the real world in New York.[1] His chance at normalcy came through the Center for Employment Opportunities (CEO), which helps those with criminal backgrounds find jobs in fields like maintenance or construction and give them the tools to retain those jobs. His first job was scrubbing toilets for $30 a day at City Hall. Next was a moving company where he was promoted to supervisor. Most recently he has had help starting his own business. It still will not be enough to support him long term – the time in prison left him without the ability to save for retirement or have a pension: "When it's over, it's over. I have no 401(k). I have no pension. I have nothing," he said, "All I've been looking for is a job with a pension. Something I could do for 20 years or something, and at least be able to retire."[2]

Incarceration instantly places an individual at the bottom of the economic ladder, with absolutely no hope of moving forward. Including drug crimes, economic desperation is associated with the majority of crimes for the overcriminalized, and incarceration only increases their obstacles. These citizens need direct intervention from government and civil society institutions in order to have any aspect of productivity. Some states are starting to work on legislation that bans the checkbox for criminal records on applications, something that hinders those with a record from applying for almost all positions. SUNY schools in Buffalo removed the check box from their application to help encourage those who have been in prison or juvenile detention to still apply for school.[3] "They do want a second chance and

---

[1] Elena Holodny. "'It Still Haunts Me': What It's Like to Get a Hob after Prison in America." Business Insider. July 30, 2017. Accessed August 01, 2017. www.businessinsider.com/finding-job-after-prison-2017-7.
[2] Holodny, "It Still Haunts Me."
[3] Angela Christoforos News 4. "SUNY Schools to Remove Felony Conviction Checkbox from Student Applications." Wivb.com. September 15, 2016. Accessed August 01, 2017.

they want a fresh start and they're concerned whether it's an employment application or the SUNY application it's going to keep them from being able to get in,"[4]
one school spokesperson said. Of the 2,900 people that were applying to SUNY with
a record, each year more than half would drop out before completing a degree due
to discouragement.

For many former prisoners this is a common sentiment as law-abiding employers
get a negative first impression of criminal records and the culture shock of interact-
ing with someone that was in prison. It is a problem affecting all areas of civil society
and the solution at all levels need to be equally multifaceted.

Civil society institutions, like the CEO, have been the key to African American's
thriving in America's history.[5] Because the government in the American black
experience did not serve to create or protect opportunities for black prosperity until
the Civil Rights Act of 1964, African Americans have had to rely on nongovern-
mental institutions to survive. Institutions and organizations like the black church,
black labor organizations, historically black colleges, and universities, black frater-
nities and sororities, the NAACP, the National Urban League, the family, black
sports leagues, rural food co-ops, and other predominantly African American volun-
tary associations, were vital for black thriving because blacks could not rely on the
government to create the conditions for blacks to enjoy political and economic
liberty.[6] Adjustments to criminal law alone will not bring about the type of social
and cultural reform needed to keep men and women of prison. This is the work of
civil society instructions.

Government policy does not have the capacity to create a society of more virtuous
citizens whose lives are characterized by reciprocating each other's flourishing.[7]
Cultivating a culture where people desire and seek the flourishing of one's neighbor
is what civil society institutions do best. This chapter provides an introduction to
effective civil society programs that are doing their part to dismantle the debilitating
criminal justice complex one person at a time at the local level. The criminal laws
could completely be rewritten in every state, but that will not change the individual
motivations to seek virtuous activities instead of deviance. Individuals need the right
human connections and economic freedom to thrive. What follows are examples of
some of the best designed programs that exist to work to keep people out of prison,
those that work with those incarcerated, for ex-offender entry back into
communities.

http://wivb.com/2016/09/15/suny-schools-to-removing-felony-conviction-checkbox-from-stu
      dent-applications/.
[4]   Angela Christoforos, "Suny Schools."
[5]   Brian Mc Kenzie, "Reconsidering the Effects of Bonding Social Capital: A Closer Look at
      Black Civil Society Institutions in America." *Political Behavior* 30, no. 1 (2008): 25–45.
[6]   Ibid, 30.
[7]   David Schmidtz, *Elements of Justice* (Cambridge: Cambridge University Press, 2006), 82–89.

PREINCARCERATION

South Bronx Community Connections (SBSS) – Bronx, New York

Community Connections for Youth (CCFY), a New York based–nonprofit organization, exists to curtail the school-to-prison pipeline by rerouting at-risk youth from the justice system back into their community and connecting them with adult mentors. The organization's aim is to build positive, local mentorships with at-risk youth in the hope that a stable and enduring relationship can achieve true change in the future. CCFY's South Bronx Community Connections (SBCC) project was started with a three-year $1.1 million grant from the New York State Division of Criminal Justice Services to achieve this goal in the Bronx.[8] SBCC also provides at-risk youth with alternatives to prison by connecting them with local mentors and promoting "partnerships between juvenile justice system stakeholders and local neighborhood organizations." The organization believes that local mentorships and amelioration of interpersonal problems can decrease the chances of an individual being incarcerated.

A 2016 article in the *New York Daily* reported a speech given by Ruben Austria, executive director of CCFY, at the Mott Haven Public Library in August of that year. Austria is quoted saying, "We want to get young people plugged back into the fabric of community life, and involved long-term in the neighborhood with positive youth development activities lasting beyond the short-term mandate."[9] The article also features quotes from Clinton Lacey, the deputy commissioner of CCFY, who said, "we think the people who can best serve our young people are those in the community."[10] This principle of local solutions to local problems is at the heart of the organization's mission. According to CCFY's website, their model is "built on three principles: (1) a community-driven grassroots neighborhood approach, (2) a positive development approach to youth that focuses on strengths and assets, and (3) embracing the importance of connecting youth to their communities … with mentors who are credible messengers."[11]

An independent evaluation by the John Jay College of Criminal Justice found that between 2011 and 2013, more than 100 young people living in the South Bronx had their cases redirected to the SBCC project and noted a dramatic cut in

[8] "South Bronx Community Connections." Community Connections for Youth. March 04, 2017. Accessed September 28, 2017. https://cc-fy.org/project/south-bronx-community-connections/.

[9] Corinne Lestch. "South Bronx Nonprofit Offers Ideas for Youth out of Detention." NY *Daily News*. Accessed August 08, 2016. www.nydailynews.com/new-york/bronx/south-bronx-nonprofit-offers-ideas-community-support-youth-returning-upstate-detention-article-1.1121833.

[10] Ibid.

[11] "South Bronx Community Connections." Community Connections for Youth. March 04, 2017. Accessed September 28, 2017. https://cc-fy.org/project/south-bronx-community-connections/.

recidivism rates: "only 15 percent of youth who enrolled in the program were re-arrested, and only 5 percent had new charges filed against them."[12]

In addition to focusing on fostering local relationships amongst at risk youth and mentors, CCFY provides technical assistance for organizations that want to replicate their design in other communities and produced a "10-module curriculum that guides organizations through the process of developing community-based alternatives to incarceration."[13] CCFY also offers workshops and training sessions "in community based alternatives such as Family Engagement, Positive Youth Development, Community Coaching (Mentoring), and Parent Peer Support."[14]

This program serves as a catalyst for addressing the issue of local causes and consequences of youth incarceration by using all resources available for a local solution.

Twin Cities Rise – Minneapolis–Saint Paul, Minnesota

Twin Cities R!SE (TCR) is a organization based in Minneapolis–Saint Paul, Minnesota, focused on placing recently incarcerated individuals "on the path to - long-term and stable employment."[15] The organization began in 1993 when TCR's founder, a former executive Vice President at General Mills, Steve Rothschild, sought to ameliorate the long-term poverty plaguing recently incarcerated individuals in the Twin Cities.[16] He implemented a "market-driven approach" and "sought to assist individuals find stable and well-paying employment."[17]

TCR's Reentry Connect program focuses directly on bolstering the long-term educational and occupational success of adults who are released from incarceration. According to TCR's website, it "provides a high level of support to participants, by beginning to work with them 60–90 days prior to their release from prison."[18] Case managers work with participants to build a specialized release plan who "receive personal empowerment training and work with a Reentry Connect case manager to develop their career goals and pathways."[19] Case managers then act to "connect participants to resources for housing, mental health treatment, parenting groups,

[12] Ibid.
[13] "Training & Technical Assistance." Community Connections for Youth. Accessed September 28, 2017. https://cc-fy.org/training-and-technical-assistance/.
[14] Ibid.
[15] "Who We Are." Twin Cities R!SE. Accessed September 28, 2017. www.twincitiesrise.org/who-we-are/.
[16] "History." Twin Cities R!SE. Accessed September 28, 2017. www.twincitiesrise.org/history/.
[17] Ibid.
[18] *Twin Cities R!SE Winter 2016 Newsletter*, 2–8. December 18, 2016. Accessed September 27, 2017. https://issuu.com/twincitiesrise/docs/tcr_newsletter_winter_2016_11_3_16.
[19] "Our Programs." Twin Cities R!SE. Accessed September 28, 2017. www.twincitiesrise.org/training-programs/.

mentoring and other support services."[20] In a recently published report, TCR highlighted the "13 percent one year recidivism rate"[21] of its Reentry Connect Participants.

TCR's approach is comprehensive and seeks to not only bring about greater chances of employment for its participants, but also hopes to impart a sense of self-confidence and worth in them. Ronald Baker is a program graduate that was met by a Twin Cities R!SE Engagement Leader "at a point in his life, where several bad decisions had led him to a halfway house."[22] Since his meeting with a TCR staff member, Ronald has maintained full time employment for "over two years and teaches his children everything that he learned in TCR empowerment classes."[23] As a result of the resources made available to him by TCR, Ronald now has stable employment and is able to provide full support for his family.[24]

According to Reentry Connect Case Manager, Jeff Williams, "Success happens when an individual realizes that he/she has value and that their place in society is important, as this is realized, an individual becomes motivated and most importantly consistent with their dedication to live a better life as they utilize the new tool and the resources that we provide for them."[25] This strategy and commitment helped Dylan, who had just been released upon coming to TCR; he was referred by a friend who was familiar with the work of Reentry Connect and began "three 10 week sessions of training while looking for employment, and for first time in his life learning was enjoyable."[26] Dylan no longer had probation officers in his life, but instructors and a career advisor that challenged him to achieve his goals of successful reentry. Like Ronald, Dylan also benefited from TCR's Personal Empowerment classes, which helped him to begin feeling more confident and calm, even in the midst of great personal challenges associated with reentry.

In October of 2016, Dylan graduated from TCR by marking one year of employment. According to a recent report, "during that year Dylan ... [was] promoted twice, and is now an Assistant Manager"[27] at his company where "he works over 40 hours a week and has benefits."[28]

[20] Ibid.
[21] Twin Cities R!SE Winter 2016 Newsletter, 2–8. December 18, 2016. Accessed September 27, 2017. https://issuu.com/twincitiesrise/docs/tcr_newsletter_winter_2016_11_3_16.
[22] "Testimonials." Twin Cities R!SE. Accessed September 28, 2017. www.twincitiesrise.org/testimonials/.
[23] Ibid.
[24] Ibid.
[25] Twin Cities R!SE Winter 2016 Newsletter, 2–8. December 18, 2016. Accessed September 27, 2017.
[26] Ibid.
[27] Ibid.
[28] Ibid.

Restorative Justice Project of the Midcoast – Maine

The Restorative Justice Project (RJP) of the Midcoast aids communities in Maine in responding holistically to the consequences and causes of crime. Founded in 2005, it seeks to reconcile offenders with their victims and the community at large in order to reduce recidivism rates.[29] RJP "provides restorative conferences for adult and juvenile offenders"[30] in various Maine counties "and an array of restorative justice services for the Maine Coast Regional Reentry Center and for K–12 schools."[31] RJP places a primary importance on focusing on the rehabilitation of the offenders with those whom they have harmed and their local community. The program's efforts are "based on the belief that through connection, not exclusion, balance can be restored when harm has been done."[32] Among its participants, there is only a 31 percent recidivism rate compared to the state average of 70 percent.[33]

RJP's programming encourages schools to respond to delinquent behavior without removing youth from the educational environment. As an alternative to suspension and expulsion, RJP keeps students accountable by placing them in conversation with the victims they've harmed and school leaders. The students are given opportunities to repair the damage through actions that the victim(s), school staff, and offender agree are fair and equitable.[34] Matthew Houghton, Principal of Morse and Monroe Elementary Schools, is an advocate of the RJP. He writes that "we have seen a dramatic decline in office referrals. Students are showing more empathy and understanding that their choices affect others. Trust has been established, and we are a team, problem-solving solutions together."[35]

In this model, the end goal for justice is establishing harmony. For example, a teen caught vandalizing a store might be placed in a room with his parents, the store owner, and local police officer. After the teen is informed of the monetary damage his actions have caused, the group might collectively decide that the teen must wash all the store windows daily for two weeks. The teen is shown that actions have consequences, but without it resulting in a criminal record. Additionally, the store owner feels compensated for the damages.

According to RJP, individuals "harmed take an active role in the process, while offenders are encouraged to take responsibility for their actions 'to repair the harm

---

[29] "About Us." RJPMidcoast. Accessed September 28, 2017. www.rjpmidcoast.org/about-us.html.
[30] Ibid.
[31] Ibid.
[32] "Our Philosophy." RJPMidcoast. Accessed August 08, 2016. www.rjpmidcoast.org/our-philoso phy.html.
[33] Ibid.
[34] "Restorative School Practices." RJPMidcoast. Accessed September 28, 2017. www.rjpmidcoast .org/restorative-school-practices.html.
[35] "Restorative School Practices." RJPMidcoast. Accessed August 09, 2016. www.rjpmidcoast.org/ restorative-school-practices.html.

they've done.'"[36] By taking this approach, RJP "fosters dialogue between the harmed party (victim) and offender"[37] and "holds the potential for those harmed and their families to have a direct voice in determining just outcomes and reestablishes the role of the community in supporting all parties affected by crime."[38] The assumption of responsibility not only discourages people from repeating bad choices, but it also provides them with the opportunity to see themselves as citizens, ones who can participate in their local community and pursue the common good for the sake of their neighbors.

RJP partners with the Maine Coastal Regional Reentry Center in Belfast, Maine, to provide resources for those staying at the Center that include "facilitation and support of mentor matches for all residents for a minimum of three sessions and usually for 6–12 months a five week introductory course on Restorative Justice, prosocial events/outings such as hiking, bowling, cooking and kayaking."[39]

Juvenile Detention Alternative Initiative – Nationwide

The Juvenile Detention Alternatives Initiative (JDAI) launched "as a pilot project in the early 1990s" in Baltimore, Maryland, by the Annie E. Casey Foundation. JDAI exists to address and reduce the over reliance on detention by the juvenile court process; according to the JDAI website, placement "into a locked detention center pending court significantly increases the odds that youth will be found delinquent and committed to corrections facilities and can seriously damage their prospects for future success."[40] JDAI identifies detention as a critical initial phase that juveniles often find themselves upon entering the court process. The organization combats the predominant practice of placing youth, who pose little or no threat to public safety into detention. Since its founding in the 1990s, the JDAI model "now reaches over one fourth of the total US youth population."[41] According to a recent report, "The most recent data available show that among local JDAI sites, which reported both current and pre-JDAI data, the total average daily detention population was 43 percent lower in 2011 than in the year before joining JDAI."[42] In addition, "Thirty-four percent of these reporting sites have reduced their average daily detention populations by more than half since entering JDAI," and "the data show that

---

[36] "What Is Restorative Justice?" RJPMidcoast. Accessed September 28, 2017. www.rjpmidcoast .org/what-is-restorative-justice.html.
[37] Ibid.
[38] Ibid.
[39] Ibid.
[40] Ibid.
[41] The Annie E. Casey Foundation. "Juvenile Detention Alternatives Initiative Progress Report 2014." Baltimore: The Annie E. Casey Foundation, Publication Year. Accessed October 10, 2017. www.aecf.org/m/resourcedoc/aecf-2014JDAIProgressReport-2014.pdf.
[42] Ibid., 2.

participating jurisdictions admitted 59,000 fewer youth to detention in 2012 than in the year prior to launching JDAI, a drop of 39 percent."[43]

To achieve these results, the JDAI model includes "promoting collaboration between juvenile court officials, probation agencies, prosecutors, defense attorneys, schools, community organizations and advocates; using rigorous data collection and analysis to guide decision making; [and] instituting case processing reforms to expedite the flow of cases through the system," among other tactics. Emphasis is also placed on decreasing the number of youth who are detained for "probation rule violations," addressing demographic disparities by "examining data to identify policies that may disadvantage youth of color," and "improving conditions of confinement in detention facilities."[44]

Since the inception of its first five pilot sites in the early 1990s, JDAI has expanded to "nearly 300 jurisdictions in 39 states and the District of Columbia."[45] As of 2013, over "30 percent of U.S. youth reside in jurisdictions where JDAI is active."[46] Locales where JDAI models are used have scene reductions in the "number of youth of color in detention by 40 percent."[47]

These are the primary goals of the organization and "as an outgrowth of their JDAI efforts, most participating jurisdictions have adopted reforms (such as establishing new probation practices, improving community-based programming services, etc.) in other aspects of their juvenile systems that further reduces chances of youth detainment."[48] According to the University of California Berkeley's JDAI evaluation in 2012, youth detainment has "been falling faster in those sites (down 40 percent) than occur statewide (down 29 percent) and in 15 of the 23 states examined, JDAI sites reduction in commitments outpaced the statewide average."[49]

DURING INCARCERATION

Ambassadors for Hope

According to a 2016 *Lancaster Online* article, Robert Cooper started Ambassadors for Hope (AFH) to help children in Lancaster County, Pennsylvania, "dealing with the effects: social, emotional, material of their parents' incarceration."[50]

[43] Ibid.
[44] Ibid., 34.
[45] Ibid., 8.
[46] Ibid., 12.
[47] Ibid.
[48] Ibid. 16.
[49] Ibid.
[50] The LNP Editorial Board. "Program Helping the Children of Parents Incarcerated at Lancaster County Prison Does Important Work." *Lancaster Online*. March 06, 2016. Accessed September 28, 2017. http://lancasteronline.com/opinion/editorials/program-helping-the-children-of-parents-incarcerated-at-lancaster-county/article_ae6f9ec8-e25b-11e5-95db-5b696dae1533.html.

AFH met an urgent and desperate need within the Lancaster area, "'There was nothing before,' said Bob Cooper, whose group pushed the county to start the child advocate program on a trial basis in 2015."[51] Prior to the decision to start a child support service, "there was no one to make sure the children left behind had even the basics, prison officials previously did not even know when inmates had children, much less if those kids had stable living arrangements."[52] It would take "years listening to people from the criminal justice system," before Cooper became certain "that it is critical to provide early intervention for the children left behind when a parent is jailed."[53]

The program Cooper would go on to create, AFH, is now fully funded by the inmates: "the money for it comes from a commission of about $320,000 a year that the county receives from a company that has an exclusive contract to sell inmates snacks, clothing and other commissary items."[54]

Ambassadors for Hope aims to be the "premier advocate on behalf of children of incarcerated parents and their families."[55] Through identifying the needs of children whose parents are incarcerated and advocating for solutions to those needs, AFH educates the local Lancaster County community about this issue, supports families affected by parental incarceration, and intends to mold public policy. However, the primary attention is placed upon the children of those incarcerated. On the AFH, free resources are available for family members who find themselves responsible for raising a young child. This includes a manual containing "many of the questions children ask, tips for caregivers, and suggestions on how the child might keep in contact with their parents."[56] A Family Advocate, employed by a partnership AFH has with Compass Mark, "identifies, supports and advocates for the unique needs of children with a parent in prison"[57] and begins working with and on the child's behalf as soon as possible after a parent is incarcerated.

AFH adopted the "The Children of Incarcerated Parents Bill of Rights" which includes commitments to keep children appraised of decisions made about their parents, ensure a lasting and lifelong relationship with the parent, and have the

[51] Susan Baldridge. "Helping Kids with Incarcerated Parents." *U.S. News & World Report.* June 17, 2017. Accessed October 11, 2017. www.usnews.com/news/best-states/pennsylvania/articles/2017-06-17/helping-kids-with-incarcerated-parents.
[52] Ibid.
[53] Ibid.
[54] The LNP Editorial Board. "Program Helping the Children of Parents Incarcerated at Lancaster County Prison Does Important Work." *LancasterOnline.* March 06, 2016. Accessed September 28, 2017. http://lancasteronline.com/opinion/editorials/program-helping-the-children-of-parents-incarcerated-at-lancaster-county/article_ae6f9ec8-e25b-11e5-95db-5b696dae1533.html.
[55] "Ambassadors for Hope." Ambassadors for Hope – About Us. Accessed September 28, 2017. www.ambassadorsforhope.com/aboutus.php.
[56] "Ambassadors for Hope." Ambassadors for Hope – Resources. Accessed October 11, 2017. www.ambassadorsforhope.com/resources.php.
[57] "Ambassadors for Hope." Ambassadors for Hope – Family Services Advocate Program. Accessed October 11, 2017. www.ambassadorsforhope.com/family_services_advocate.php.

opportunity to "speak with, see and touch" their parent(s), among other guarantees.[58] These measures permit the greatest amount of normalcy possible for a child whose parent is incarcerated. AFH labors to turn these guarantees into a reality by implementing a framework possible for them to take place, seeking policy changes to promote greater care for children of incarcerated people, and placing primary importance on the child's well-being.

Prison Entrepreneurship Program – Houston, Texas

Founded in 2004 in Houston Texas, the Prison Entrepreneurship Program (PEP) works to "connect the nation's top executives, entrepreneurs, and MBA students with convicted felons."[59] The program offers an entrepreneurship boot camp for inmates, instructing them in basic business education and culminates in the awarding of a certificate from Baylor University. According to the PEP website, "The selection process begins when the Texas Department of Criminal Justice provides PEP with a list of inmates who are eligible to apply"[60] to the program. After this step, postcards are sent "to approximately 10,000 candidates inviting them to request an application" to the program. For the group that responds to the invitation, "PEP then sends a 20-page application that includes essay questions."[61] Typically "2,000 candidates will complete the applications and return them to PEP."[62] Once all completed applications are turned in, PEP staff then "carefully reviews the applications and selects the top 1,500 candidates."[63] This group of individuals "receives a study packet that includes the AP Writing Style Guide, PEP's Ten Driving Values, and a Basic Business Vocabulary reference."[64] After study packets are sent, a PEP official will visit the prison to conduct a short test, and each individual who scores 70 percent completes an in-person interview for PEP officials to decipher work ethic and chances of success.[65] After all these steps are completed, PEP will have "identified the top 450 to 500 men for the program."[66] These candidates are then transferred to "the Cleveland Unit near Houston, TX or the Estes Unit near Dallas, TX" where "they have a final round of interviews with in-prison program manager and our recently released graduates."[67]

[58] The LNP Editorial Board. "Program Helping the Children of Parents Incarcerated at Lancaster County Prison Does Important Work." *LancasterOnline*. March 06, 2016. Accessed September 28, 2017.
[59] "About Us." PEP. Accessed September 28, 2017. www.pep.org/about-us/.
[60] "Empowering Innovation." PEP. Accessed October 11, 2017. www.pep.org/empowering-nnovation/.
[61] Ibid.
[62] Ibid.
[63] Ibid.
[64] Ibid.
[65] Ibid.
[66] Ibid.
[67] Ibid.

The program is funded by the private sector and has a recidivism rate of less than seven percent.[68] In addition, program graduates have started over one hundred sixty-five businesses, with at least two grossing over 1 million dollars annually.[69]

PEP believes in instilling the posture of a fresh start in program participants with a "comprehensive solution to re-entry in a structured environment of accountability."[70] The program is guided by its overriding principle to "to serve all those with whom we come in contact, especially our participants."[71]

PEP is guided by ten principles, which include having a "servant-leader mentality," and placing on an emphasis on "innovation" and "accountability."[72] PEP actualizes its values by working with participants from the first moments they are released. Staff members from PEP "pick up participants at the release gate the minute they are released from prison."[73] Nearly "65 percent of PEP graduates choose to live in one of five transition homes managed by PEP in Houston and Dallas."[74] upon release.

After the transition process starts, PEP continues to provide resources to its participants in order to provide them with as much opportunity for future success and stability as possible. This includes "transportation, regular counseling and advice, a support network, social events and emergency financial assistance" and "access to bus passes, phone cards, reduced-cost dental services, medical services and eye exams/glasses through partnerships with other service providers."[75]

The aggregate of PEP graduates comprise the following statistics: "100 percent of PEP graduates are employed within 90 days of release from prison."[76] Program graduates "have an $11.50+ hour average starting wage and almost "100 percent of PEP graduates are still employed after 12 months."[77]

Prison University Project – San Quentin, California

In 2003 Prison University Project (PUP) was established to "provide material, administrative, and financial support to the College Program at San Quentin."[78] Today it provides quality educational opportunities to incarcerated individuals in order to prepare them for reentry by offering college level courses in prison.

---

[68] "PEP Results." PEP. Accessed September 28, 2017. www.pep.org/pep-results/.
[69] Raymond Tse, "Prison Entrepreneurship: A Program That Works." Tech.Co. 2015. Accessed August 09, 2016. http://tech.co/prison-entrepreneurship-program-works-2015-03.
[70] "Releasing Potential." PEP. Accessed September 28, 2017. www.pep.org/releasing-potential/.
[71] "10 Driving Values." PEP. Accessed September 28, 2017. www.pep.org/10-driving-values/.
[72] Ibid.
[73] "Releasing Potential." PEP. Accessed September 28, 2017. www.pep.org/releasing-potential/.
[74] Ibid.
[75] Ibid.
[76] "PEP Results." PEP. Accessed September 28, 2017. www.pep.org/pep-results/.
[77] Ibid.
[78] "ABOUT US." Prison University Project. Accessed September 28, 2017. https://prisonuniversityproject.org/about-us/our-mission/.

According to PUP's website, their "college program at San Quentin State Prison provides 20 intellectually rigorous courses each semester in the humanities, social sciences, math, and science, as well as intensive college preparatory courses in math and English."[79] In addition, "textbooks and school supplies are provided by ... [the] program and through donations from publishers."[80] PUP's staff "of 130 volunteers from universities like Stanford, UC–Berkeley, and San Francisco State are asked to teach the same way ... they would at their home institutions."[81]

The second pillar focuses on advocacy for continued success of PUP students. This includes "humanizing the image of incarcerated people in the public imagination, seeking a transformed criminal justice system, and developing leaders in the incarcerated community."[82] Advocacy for these initiatives is pursued in order to make a more permanent and enduring change in the public posture toward how those with criminal backgrounds are viewed.

Finally, PUP focuses on outreach and supports the expansion of similar programs nationwide. Through their Technical Assistance program, PUP "aims to develop a skilled, knowledgeable and professional community of higher education practitioners by offering resources and services that any college, university or prison can access"[83]

A 2015 National Public Radio article quoted PUP executive director Jody Lewen, saying, "In California, about 65 percent of released prisoners return to prison within three years, and the rate for PUP participants was 17 percent after three years, none was for a violent crime."[84]

Defy Ventures – New York City, New York

Catherine Hoke started Defy Ventures in New York City in 2004 with the mission to transform "the lives of business leaders and people with criminal histories through their collaboration along the entrepreneurial journey."[85] She wanted to place them

[79] "Education." Prison University Project. Accessed September 28, 2017. https://prisonuniversity project.org/what-we-do/education/.
[80] Ibid.
[81] Vincent J. Cannato, Barbara Will, Daniel Feller, Danny Heitman, and Steven Nadler. "Prison University Project." National Endowment for the Humanities. Accessed October 11, 2017. www.neh.gov/humanities/2016/fall/feature/prison-university-project.
[82] "Advocacy." Prison University Project. Accessed September 28, 2017. https://prisonuniversity project.org/what-we-do/advocacy/.
[83] "Outreach." Prison University Project. Accessed September 28, 2017. https://prisonuniversity project.org/what-we-do/outreach/.
[84] Westervelt, Eric. "Why Aren't There More Higher Ed Programs Behind Bars?" *NPR.* September 07, 2015. Accessed September 28, 2017. www.npr.org/sections/ed/2015/09/07/436342257/prison-university-project.
[85] "Our Mission." Defy Ventures Inc. Accessed September 28, 2017. https://defyventures.org/what-we-do/our-mission/.

into dialogue with one another in order to promote more stable and lasting employment for recently incarcerated individuals. By placing recently incarcerated individuals into community with business leaders, Defy aims to reduce recidivism and increase the long-term stability of those recently released from prison. The program harnesses "the innate entrepreneurial talents of people with criminal histories and … [redirects] them toward the creation of *legal* businesses and careers."[86] Defy contends that pairing "senior business executives, entrepreneurs, and other influencers with … EITs (people who formerly led drug rings and gangs)," will enable EITs "to become successful business owners, employers, parents and community leaders."[87]

Wired Magazine reported in 2015 that "so far the organization has incubated and funded more than one hundred new businesses with the help of venture capitalists, tech leaders, investment bank executives, and Fortune 500 managers."[88] In addition, it offers a "suite of services that includes intensive personal and leadership development, competition-based entrepreneurship training, executive mentoring, financial investment, and business incubation."[89] The goal is to prove those with a criminal record needed skills to compete and thrive in business and employment after being released from prison.

The organization also focuses on "engaging top corporate executives, investors, and entrepreneurs nationally," catalyzing "broad scale personal and economic opportunities for people with criminal histories, and shatters perceptions of one of the most stigmatized and overlooked populations in America."[90]

According to a recent report, as of February 2017, Defy has over 550 "formerly incarcerated Entrepreneurs-in-Training (EITs) across 24 states (majority in NY/CA),"[91] and currently serves (as of February 2017) "1,400+ currently incarcerated EITs across 25 correctional facilities."[92] Rates of recidivism for "EITs is less than 5 percent," graduates have procured financing for "over 165 startups … which created 350+ jobs in their communities," and "report an 83 percent income increase and 95 percent employment rate within 7 months of enrolling in Defy."[93]

---

[86] "Our Solution." Defy Ventures Inc. Accessed October 11, 2017. https://defyventures.org/what-we-do/our-solution/.

[87] "Our Mission." Defy Ventures Inc. Accessed September 28, 2017. https://defyventures.org/what-we-do/our-mission/.

[88] "Transforming the Incarcerated into Entrepreneurs." Wired.com. Accessed August 09, 2016. www.wired.com/brandlab/2015/10/transforming-the-incarcerated-into-entrepreneurs/.

[89] Ibid.

[90] Ibid.

[91] "Our Impact." Defy Ventures Inc. Accessed October 11, 2017. https://defyventures.org/what-we-do/our-impact/.

[92] Ibid.

[93] Ibid.

Prison-to-College Pipeline – New York, New York

The Prison-to-College Pipeline (P2CP) exists to help incarcerated individuals complete their college education upon their release. Baz Dreisinger, Professor at John Jay College, started the organization in 2011.[94] P2CP is affiliated with the Prison Reentry Institute at John Jay College in New York City. To be eligible for the program, applicants must meet specific qualifications: "(i) have their high school diplomas or GEDs; (ii) are eligible for release within five years; and (iii) pass City of New York (CUNY) reading and writing assessments, are evaluated based on written essays and interviews to determine admission in a competitive process."[95]

According to the organization's website, P2CP partners with John Jay College to bring "CUNY professors to Otisville Correctional Facility to teach accredited college courses in a variety of liberal arts disciplines including English, Sociology, Anthropology, and more."[96] The primary focus to bolster student's reading and writing skills is a critical aim of P2CP's work as these skills will be critical for employment success after being released. In addition to these classes, P2CP also offers an educational development program that augments participants reading, writing, and analytical skills for success in passing the CUNY Assessment Test.[97]

P2CP offers workshops "designed to support reentering students' successful transition into postsecondary education in the community."[98] This is done by providing support networks and encouraging students to build interpersonal skills critical for success in higher education. According to John Jay College, research indicates, "that prisoners who engage in higher education while incarcerated have lower return to custody rates and higher levels of employment and wages upon release."[99] This educational investment during an individual's time in prison is an "investment that results in cost savings through long term crime prevention."[100] The P2CP organization "provides prisoners with college level work in the three to five years prior to their release, which can be pivotal in making it more likely that someone will pursue educational opportunities when released and, ultimately, succeed in college and a career."[101] In its essence, the organization wishes to impart life-long educational

---

[94] "Prison-to-College Pipeline." Prisoner Reentry Institute. Accessed September 28, 2017. http://johnjaypri.org/educational-initiatives/prison-to-college-pipeline/.
[95] "How P2CP Works." Prisoner Reentry Institute. Accessed September 28, 2017. http://johnjaypri.org/educational-initiatives/prison-to-college-pipeline/how-p2cp-works.
[96] "How P2CP Works." Prisoner Reentry Institute. Accessed September 28, 2017. http://johnjaypri.org/educational-initiatives/prison-to-college-pipeline/how-p2cp-works.
[97] Ibid.
[98] Ibid.
[99] "Prison-to-College Pipeline." Prisoner Reentry Institute. Accessed October 11, 2017. http://johnjaypri.org/educational-initiatives/prison-to-college-pipeline/.
[100] Ibid.
[101] Ibid.

skills to inmates in the hopes that more education can prevent a return to prison by fueling opportunities for employment once released.

P2CP is composed of "a dynamic partnership between two major public institutions: the New York State Department of Corrections and Community Supervision (DOCCS) and CUNY, a public university system with a rich history of providing quality education to typically underserved communities."[102] Since starting in 2011, "P2CP has been delivering classes at the Otisville Correctional Facility, a medium security federal men's institution approximately two hours from New York City."[103]

According to John Jay College, "95 percent of P2CP students in the community are currently employed, enrolled in training programs, or working in internships."[104] More than "50 percent of released P2CP students have enrolled or are in the process of enrolling in college in the community,"[105] and only "12.5 percent P2CP students have been reincarcerated, compared to 42 percent statewide."[106]

Bard Prison Initiative – Hudson, New York

Started in 1999 by Max Kenner, Bard Prison Initiative (BPI) in New York "enrolls . . . incarcerated men and women across a full spectrum of academic disciplines."[107] BPI's website notes that the initiative was originally focused on organizing current Bard students to volunteer in local prisons as tutors.[108] However, "In 2001, BPI outgrew its role as a student organization and became an academic program of the College . . . and awarded the first Bard College degrees to incarcerated candidates" in 2005. Today, BPI "now operates a network of 6 satellite campuses across New York, engaging students up through their release and after."[109]

The Bard Prison Initiative is funded through private philanthropy and in 2009 it received a private grant that supported the creation of the Consortium for the Liberal Arts in Prison.[110] This Consortium has allowed BPI to help several colleges, including Wesleyan University in Connecticut, Grinnell College in Iowa, Goucher College in Maryland, the University of Notre Dame, and Holy Cross College in Indiana, replicate this in-prison college program.[111]

---

[102] "Prison-to-College Pipeline." Prisoner Reentry Institute. Accessed October 11, 2017. http://johnjaypri.org/educational-initiatives/prison-to-college-pipeline/.
[103] Ibid.
[104] "Higher Education and Reentry." Prisoner Reentry Institute. Accessed October 11, 2017. Available at: http://johnjaypri.org/wp-content/uploads/2016/09/P2CP-One-Pager-June-2016.pdf.
[105] Ibid.
[106] Ibid.
[107] "What We Do." Bard Prison Initiative. Accessed September 28, 2017. http://bpi.bard.edu/what-we-do/.
[108] "What We Do." Bard Prison Initiative.
[109] Ibid.
[110] Ibid.
[111] Ibid.

Classes in the liberal arts tradition, which are the same as those taken by regular undergraduate students at Bard College, are taught by the Bard faculty and professors from local, regional colleges and universities, Columbia University, and NYU.[112] According to Bard's website, "Through rigorous study in the humanities, sciences, and the arts, BPI students discover new strength and direction, often fundamentally rethinking their relationship to themselves, their communities, and the world in which we live."[113] By engaging students prior to their release from prison, and continuing afterwards, program participants return "home with confidence and hope … [and] are able to find and hold satisfying jobs in a range of fields."[114] Some participants of the program "go directly to work in the private sector or social services, while others pursue further education, enrolling in colleges and universities."[115]

According to a *Miami-Dade Matters* article, "The Bard Prison Initiative has expanded to offer college inside three long-term, maximum-security prisons and two transitional medium-security prisons."[116] The spotlight also cites BPI's recidivism rate at "approximately 4 percent."[117]

EX-OFFENDER RE-ENTRY

EDWINS Restaurant

Founded in 2007, EDWINS is a restaurant in Cleveland, Ohio, started by Brandon Chrostowski; it specializes in French cuisine and deliberately gives previously incarcerated individuals employment in the hopes of a more stable and prosperous reentry. "EDWINS Leadership and Restaurant Institute stands for 'Education Wins' and created … in order to make it, in Chrostowski's words, 'an everlasting, self-sustaining operation.'"[118] The recidivism rate of program graduates is only 1.2 percent.[119]

---

[112] "FAQs." Bard Prison Initiative. Accessed August 09, 2016. http://bpi.bard.edu/faqs/.
[113] Ibid.
[114] Ibid.
[115] Ibid.
[116] Matters, Miami-Dade. "Bard Prison Initiative." *Miami-Dade Matters*: Promising Practices: Bard Prison Initiative. Accessed October 11, 2017. www.miamidadematters.org/index.php?module=promisepractice&controller=index&action=view&pid=3215.
[117] Ibid.
[118] Joe Crea. "Edwins Restaurant, Outreach to Former Prisoners Returning to Workforce, Opening Nov. 1." Cleveland.com. October 22, 2013. Accessed October 11, 2017. www.cleveland.com/dining/index.ssf/2013/10/edwins_restaurant_outreach_to.html.
[119] "Edwins Restaurant in Cleveland Offers Ex-Offenders a New Start." Pastemagazine.com. Accessed October 11, 2017. www.pastemagazine.com/articles/2017/02/or-edwins-restaurant-in-cleveland-offers-ex-offend.html.

Nearly everyone on staff at EDWINS was previously incarcerated.[120] Chrostowski, an experienced chef who has worked in New York, Chicago, and Paris, aims to push against the stigma of employing those with a prison record. During his youth, he "spent a few days behind bars . . . for eluding an officer and he credits his success to a chef who mentored him despite his past."[121] It is this experience that showed him the critical importance of help upon release. According to *Paste Magazine*, "'he says it's about paying forward' the break he was given as a young adult in Detroit. He was received probation instead of a prison sentence. That 'aha' moment primed him to take stock, find a mentor and launch a fine-dining career that brought him to restaurants including Charlie Trotter's in Chicago, Lucas Carton in Paris and NYC's Le Cirque."[122]

His institute "is a 501(c)(3) organization that gives formerly incarcerated adults a foundation in the hospitality industry while providing a support network necessary for long-term success."[123] The specific aspects of his program focusing on reentry are "a six-month program conducted at EDWINS restaurant in Cleveland, Ohio as well as in prison."[124] Participants commit around forty-five hours a week to the program and learn "the essentials of high-end cuisine, from culinary math to wine selection, and then apply their new skills working in the restaurant."[125]

Chrostowski charges no cost to the participant in his institute. In fact, students receive "a stipend of about $300 every two weeks."[126] The point of the program is to "arm those reentering society with a skill set and a smile through training in Culinary Arts and the Hospitality Industry."[127] Participants also receive support and help procuring employment, have access to free housing, and receive medical care if needed. EDWINS now graduates around 100 participants each year from its institute.[128] Chrostowski wants program participants to have a fair chance at escaping

---

[120] Kathleen Toner. "Restaurant Gives Ex-Offenders a Recipe for Success." CNN. July 21, 2016. Accessed October 11, 2017. www.cnn.com/2016/03/17/us/cnnheroes-brandon-chrostowski-edwins-cleveland/index.html.

[121] Sarah Ruiz-Grossman. "Chef Who Spent Time in Jail Now Trains Other Ex-Offenders in Culinary Arts." *The Huffington Post*. June 30, 2016. Accessed October 11, 2017. www.huffington post.com/entry/brandon-chrostowski-edwins-leadership-restaurant-institute_us_576c53b3e4b017b379f564d9.

[122] "Edwins Restaurant in Cleveland Offers Ex-Offenders a New Start." Pastemagazine.com. Accessed October 11, 2017. www.pastemagazine.com/articles/2017/02/or-edwins-restaurant-in-cleveland-offers-ex-offend.html.

[123] "Our Mission." Edwins Leadership Restaurant. Accessed October 11, 2017. http://edwinsrestaurant.org/about-us/.

[124] Ibid.

[125] Sarah Ruiz-Grossman. "Chef Who Spent Time in Jail Now Trains Other Ex-Offenders in Culinary Arts." *The Huffington Post*. June 30, 2016. Accessed October 11, 2017. www.huffingtonpost.com/entry/brandon-chrostowski-edwins-leadership-restaurant-institute_us_576c53b3e4b017b379f564d9.

[126] Ibid.

[127] Ibid.

[128] Ibid.

the cycle of recidivism through his institute's job and skills training in the culinary and hospitality fields. However, participants do not exclusively receive culinary and hospitality skills.

Much of the work of the program begins while participants are still in prison. EDWINS prison program was inaugurated in 2011 in Ohio at Grafton Prison.[129] The aim of the prison program is to teach the most essential skills needed to be successful in the culinary industry, like "how to use knives, burners, [and] select wines."[130] These graduates "have gained employment in Cleveland's finest restaurants after finishing the program or after release from prison" and 95 percent of participants have gained employment after graduating.[131] The program has been so successful that Chrostowski "plans to expand with an EDWINS campus ... [that would include] a 30 bed apartment building and a fitness center and library."[132]

Thomas Lennon, a documentary filmmaker, featured EDWINS in his documentary *Knife Skills* after a chance meeting in New York City where Chrostowski told Lennon his idea for starting a restaurant in Ohio specifically for aiding recently released prisoners. Chrostowski was skeptical about media attention but saw a special opportunity to showcase EDWINS with Lennon. He believed Lennon was a "filmmaker not interested in ratings or celebrity attention" and gave him permission to film in his restaurant where he would produce a short documentary on the project started by Chrostowski.[133]

To enroll at EDWINS, participants must be at least eighteen years of age, but no education or employment experiences are required for matriculation. In addition, the organization never asks participants to disclose information pertaining to their arrest, sentencing, and incarceration. In addition, individuals from any geographic location can apply and matriculate, if accepted. These students are asked to provide their own transportations and lodging costs to travel to Cleveland. According to EDWINS website, if "you are ready to move forward, work hard, dedicate yourself and adhere to our strict attendance policy, you are welcome at EDWINS."[134]

The program has been so successful that the number of participants is growing alongside its campus size and in 2016, the EDWINS "launched a three-building Life

---

[129] Sarah Ruiz-Grossman. "Chef Who Spent Time in Jail Now Trains Other Ex-Offenders in Culinary Arts." *The Huffington Post*. June 30, 2016. Accessed October 11, 2017. www .huffingtonpost.com/entry/brandon-chrostowski-edwins-leadership-restaurant-institute_us_ 576c53b3e4b017b379f564d9.

[130] Ibid.

[131] "Our Mission." Edwins Leadership Restaurant. Accessed October 11, 2017. http://edwinsrestaur ant.org/about-us/.

[132] "About Us." Edwins Leadership & Restaurant. Accessed October 11, 2017. https://edwinsrestaur ant.org/about-us/brandon-edwin-chrostowski/.

[133] Marc Bona. "Edwins Beginnings in Shaker Square Captured in 'Knife Skills' Documentary." Cleveland.com. October 03, 2017. Accessed October 11, 2017. www.cleveland.com/entertain ment/index.ssf/2017/10/edwins_beginnings_in_shaker_sq.html.

[134] "Interested in Joining the EDWINS Program?" Edwins Leadership & Restaurant. Accessed October 11, 2017. https://edwinsrestaurant.org/interested-in-joining-the-edwins-program/.

Skills Center that includes a test kitchen, culinary library, fitness center and housing for students and alumni who may have nowhere else to go."[135]

At its zenith, however, EDWINS aims to be a stable, dependable, and encouraging network of support, buttressed by resources and case managers, for those facing the daunting challenges of reentry. Graduates are not only just learning food skills, they will be equipped with a passion and deeper understanding of the business and logistics aspects of the industry: "while participants indeed learn a perfect braise, they also get help with everything from reinstating their driver's license to securing medical care."[136]

Chrostowski understands the challenges of seeking employment after his experience with the justice system. Through EDWINS, he humanizes and equips individuals for successfully escaping the recidivism trap.

Homeboy Industries – California

Started in 1988 by Father Gregory Boyle of Los Angeles, Homeboy Industries brought together "a few caring business owners willing to hire former gang members."[137] They created the organization that has since become Homeboy Industries.

Formerly incarcerated individuals "are welcomed into a community of mutual kinship, love, and a wide variety of services ranging from tattoo removal to anger management and parenting classes."[138] In addition, "employment is offered for more than 200 men and women at a time through an 18-month program that helps them re-identify who they are in the world," according to Homeboy Industries' website.

The organization provides training programs, which give participants the ability to work in one of six social enterprises.[139] Homeboy Industries sustains itself through these social enterprises, which in 2016, was the source of 37 percent of the required operating funding.[140]

While the replications of this program differ according to the specific needs of the locality, the primary aim is that community and the dignity of honest work provide a worthwhile antidote to criminal ties. In addition, a study from

[135] "Edwins Restaurant in Cleveland Offers Ex-Offenders a New Start." Pastemagazine.com. Accessed October 11, 2017. www.pastemagazine.com/articles/2017/02/or-edwins-restaurant-in-cleveland-offers-ex-offend.html.
[136] Ibid.
[137] "History." Homeboy Industries. Accessed September 28, 2017. www.homeboyindustries.org/life-at-homeboy/history/.
[138] "Why We Do It." Homeboy Industries. Accessed September 28, 2017. www.homeboyindustries.org/why-we-do-it/.
[139] Homeboy Industries, 2016 Annual Report, 2016, http://homeboyindustries.org/hb_adm/img/news-events/HB-2016-AnnualReport.pdf.
[140] Ibid.

UCLA found that seventy percent of the former gang members who participate in the program do not recidivate.[141]

This training program allows participants to work in one of six social enterprises which include a bakery, grocery, and farmer's market. Homeboy Industries sustains itself through its social enterprises, which, in 2015, was the source of 40 percent of the needed funding, as well as fundraising events, private and corporate donations, and some government funding. In 2015 alone, over 9,200 people were helped, and more than 370 families were reunited. In addition, a study from UCLA found that 70 percent of the former gang members who participate in the program do not recidivate.

Father Gregory explains the success of the program by saying that Homeboy Industries "has been the tipping point to change the metaphors around gangs and how we deal with them in Los Angeles County."[142] He says that the "organization has engaged the imagination of 120,000 gang members and helped them to envision an exit ramp off the 'freeway' of violence, addiction and incarceration."[143] He also states that Homeboy Industries has "helped more than forty other organizations replicate elements of our service delivery model, broadening further the understanding that community trumps gang activity."[144]

Emerge Connecticut – New Haven, Connecticut

Emerge Connecticut provides transitional work for individuals recently incarcerated and on the path to reentry. According to their website, the "Community Offender Re-Entry Experience (C.O.R.E.) is ... [the] transitional employment component and it is the flagship program that makes EMERGE unique among Connecticut nonprofits."[145] Once being released and undergoing initial vetting, "participants are eligible to work up to six months, where they earn between $10 to $12 per hour, based on experience and performance."[146] Emerge places work into the lives of previously incarcerated individuals in order to prevent them from returning to prison and providing an opportunity to support themselves through wages.

Emerge has contracted with Urban Resource Initiative, a nonprofit affiliated with the Yale School of Forestry and Environmental Studies. Emerge "crewmembers" (the employed and formerly incarcerated workers) work together with Yale students

---

[141] Homeboy Industries, 2015 Yearbook, 2015, http://homeboyindustries.org/hb_adm/img/news-events/Homeboy_Yearbook_2015.pdf.
[142] "Why We Do It." Homeboy Industries. Accessed August 09, 2016. www.homeboyindustries.org/why-we-do-it/.
[143] Ibid.
[144] Ibid.
[145] "C.O.R.E. PROGRAM." C.O.R.E.. Skills. Accessed September 28, 2017. www.emergect.net/c-o-r-e-skills.
[146] Ibid.

to plant elm trees, replacing trees destroyed by Dutch elm disease.[147] Regarding the partnership, Colleen Murphy-Dunning, director of the Urban Resources Initiative, said that "the Yale students are just everyday people. They may be smart, but the Yale students are digging right alongside of [the Emerge employees]. I think it breaks down walls that exist in our society around race and economics. I think it's very powerful for both the guys from Emerge as well as the Yale students that are able to have these interactions."[148]

C.O.R.E. acknowledges that many individuals coming out of the criminal justice system have limited reading, writing, and math skills, which hurt their chances to gain meaningful employment. Emerge Connecticut's defining characteristic is its focus on developing participants literacy and numeracy skills as a means to combat this trend. C.O.R.E.'s mandatory literacy and numeracy program relies on an assessment that pinpoints specific areas of needed learning, individualized learning plans, free online math videos from Khan Academy, and individual tutoring by local volunteers.[149] In addition to the paid employment and learning program, Emerge Connecticut also hosts parenting classes and life coaching.[150]

Emerge hosts a weekly forum called *Real Talk*, where program participants take turns picking discussion topics relevant to them and reentry.[151] It also offers special workshops on parenting via "a partnership with the Fair Haven Community Health Center ... EMERGE supports parents and children in New Haven with the goal of preventing child maltreatment by strengthening families through reunification, fatherhood outreach and group support."[152] The organization offers a Trauma Informed Men's Group that "focuses on exploring the unresolved childhood traumas that play into behavior and attitudes as adults. This includes "Traumatic stress and Adverse Childhood Experiences (ACES) [which] are high among many who have been incarcerated, and this group raises awareness and offers strategies to navigate the feelings and behaviors associated with many of these issues."[153] As a result of these programs and the skills they are designed to develop, Emerge participants maintain a recidivism rate of only twelve percent.[154]

[147] Theresa Sullivan Barger. "Ex-Cons and Yale Students Team Up to Plant Trees." Courant.com. May 19, 2016. Accessed October 11, 2017. www.courant.com/new-haven-living/upfront/hc-nh-tree-planting-ex-convicts-and-yale-20160522-story.html.

[148] "Ex-Cons and Yale Students Team Up to Plant Trees."

[149] "Program." EMERGE Connecticut, Inc. Accessed August 09, 2016. www.emergect.net/program.html.

[150] "Our Philosophy." Accessed September 28, 2017. www.emergect.net/our-philosophy.

[151] "C.O.R.E. PROGRAM." C.O.R.E. Skills. Accessed September 28, 2017. www.emergect.net/c-o-r-e-skills.

[152] Ibid.

[153] Ibid.

[154] Ibid.

The Doe Fund – New York, New York

Founded in 1985, The Doe Fund works to transform the lives of individuals who have experienced "homelessness, incarceration, poverty, substance abuse, and HIV/AIDS."[55] Ready, Willing and Able (RWA) is the centerpiece of The Doe Fund's transitional work efforts – since 1990 transitioning "more than 22,000 men back into mainstream society after incarceration and homelessness."[56] It exists to bolster the chances of successful reentry for recently incarcerated individuals by placing them into stable employment and disincentivizing criminal activity.

Today, RWA serves more than 1,000 men from three different residential facilities located in New York City's Harlem neighborhood and Brooklyn borough.[57] According to RWA's website, after one month of stabilization after release from incarceration, participants begin "approximately seven months of paid work cleaning streets and sidewalks throughout New York City."[58] Participants continue to complete four to six "months of paid occupational training in one of several growth industries, including the culinary arts, commercial driving, pest control, building maintenance, and fleet management."[59] undertake required educational "classes throughout the program," which "cover a variety of essential skills, including adult literacy, financial management, relapse prevention, conflict resolution, and parenting (for those with children under 18)."[60]

In addition to these required courses, optional "opportunities are also available, including the chance to achieve high school equivalency diplomas and pursue post-secondary coursework and degrees."[61] This culminates in the final months of the program, when the participants are "connected with employment opportunities and assisted in applying for self-supported apartments."[62] Participants who complete Ready, Willing and Able's program "are 56 percent less likely to commit a violent crime three years later" and cut "the risk of future police contact by a third."[63]

The standards for conduct are very high within the program. Wages from work are deposited automatically into a savings account managed by RWA. Further, from the participant's first paycheck, they "must pay child support, set aside savings, and remit nominal fees for room and board."[64] In addition all "Ready,

---

[55] "About." History. Accessed September 28, 2017. www.doe.org/programs/ready-willing-able.
[56] Ibid.
[57] "Programs." Ready, Willing & Able. Accessed September 28, 2017. www.doe.org/programs/ready-willing-able.
[58] Ibid.
[59] Ibid.
[60] Ibid.
[61] Ibid.
[62] Ibid.
[63] Ibid.
[64] Ibid.

Willing & Able participants must abstain from substance and alcohol use and are drug tested randomly, twice a week."[165]

During the closing weeks of the program, participants are able to practice interview skills via mock interviews that include individuals from corporate backgrounds. The program's graduate services department, which is on campus, connects participants with employment opportunities through its network of over 400 employer connections. After their first year is over upon graduating, RWA contributes $1,000 in installments as part of its savings matching grant. These payments are only disbursed from RWA if a graduate has met with their caseworker and had adequate updates on their employment and living status as well as compliance with no criminal activity. An installment is paid only when a graduate checks in with their caseworker and reports on their employment, housing, and criminal justice status.

Changing Together – Asheville, North Carolina

In 2011, "community members, faith leaders, law enforcement and human service agencies"[166] came together in Buncombe County, North Carolina, to focus on the small percentage of the population committing violent and serious crime. Changing Together is a "project of The SPARC Network, a nonprofit with branches in Charlotte and Asheville ... [and] works in partnership with local law enforcement."[167] The efforts came to be "known as Asheville-Buncombe Violent Crime Initiative (VCI)" and "applies the principles of Focused Deterrence, a violence reduction strategy developed by David Kennedy of John Jay College of Criminal Justice in order to reduce recidivism rates of violent crimes by the few select individuals most responsible for their occurrence."[168] The program seeks a local amelioration of the problem with those who have a record of, or proclivity to violent crime in the area. The solution, according to Changing Together, rests in placing the offender into contact with key neighborhood personnel placing community authority personnel into contact with offenders in order to build trust, open communication, and to clearly convey the devastating consequences of committing crime and offer reasons for abiding by the law.

According to VCI's website "offenders are invited to a Call-In where VCI participants complete a needs assessment and listen to a specific message from a panel of community members, clergy, law enforcement and others discuss the main message of focused deterrence to the invited individuals."[169] After these initial steps,

[165] Ibid.
[166] "Programs." Changing Together. Accessed September 28, 2017. http://thesparcfoundation.org/.
[167] Boyd, Leslie. "Changing Together gives Felons Second Chance." Mountain Xpress. Accessed October 11, 2017. https://mountainx.com/news/changing-together-gives-felons-second-chance/.
[168] Ibid.
[169] Ibid.

"Participants are then asked to never commit a violent trigger crime again and are introduced to … the Life-Skills programs that Changing Together offers and Changing Together staff including dedicated case managers."[170] A North Carolina news outlet captured Tim Splain, a Changing Together staffer, speaking about the program in 2016. Splain says, "'We ask them not to commit any more violent crime, and then we offer to help them,' continues Splain. 'It's very stick-and-carrot: The violence has to stop, and we're here to help you.'"[171]

According the programs director in 2016, "'It's hard to ask people to stop violent behavior and then send them out with a piece of paper with some phone numbers. You have to connect them to what they need.'"[172]

The organization attempts to take a holistic approach to solving local crime: "Changing Together and the VCI also houses a Domestic Violence Focused Deterrence strategy to make sure that offenders who are convicted of domestic violence crimes and placed on probation are receiving instruction and education about breaking cycles of violence within themselves and their family systems."[173]

In Asheville and Buncombe County, program participants "have had an 82 percent success rate … [as] in 82 percent of the folks that have been called in have not committed another violent crime since."[174]

POLICY/ADVOCACY

Pennsylvania Prison Society – Philadelphia, Pennsylvania

Started in 1787, the Pennsylvania Prison Society promotes humane and restorative jail conditions as it serves thousands of inmates, returning citizens, and their family members.[175] Its services include transportation for visitation, parenting classes, and a Prisoner Reentry Network that helps both local agencies and returning citizens.[176]

The organization also advocates for policy changes. For example, since 1990 when the Pennsylvania General Assembly guaranteed Prison Society Official Visitors access to all Pennsylvania correctional facilities, more than four hundred volunteer Official Visitors make approximately three thousand visits to jails and prisons each year.[177] According to the organization, "The cornerstone of the Society's work is a

[170] Ibid.
[171] Ibid.
[172] Ibid.
[173] "Programs." Changing Together. Accessed September 28, 2017. http://thesparcfoundation.org/.
[174] Ibid.
[175] "Pennsylvania Prison Society." Pennsylvania Prison Society. Accessed September 28, 2017. www.prisonsociety.org/about_us.
[176] Ibid.
[177] "Pennsylvania Prison Society." Pennsylvania Prison Society. Accessed August 09, 2016. www.prisonsociety.org/#!prisoner-advocacy/c236c.

network of volunteers, known as Official Visitors, who visit prisoners throughout Pennsylvania."[178] State law "authorizes the Prison Society to designate volunteers to visit any prison or jail in the Commonwealth. Prison Society volunteers (i.e. Official Visitors) have authority to privately interview any inmate in any prison or jail for any reason."[179]

During these visits, they talk to inmates about their concerns and complaints. This program helps hold correctional facilities responsible in the hopes of lowering instances of abuse and negligence, while bringing attention to issues like under-funding and overcrowding.

According to its website, "The Society is the oldest organization in the country dedicated to sensible and humane criminal justice."[180] It "advocates for systemic policy change, responds to the concerns of inmates and their families, provides subsidized bus service for Philadelphia families visiting loved ones incarcerated in different parts of the state, and provides assistance to individuals returning home from incarceration."[181]

In addition to visits, "The program helps prepare incarcerated individuals for successful re-entry mentally, emotionally, and logistically" through its workshop series on topics directly relevant for reentering individuals. Participants receive mentors and agree to meet for "at least six months to develop and achieve a personalized goal plan.[182]

Root and Rebound – Oakland, California

Root and Rebound (RAR) was started in 2014 by a team of lawyers in order to "reduce the devastating impacts of collateral consequences, and help clients navigate a complicated system that they were not at all prepared for during incarceration."[183] The founders behind RAR believed that if understanding the legal complexities were difficult for them, the average citizen could not be expected to navigate such convoluted nuances during most phases of the criminal justice process.

After fourteen months of research, Root and Rebound published the *Roadmap to Reentry: A California Legal Guide* which is designed to be "an easy-to-use navigation tool covering the major barriers in reentry intended for a broad audience," including "people preparing for reentry as well as their families, social workers and case

---

[178] Pennsylvania Prison Society." Pennsylvania Prison Society. Accessed September 28, 2017. www.prisonsociety.org/about_us.
[179] Ibid.
[180] Ibid.
[181] Ibid.
[182] Ibid.
[183] "Mission and Vision." Root & Rebound. Accessed September 28, 2017. www.rootandrebound .org/mission-and-vision/.

managers, teachers, community supervision officers, and attorneys."[184] The roadmap is over one-thousand pages in length and "covers the major barriers in reentry in nine areas of law and civic life: housing, public benefits, parole & probation, education, understanding & cleaning up your criminal record, ID & voting, family & children, court-ordered debt, and employment."[185]

In addition to the published guide and other printed resources, RAR also operates a hotline where callers can seek advice as they navigate the legal challenges of reentry; through participation in coalitions and advocacy groups in California and nationally, Roots and Rebound advocates for better reentry policies at the federal, state, and local levels.[186]

In its essence, RAR aims to help those reentering society after being incarcerated to fill the information gap about questions regarding achieving normalcy. The guide encourages individuals to be forward looking and equips them with knowledge on topics and questions that are often difficult and nuanced.

By codifying these answers, RAR supports all those reentering with the necessary information needed to be successful in the long term. It also allows individuals to understand their background more clearly and guides them on what they can do to ensure a past conviction and any criminal record will not prove to be a hurdle for employment, housing, and other essential aspects of daily living.

CONCLUSION

In order for criminal justice reform to be effective, civil-society institutions must not only be invited to make contributions to the discourse on solutions, they need to be mobilized for action in local communities to reduce the number of people incarcerated. Personalism calls for an ever-increasing presence of civil-society institutions fill in the gaps where the state fails so that the real needs of the human person are met. Therefore, every state needs more and more institutions like the church, nonreligious nonprofits, and specific programs to complete the work that government agencies are not equipped or intended for. While criminal laws and adjudication procedures are reimagined to reduce prisoner numbers, it will be the work of civil society institutions to keep offender numbers dropping and bring the type of cultural change needed to end mass incarceration.

Solutions are plentiful, and evidence of effectiveness is abundant. With a collective determination to increase the application of proven methods, this national

[184] Ibid.
[185] "Root & Rebound Offers Help to People with Criminal Records Attempting to Overcome Legal Barriers." Root & Rebound. Accessed September 28, 2017. www.rootandrebound.org/news-1/2016/5/3/root-rebound-offers-help-to-people-with-criminal-records-attempting-to-overcome-legal-barriers.
[186] "Our Model for Change." Root & Rebound. Accessed September 28, 2017. www.rootandrebound.org/model-for-change.

wound of overcriminalization will heal. When the community engages with good intentions to help their fellow human, the outcome is markedly better. It is these conclusions which must finalize the argument that methodically comprehensive reform must be applied to every facet of every criminal justice system in every state. Each broken system can be improved. We need more people creatively developing more solutions like the ones listed in this chapter if we truly want effective criminal justice reform. These institutions provide us hope for sustainable change.

Conclusion

Evidence has grown within the scientific and academic world about the human dynamic and optimization of social and individual productivity. The biosocial and psychological factors of crime directly point to a personalist-like approach to criminal justice reform. Modernizing the criminal justice system to become operationally efficient is actually a discourse about the best way to reform and develop individual persons who are interdependent and connected to our communities. The inviolable nature of our humanity includes the guarantee of imperfection, corruption, and deviance – nobody's perfect. In addition to the necessary role of reforming the role of institutions, we must remember that the human organism is at the center. The roles of criminal justice professionals are just as important as family, education, and civil society organizations. Key leaders and thinkers from all spaces across the community must be included in all reforms so that changing criminal justice policy and procedure can actually create the conditions for well-being, thriving, and human flourishing. The occurrence of deviant criminal activities represents a complex matrix of causal variables that require an "all hands on deck" approach if we are to make any progress towards solving the problem.

Civil society institutions matter in the community, courtroom, and prison, and are ground zero for changing the criminal justice system. Many argue that civil society institutions have broken down, leading to economic deprivation and loss of individual freedoms with strong correlations between marginalization from the marketplace, the crumbling of community institutions and increases in deviance and criminal activity.

From a personalist perspective, the requirement of our communities is to create a context that appropriately mediates between punishment and restoration of the person so they can contribute to the community. A system that brings justice to victims seriously recognizes that some offenders are good candidates to receive aggressive rehabilitation, mercy, and a second chance. To do this effectively and humanely, we need to understand basic human interests, motivations, and social needs. Christian Smith is helpful; by "basic," Smith means a motivation "that generates actions intended to produce a result that is valued for its own sake. The ends of basic motivations are taken to be goods of intrinsic and fundamental value, not merely instrumental goods that serve some other more primary purpose or benefit."[1] After synthesizing various accounts of basic human needs, drives, desires, interests, values, and goods from scholars such as H. A. Murray, Jacob Alsted, Erich Fromm, Jonathan Turner, Susan Fiske, Abraham Maslow, Edward Deci and Richard Ryan, Maureen Ramsay, Manfred Max-Neef, Kai Nielson, Ervin Staup, Paul Lawrence, Michael Argyle, Steven Reiss, Roy Baumeister, Martin Ford, Marth Nausbam, Carol Ryff, Mozaffar Qizilbash, James Griffin, and John Finnis, Smith proposed six distinct basic, natural human goods and interests as follows:

1. *Bodily Survival, Security, and Pleasure*: avoiding bodily death, injury, sickness, disease, and sustained vulnerability to harm; maintaining physical and bodily health and safety; sensual enjoyment, satisfaction, delight, or gratification of appetitive and perceptual desires of the body, and the absence of physical pain and suffering.

2. *Knowledge of Reality*: learning about the world and one's place and potential in it; increasing awareness and understanding of material and social realities; developing or embracing believed-in truths about what exists and how it works that provide order, continuity, and practical know-how to life experience.

3. *Identity Coherence and Affirmation*: developing and maintaining continuity and positive self-regard in one's sense of personal selfhood over time and in different contexts and situations.

4. *Exercising Purposive Agency*: exerting influence or power (broadly understood as transformative capacity) in the social and material worlds, through the application of personal capabilities for perception, reflection, care, evaluation, self-direction, decision, and action, which causes desired (and unanticipated) effects in one's environment.

5. *Moral Affirmation*: believing that one is in the right or is living a morally commendable life, by being, doing, serving, thinking, and feeling what is good, correct, and admirable; avoiding moral fault, blame, guilt, or culpability.

6. *Social Belonging and Love*: enjoying recognition by, inclusion and member-ship in, and identification with significant social groups; loving and being loved by others in significant relationships.[2]

Smith recommends that these be view as a sociological "periodic table" of sorts that provide the building blocks for human life much like in the biological sciences. We know that life on earth would cease to exist without carbon, hydrogen, oxygen, phosphorus, and sulfur. By extension, human flourishing will not happen without Smith's six minimal elements. The implications of this concept on criminal justice reform point us to deeper more comprehensive questions beyond simply reducing

[1] Smith, *Flourish*, 159.
[2] Smith, *Flourish*, 162–182. Italics his.

prison numbers and procedural justice. These six motivations help us construct new imaginations regarding what it means to keep the human person as the center of our criminal justice system. They help us clarify that if criminal justice reform is going to be effective, based on what it means to be human, criminal law cannot do the heavy lifting alone. Effective, sustainable criminal justice reform requires acceptance of the fact that ending overcriminalization and mass incarceration demands that we take seriously the realities of human deviance and systemic/structural dehumanizing. A criminal justice system that is primarily concerned with criminal procedure rather than the personhood of victims and offenders create incentives which lead to over incarceration. Civil society institutions provide much needed hope because, as Smith maintains, people's natural motivations are always mediated through culture, motivated human actions are always facilitated, governed, and constrained by the ordering causal powers of social institutions and structures, and, finally, human motivations for action are also always mediated at the level of personality through specific structures of personal beliefs, desires, and emotions.[3] The most effective method of reforming the criminal justice system is unlocking the civil-society institutions that best provide context for the six basic differentiated natural human goods, interests, and motivations to flourish.

First, *bodily survival, security, and pleasure.* Taking bodies seriously, because offenders are persons, helps us reimagine the sorts of interventions that can reduce the number of people entering the criminal justice system in the first place. These include the basics like food, water, and shelter. One of the great weapons against deviance and criminal activity in gainful, humanizing long-term employment that provides opportunities for people to learn, grow, and advance. Taking bodies seriously also challenges us to think about the limitations of policy to address certain kinds of issues. For example, the causes and solutions to juvenile delinquency continue to be a mystery for those involved in the juvenile justice system.[4]

We live in a culture with fairly widespread levels of juvenile delinquency. According to the Juvenile Offenders and Victims: 2014 National Report issued by the National Center for Juvenile Justice, 33 percent of high school students said they had been in one or more physical fights during the past twelve months.[5] In fact, the report continues to reveal troubling statistics about delinquency behavior among juveniles: Nationwide, 12 percent of high school students had been in a physical fight on school property one or more times in the twelve months; nearly half (48 percent) of all seniors said they had at least tried illicit drugs; 44 percent of high school seniors

---

[3] Smith, *Flourish*, 188–189.
[4] The next phase of the application of personalism to criminal justice reform will be to unpack the implications of all six of these human goods for effective criminal justice reform. The detailed psychological application I provide for the first stated good only serves as an example of the direction and solutions a personalist perspective brings to the surface.
[5] Melissa Sickmund and Charles Puzzanchera. *Juvenile Offenders and Victims: 2014 National Report.* Pittsburgh, PA: National Center for Juvenile Justice, 2014.

said they had tried marijuana; seven in ten high school seniors said they had tried alcohol at least once; and two in five said they used alcohol in the previous month.

Based on the 2012 National Youth Gang Survey (NYGS), there were an estimated 30,700 gangs and 850,000 gang members throughout 3,100 jurisdictions with gang problems (down from 3,300 in 2011) (National Gang, 2012). The report explains that gang-related homicides are on the rise. For example, the number of reported gang-related homicides increased 20 percent from 1,824 in 2011 to 2,363 in 2012 (National Gang, 2012). The survey reports that approximately 85 percent of gangs are in larger cities, 50 percent of suburban counties, and 15 percent of rural counties. With a male population of 92.6 percent, juveniles account for 35 percent of gang membership (National Gang, 2012). Gangs generally commit crimes like aggravated assault (34.6 percent), firearms use (34.1 percent), drug sales (30.4 percent), robbery (30.8 percent), burglary/breaking and entering (22.8 percent), motor vehicle theft (21.5 percent), and larceny/theft (21.0 percent).

These are the types of juvenile delinquent behaviors that result in being taking into custody by law enforcement. According to the Survey of Youth in Residential Placement (SYRP) there are approximately 101,040 juvenile ten- to twenty-year-olds in custody for the types of delinquent behaviors mentioned above and more. According to the survey, the greatest percentages of youth crime reported property offenses (45 percent), person offenses (43 percent), and status offenses (42 percent). For these juvenile offenders who commit such acts resulting in being taken into custody, researchers have been attempting to isolate the variables that might be cause for such behavior to reduce incarceration and juvenile offender recidivism rates, especially as it relates to juvenile delinquency to adult prison pipeline. With an understanding of what causes delinquent behavior, rehabilitation strategies can be developed for implementation during custody to put juveniles in the best position to habituate prosocial behaviors upon release.

SENSORY DEPRIVATION, NEGLECT, AND DELINQUENCY

Research has shown the sensory neglect and early childhood neglect risk factors for aggression and violence in youth and children.[6] Some researchers highlight that criminal justice systems often overlook the role of child welfare. Most of the research highlights the role of abuse, although 78 percent of child protection services cases are neglect. When juveniles are both in the child welfare system and juvenile court system they are under more scrutiny and are more likely to be rearrested. Research shows that neglect impairs cognitive functioning, which makes neglected juveniles more likely to get trapped in cycles of reoffending.

[6] Joseph P. Ryan, Abigail B. Williams, and Courtney, Mark E. Adolescent Neglect, "Juvenile Delinquency and the Risk of Recidivism." *Journal of Youth and Adolescence*, 42(3) (2013): 454–465.

There is a strong association between parental neglect and later delinquency. Research shows that variables like the role of parental separations, disorganized and chaotic homes, marital harmony and father involvement, and parental supervision are predictors of delinquency. The study concluded that parental separations and disorganized homes showed the greatest impact compared to other variables. Chaotic and leaderless home environments were particularly linked to future delinquent activity in juveniles and adults. These environments also negatively affected the development of prosocial peer skills. According research reviewed by Logan-Green and Jones, several studies have found that children who had been neglected were at greater risk for juvenile drug and alcohol offenses and other juvenile offenses and aggressive or violent behavior in adolescence, as well as later involvement with criminal justice systems as adults, compared to those who had not suffered neglect.[7]

INTERVENTIONS

Massage therapy has been shown to alleviate pain, increase alertness, reduce stress symptoms, and reduce stress hormones. Child abuse has increased in Sweden likely due to changes in family structure, exposure to violence, and parental drug abuse. In daycare settings, aggressive behavior in boys has become a particular problem. The study investigated the effects of massage over a longer period of time than previous studies. The study was conducted on 110 four- to five-year-olds at daycare centers in two different cities. The massages lasted from five to ten minutes. Researchers studied massage therapy as a protective intervention against future aggression in juveniles in grades 9–12. Aggression is associated with acting out in hostility, fear, anger, and violence. Because aggression is generally not treated as a disorder there are no effective strategies for reducing its onset in high frequency. This study found that daily massages of aggressive children over a six-month period resulted in decreases in aggression and social problems, and overall, massaged children improved their behavior in their respective daycare settings. The greatest change in aggression occurred in the three- to six-month time frame. Six months after the study concluded – that is, one year after massages were initiated – the massage group continued to show decreases in aggression.

Diego et al. issued a report that massage therapy has been shown to be successful at reducing stress and depression, where researchers studied its effects on highly aggressive teens.[8] In one study group of violent teens were given twenty-minute chair massages for five weeks. A control group watched relaxation videos. At the end of five weeks, the massage group reported fewer feelings of aggression

[7] P. Logan-Greene and A. Jones, "Chronic Neglect and Aggression/Delinquency: A Longitudinal Examination." *Child Abuse and Neglect* 45(2015) : 9.
[8] M. Diego, T. Field, M. Hernandez-Reif, J. Shaw, E. Rothe, D. Castellanos, D. and L. Mesner, "Aggressive Adolescents Benefit from Massage Therapy." *Adolescence*, 37(147), (2002): 597–607.

and hostility. Their parents also reported less aggression after the study was completed. The control group showed no change.

In another study reported by Field, thirty-minute back massages were given over a five-day period to fifty-two institutionalized adolescents with conduct disorders.[9] In the posttest phase of the study, the control group, who watched relaxation videos, showed no change while the massage group reported being less depressed and less anxious, displaying lower cortisol levels (the stress hormone), and experiencing better sleep patterns. Nurses also observed that the adolescents were less aggressive and more cooperative by the end of the study.

IMPLICATIONS FOR JUVENILES IN CUSTODY

Research seems to point to a link between early childhood maltreatment and juvenile delinquency.[10] The types of delinquent behaviors that are associated with touch privation are the ones that normally result in juveniles being taken into custody. While increasing empathy, massage therapy seems to also be immediately effective in lowering aggression and violent behaviors in children and adolescents. Touch therapy needs to be added as a basic rehabilitative model. While treatment models usually include some form of insight-based therapy, behavior therapy, cognitive-behavioral therapy, group programs, and substance abuse interventions have their respective merits, and if 78 percent of abuse cases are neglect and deprivation cases, touch therapy may prove more promising and more effective as a treatment model in the juvenile justice process. Sensory deprivation and neglect are strong predictors of aggression, low impulse control, and violence. It is strategically important to address the sensory needs as a means for facilitating greater treatment success. More touch studies are needed with greater populations in custody to test the generalizability and applicability of previous research.

Juveniles are persons and have basic human motivations, it stands to reasons then that sensory neglect is correlated with deviance and early incarceration because, as Smith proposes, a basic human good is "bodily survival, security, and pleasure." Changing sentencing laws, keeping prosecutors accountable, giving judges more discretion, and the like will not directly address the physical needs of offenders (and

---

9 Tiffany Field, " Violence and Touch Deprivation in Adolescents." *Adolescence*, 37(148), (2002): 735–49.

10 Yu-Ling Chiu, Joseph P. Ryan, and Denise C Herz, "Allegations of Maltreatment and Delinquency: Does Risk of Juvenile Arrest Vary Substantiation Status?" *Children and Youth Services Review*, 33(6), (2011): 855; C. Mallett, "Youthful Offending and Delinquency: The Comorbid Impact of Maltreatment, Mental Health Problems, and Learning Disabilities." *Child and Adolescent Social Work Journal*, 31(4), (2014): 369–392, Ilhong Yun, Jeremy D Ball, and Hyeyoung Lim, "Disentangling the Relationship between Child Maltreatment and Violent Delinquency: Using a Nationally Representative Sample." *Journal of Interpersonal Violence*, 26(1), (2011): 88–110.

preoffenders) who often find themselves participating in deviant behavior in response to sensory neglect. An ideal criminal justice reform objective is to enlist institutions in society that are best at meeting basic human needs like bodily survival, security, and pleasure in order to keep people out of prison, humanize incarcerated prisoners, and keep ex-offenders from re-offending. Additional partners to the parole and probation process need to be maximized in order to sustain the lowest number of incarcerated men, women, and youth as possible while maintaining public safety.

The relationship between sensory neglect and deprivation naturally point to the need for thriving families.[11] While it is true that family provides an important as aspect of how children rationally bind themselves to the prosocial norms of society it is also true that those bonds are habituated and reinforced physically through warmth or trauma. Can government policy make parents more physically and emotionally available for their children in order to stave off deviance? Is sensory neglect and touch deprivation properly resolved by our penal system? Do government programs have a proven success record in this area? Why is it that we assume a government policy can effectively address something so intimate and personal? A personalist perspective relies on and invites civil society organizations into the solution matrix, with government agencies stepping aside to allow those institutions to be truly effective. If affectionate touch thwarts aggression and deviance, there is a responsible way to see that this happens in the homes of America's children as well as for children in the foster care system.

Second, *Knowledge of Reality*. The connections here to civil society are obvious when it comes to thinking about education. We will not have criminal justice reform without education reform targeted toward the truly disadvantaged. The school-to-prison pipeline must be completely dismantled, not from the policy down but from the person up. The needs of children and their families must be above desires to have a preferred ideologically driven public policy initiative. Building an education system from the person up requires accepting the fact that education outcomes, regardless of relative socioeconomic status is largely dependent on the structure and stability of families and participation in virtue forming institutions like the church. More funding to low-performing schools does not itself address the core issues that allow the school-to-prison pipeline to thrive – issues like the breakdown of the family and lack of bonds to social stabilizing institutions in disadvantaged neighborhoods.

Third, *Identity Coherence and Affirmation*. The critical question is: In what institutions in society do people first discover what it means to be human? In the American context there are three spaces where children first experience positive

---

[11] Cusick, G. R., Havlicek, J. R., and Courtney, M. E., "Risk for Arrest: The Role of Social Bonds in Protecting Foster Youth Making the Transition to Adulthood." *The American Journal of Orthopsychiatry*, 82(1), (2012): 19–31. See also Jonathan Intravia, "The Roles of Social Bonds, Personality, and Rational Decision-Making: An Empirical Investigation into Hirschi's "New" Control Theory" (2009). Graduate Theses and Dissertations.

self-regard: (1) the family and familial-like social networks like vulnerable friend-ships; (2) value-forming institutions like schools, churches, clubs, etc.; and (3) co-curricular and extracurricular activities like involvement in the art, music, and sports. When there are gaps in desirable affirmation, the community must have the resources and flexibility to address the development of the full human, so that disadvantage will dissipate.

Fourth, *Exercising Purposive Agency.* The exercise of agency is lived out in the family and social networks, value-forming institutions, co-curricular and extracurri-cular activities, and especially in the marketplace. Those who are disadvantaged must be connected to mediums of exchange in the marketplace so they can sustain themselves and their families financially. The world of work allows people's lives to make a difference in the world. Each individual's gifts, interests, decisions, and actions bring about a tangible effect in the immediate sphere of influence. For children, purposive agency is first exercised within the family and then school. When families thrive, so does the purposive agency of those in the community from those families.

Fifth, *Moral Affirmation.* Morals matter and values matter. In our earnest resolve to free American society from the influence of religion we have opened our culture up to a form of moral relativism that reduces virtue to the utility of the pursuit of personal moral autonomy as long as it avoids harming another. The West is heavily influenced in the politics and social life of Judeo-Christian traditions. In our pluralistic, multicultural society, from where do we derive our values that encourage us to care about our neighbors? From where do we foster this type of reciprocity? David Schimidtz argues, "when people reciprocate, they teach people around them to cooperate. In the process, they not only respect justice, but also foster it. Specifically, they foster a form of justice that enables people to live together in mutually respectful peace." Understanding reciprocity this way is vital for creating the right kinds of conditions that will reduce deviance and crime. Schmidtz observes that reciprocity requires the types of relationships that do not exhaust the demands of justice but provide an essential thread to the fabric of a virtuous community.[12] The clearest expression on the principle is articulated as "transitive reciprocity."[13] Personalism values this type of reciprocity because it fosters the type of community solidarity that ennobles mutual human dignity from the person up. Schmidtz describes it this way:

> When a teacher helps us, we are grateful. However, it is both odd and ordinary that we acknowledge debts to teachers mainly by passing on benefits to those whom we can help as our teachers helped us. I call this transitive reciprocity. Having received unearned windfall. We are in debt. The moral scales are out of balance. The canonical way to restore a measure of balance is to return the favor to our

[12] Scdmidtz, 81.
[13] Ibid., 82.

benefactor, as per symmetrical reciprocity. However, the canonical way is not the only way. Another way is to pass the favor on, as per transitive reciprocity. Transitive reciprocity is less about returning a favor and more about honoring it – doing justice to it. Passing the favor on may not repay an original benefactor, but is can be a way of giving thanks.[14]

There will be no effective long-term criminal justice reform without teaching the values that foster reciprocity and allowing civil institutions to inculcate those values so every citizen can thrive and flourish. People will not be motivated to "pay it forward" with a moral defense for added value to oneself in caring for our neighbors.

Perhaps there is a need to retrieve formation in the cardinal virtues within value-shaping institutions, especially in those areas where people are geographically and socially isolated from social contexts that value, affirm, reinforce, and celebrate Aristotle's four cardinal virtues: prudence, justice, temperance, and fortitude. Personalism wants to invite civil society institutions to teach virtues; people matter more than ideology. The best crime control and criminal justice reform mechanism available to us is a society that is more virtuous. The practice of virtue fosters a type of reciprocity that dismantles deviance, changes police practice, restructures corrections, and provides the foundation for successful and sustainable reentry. Using shame and guilt as a means of deterrence from deviance and crime will never be as successful as the practice and habits of reciprocated virtue of the common good.

John Rawls incorrectly presents an account of human motivations that leave no direction to guide our conceptions of well-being. The social sciences falsely believed that Rawlsian conceptions of justice can do all the justificatory work. With Rawls there is no longer a normative account of justice as proper order.[15] Personalism provides an account of justice that take human motivations and needs seriously, then proposes methods to accommodate the accompanying realities. Personalism challenges the notion that public policy and government programs are the most effective means to operationalize virtue and inspire transitive reciprocity. This is the work of civil society institutions.

Finally, *Social Belonging and Love*. There is no public policy that can incentivize the type of connection and love needed for human flourishing. By extension, there will be no effective long-term criminal justice reform until our society retrieves an emphasis on love fueled by belonging and connection. Loving and being loved is a need that all humans have. Abuse and neglect can make the search for love and being loved vulnerable to deviance and crime. Smith is right to point out that social scientist are working from a flawed view of human nature that ignores the importance of love. Criminological theories that fail to take the role of love into account also fail to point people in the most helpful and effective direction. Criminal justice

[14] Ibid., 83.
[15] Thanks to my colleagues Joshua Blander for this insight on the limitations of Rawls.

reform must consider humans as fundamentally interest-driven and concerned with the basic goods of personhood. Implementation of punishment needs a better account in light of human personhood.

HUMAN FLOURISHING AND PUNISHMENT

For Smith, personalism says that there is larger framework or purpose within which the intersection of the six basic goods described as "the flourishing of human personhood."[16] The starting point of criminal justice reform, "concerns the proper human telos: to flourish as the kind of beings that we are *as persons*."[17] The features and capacities of what it means to be human come with constraints and limitations but it does not limit the possibility of flourishing. A flourishing life is achieved when we are free to be truly human. We flourish when we are free to grow, learn, develop, and realize our "potentials, powers, capacities (and limitations)" in connectional relationships with other people.[18] Smith astutely observes, "that we cannot thrive without truly and genuinely seeking the thriving of other people."[19] How do we embed this reality into our curtailing of deviance, into our offender intake procedures, into the courtroom, into jails and prisons, and into how we construct our systems of probation and parole? Smith argues:

> Virtues are hard-won dispositions and practices of excellence that lead to a flourishing, truly happy life. Virtues are not naïve or innocent or smug. They are difficult and experienced and satisfying. Learning and practicing virtues demands discipline and practice, which pays off in human excellence.[20]

What do we do with people, namely offenders, who take actions that ultimately undermine or destroy the flourishing of others? We must get a better understanding of what criminals deserve.

Beyond the classic distinctions between punishment as deterrence, retribution, or rehabilitative, different conceptions of what criminals deserve must be addressed. Douglas Husak believes that we need to wrestle with how we morally and philosophically justify punishments given to offenders. Husak believes that we need to distinguish between two important questions, (1) What do criminals deserve? and (2) Should the state actually treat criminals as they deserve?[21] According to Husak:

> On my view, deserving may be all that is needed to justify punishment in a divine realm, but it provides an extraordinarily weak reason to create earthly institutions

---

[16] Smith, 202.
[17] Ibid. Italics his.
[18] Ibid., 204.
[19] Ibid., 205.
[20] Ibid., 207.
[21] Douglas Husak: "Why Punish the Deserving?" in Husak, ed.: *The Philosophy of Criminal Law: Selected Essays* (Oxford: Oxford University Press, 2010), p. 393.

that treat persons as they deserve. Systems of penal justice in the real world are notoriously problematic: they are astronomically expensive, prone to error and mistake, and subject to enormous abuse by the officials they empower. Citizen-taxpayers need much better reasons to create such institutions than that they treat offenders as they deserve. What additional reasons should citizens demand? Systems of criminal justice promote several worthy objectives,[22] but the protection of society through deterrence – both general and special – is the most important of these purposes. Thus I agree that penal institutions should not be created simply on grounds of deserving; we must also have reason to believe they will protect rights by reducing crime. Here, then, is the legitimate place of crime-reduction in a theory of justified punishment: it provides the most important rationale for creating institutions that treat persons as they deserve.[23]

Given the brokenness in the American criminal justice system, can we even make a case to justify the current punishment in our system? Until we properly define what punishment is how do we know that offenders deserve it? Is punishment simply shaming and stigmatizing deviant actions for the sake of public safety or are we trying to do something more? Husak argues that we impose a punishment when "when it deliberately expresses condemnation and imposes a deprivation or hardship."[24] The purpose of the punishment must be to both deprive and to condemn in order for it to be true punishment. This raises even more questions. For example, if when we punish we want to condemn and deprive is it necessary that the state criminal justice system do all the condemning and depriving? Are there alternative ways to achieve condemnation and deprivation using institutions in civil society that successfully convert an offender from being merely someone who desists from deviance to being a person who acts on behalf of his or her neighbor's flourishing and thriving? Is restoration and reconciliation enough? Is not a truly virtuous society one where we have interest in our neighbor's flourishing because we are interdependent? What is the rationale for our penal system and the new criminal laws that we continue to pass at the state and federal levels? If we want punishment to change behavior, what is the best way to achieve that goal and what institutions in society have proven track records at changing behaviors in a sustainable way in the long run? It is difficult to have effective criminal justice reform of we do not have a justification for a penal system and the goals we want to achieve for offenders, victims, and the common good.

---

[22] Douglas Husak recommends reading Joel Feinberg, "The Expressive Function of Punishment," in Feinberg, ed.: _Doing and Deserving_ (Princeton: Princeton University Press, 1970), 95.

[23] Douglas Husak, "What Do Criminals Deserve", in _Legal, Moral, and Metaphysical Truths: The Philosophy of Michael S. Moore_, eds Kimberly Kessler Ferzan and Stephen J. Morse (Oxford, United Kingdom: Oxford University Press, 2016), 50.

[24] Husak, "What Do Criminals," 51.

NEW VISTAS

The state penal system and other state agencies cannot develop human character to reduce crime. Civil society institutions must be used to reduce the number of arrests, reimagine the courtroom, provide quality defense for truly disadvantaged offenders, dismantle the school-to-prison pipeline, and handle the ancillary social costs of incarceration. Love is a basic human need that both victims and offenders need but tends to be absent in the criminal justice reform legal theory and philosophy. Personalism and civil-society institutions remind us that human life has a "natural teleological end," and the realization of that, beginning in childhood and extending to one's death bed, is mediated through love experienced in interpersonal relationships.[25]

The most powerful weapon and deterrent against deviance and criminal activity is love. The human body requires love for survival. Our best social and institutional contexts that nurture and facilitate wellbeing involve love. Our worst offenders need to be oriented toward love and mercy.[26] The contexts in which men and women come to know the fullness of their agency and self-efficacy require love. Smith observes, "loves fosters trust, interpersonally and institutionally, and trust promotes human flourishing."[27] "What is the policy implication of theory or proposal X" cannot be our first question if we want to humanize our criminal justice system, significantly reduce numbers, and infuse the entire penal system from police officers to prosecutors to judges to corrections/parole officers. Government policies do not create affection for one's neighbor. Government policies do not inspire love. We shall drastically reduce the amount of incarcerated in this country through a personalist conceptual framework and institutional partners dedicated to caring for our neighbor's well-being. The manifestation of this nurturing of our neighbor will unlock the potential of our republic and we will all enjoy the bloom, which will be a beacon to the world. Pursuing well-being with the right anthropology is the birth place of a criminal justice system that honors the dignity of victims and offenders alike.

[25] Smith, 278.
[26] Bryan Stevenson, *Just Mercy: A Story of Justice and Redemption* (New York: Spiegel & Grau, 2014).
[27] Ibid.

Index

ABA. *See* American Bar Association
Adult Transition Centers (ATCs), 157
AFH. *See* Ambassadors for Hope
African Americans
  civil society institutions for, 174
  class segregation of, 109
  with disabilities, 105–106
  disciplinary actions against students
    with disabilities, 105–106
    income level as factor for, 109
    suspension rates for, 110
    unequal distribution of, 105–106, 110
  incarceration of, 62–63
  in school-to-prison pipeline, 108–109
aggression, massage therapy interventions and,
    204–205
Alabama, state prisons in, 154–157
  CCPs and, 155
  JRI and, 154–156
  parole reform and, 155–156
  prison population in, 154
  recidivism rates in, 156
  reform of, 155–156
  under SB 67, 154–155
  sentencing reform, 156–157
Alexander, Michelle, 1–2
Alsted, Jacob, 201
Alvarez, Gerald, 173
Ambassadors for Hope (AFH), 180–182
American Bar Association (ABA), 88, 90–91, 94–95,
    111, 170
American College of Pediatrics, 131
ancillary offenses, 29–32
  aggressive prosecution of, 30–32
  complementary, 29–30
  supplementary, 29–30

anthropology
  in criminal justice reform, 10–11
  of criminalization, 32–34
    Hammurabi code and, 32
    Nuremberg Trials and, 33
Argyle, Michael, 201
assigned counsel public defense system, 94
ATCs. *See* Adult Transition Centers
Atlantic, 122
attitudinal theory, judicial discretion and, 72

Ballan, Steven G., 99
Bard Prison Initiative (BPI), 187–188
Baumeister, Roy, 201
Beaufils, Vladimir, 35
Bennett, Mark W., 67
Bentley, Robert, 154–155
Beria, Lavrentiy, 17
Bibas, Stephanos, 48
BJS. *See* Bureau of Justice Statistics
Blankley, Tony, 28
Bodenkircher v. Hayes, 48
bodily survival, security and pleasure,
    202–203
Booker v. United States, 68
Boy Scouts, 135
Boyle, Gregory, 191–192
BPI. *See* Bard Prison Initiative
Bureau of Justice Statistics (BJS), 88, 142

Caplan, Lincoln, 88, 92
CAPPS. *See* Citizens Alliance on Prisons &
    Public Spending
CCFY. *See* Community Connections for Youth
CCPs. *See* Community Corrections Programs
Changing Together program, 195–196